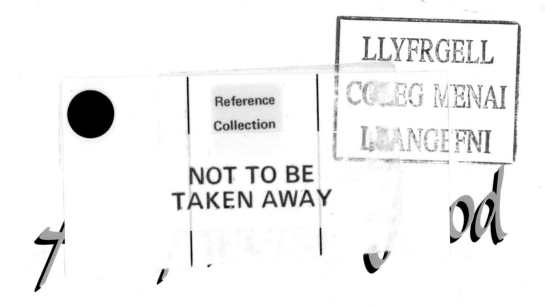

Helen McGrath

OXFORD

RESS

D0873601

Oxford University Press, Great Clarendon Street, Oxford OX2 6DP

Oxford New York
Athens Auckland Bangkok Bogotá Bombay
Buenos Aires Cape Town Dar es Salaam
Delhi Florence Hong Kong Istanbul Karachi Kolkata
Kuala Lumpur Madras Madrid Melbourne
Mexico City Nairobi Paris São Paulo Shanghai Singapore
Taipei Tokyo Toronto

and associated companies in

Berlin Ibadan

Oxford is a trade mark of Oxford University Press

© Oxford University Press 1997

First published 1982
Second edition 1988
Third edition 1997 reprinted 1999, 2000, 2001

ISBN 0 19 832767 6

A CIP catalogue record for this book is available from the British Library.

Typeset by Pentacor plc

Printed in Italy by G. Canale & C. S.p.A. - Borgaro T.se (Turin)

Acknowledgements

The publishers would like to thank the following for permission to reproduce their photographs:
p. 14 J Allan Cash Photo Library; pp. 40, 50 Telegraph Colour Library;
pp. 68, 74 Anthony Blake Photo Library; p. 106 (right) Robert Harding Picture Library;
pp. 110, 111 (all) Anthony Blake Picture Library; p. 122 Birds Eye.

Additional photography by Martin Sookias and Steven Lee.

Front cover image by Mark Mason.

Illustrations are by Stefan Chabluk, Valerie Hill, and Judy Stevens,
based on original drawings by Kate Simunek.

The publishers would also like to thank:

The Consumers' Association for the chart on p. 63 taken from *Which?* December 1995.
Which? is published by the Consumers' Association and is available only on subscription.
For details write to *Which?* Freepost, Hertford SG14 1YB, UK.

Tesco plc for the flow chart on p. 104.

McVitie's for the diagram on pp. 112–13.

Hotel and Catering International Management Association for the flow chart on p. 115.

Preface

This new edition of *All About Food* has been completely revised and updated to provide students with a sound foundation for GCSE examinations in *Home Economics: Food and Nutrition*. The addition of two new chapters – on designing and making food products, and food manufacture and processing – means that it is also highly suitable for *Design and Technology: Food Technology* at Key Stages 3 and 4.

Nutrition information and guidelines are based on the COMA (Committee on Medical Aspects of Food Policy) report of 1991 on *Dietary Reference Values for Food Energy and Nutrients for the United Kingdom*. This report made clear the changes needed in the nutritional balance of the diet. The targets set in the Government's *The Health of the Nation* were set in the overall context of this advice.

All About Food offers practical guidance on eating for health and providing food for people with special dietary needs. The revised and extended recipe section contains many inexpensive recipes based on pasta, pulses, rice, and vegetables, in accordance with the dietary guidelines. Many vegetarian and vegan recipes are included. Some recipes are marked with the following symbols:

V recipes for vegetarians;

V recipes that can easily be adapted for vegetarians.

Quick, low-fat, stir fry recipes are included for both meat and vegetables. All of the recipes can be prepared and cooked in a one-hour teaching session, making them highly suitable for classroom use.

Contents

Food for a healthy life

The food we eat has a great influence on our health and our quality of life. We are fortunate in most Western countries in having no shortage of food to eat. Rather, we have such a huge range of foods to choose from that we tend to eat not only too much but also too much of the wrong kind of food. This can and often does lead us to overweight, ill health, and even premature death.

In 1992 the Government in the UK introduced a White Paper, *The Health of the Nation*. This set targets for diet and nutrition based on a report published by the Committee on Medical Aspects of Food Policy (COMA). These targets aimed to improve the health of people in the UK by promoting a healthier life-style. This is not just so that we can live longer, but so that throughout our lives we are more healthy, feel better, and so enjoy life more. The *Health of the Nation* paper made suggestions for improving the general health of the population in several areas. Our national diet is one of them.

The balance of good health

The Government suggests eight guidelines for a healthy diet. Following these guidelines as far as we can will help us feel well, look good, and enjoy life.

They are:

- enjoy your food
- eat a variety of different foods
- eat the right amount to be a healthy weight
- eat plenty of foods rich in starch and fibre
- don't eat too much fat
- don't eat sugary foods too often
- look after the vitamins and minerals in your food
- if you drink alcohol, keep within sensible limits

O 5 1 1 4 O

The 'healthy plate' shows the different types and proportions of foods which make up a healthy diet. The proportions are important: plenty of starchy foods like bread and potatoes, plenty of vegetables and fruit, small amounts of other foods, and not too many fatty or sugary foods.

How does our food affect our health?

Coronary heart disease (CHD) and stroke are major causes of death and ill-health in the UK. Many of these deaths are premature, that is, the people who die have not reached old age. One of the things that makes us more likely to suffer from heart disease is a diet containing a lot of fat, especially animal fat. Page 22 explains how this happens.

The food we eat or don't eat can cause other problems such as overweight, decayed teeth, poor skin, diabetes, rickets, and anaemia. Most of these develop over a period of time, so it is important for young people to try to develop healthy eating habits.

A healthy diet includes not too much fat, sugar, or salt, but plenty of starchy foods such as bread, potatoes, pasta, cereals, beans, rice, fruit, and vegetables. Most of these foods have the advantage of being cheap, filling, and easy to buy, store, and cook. They are also high in NSP (dietary fibre) and low in fat and calories.

Eat more of these

More bread and cereals

More potatoes with your meals

More vegetables and fruit

More pasta, rice, and beans

QUESTIONS

1 What is the purpose of trying to have a healthy lifestyle?
2 List the eight guidelines for a healthy diet.
3 Which would you feel were the three worst health problems you could suffer as a result of poor eating habits?
4 Will a healthy diet cost you a lot more money?
5 List five foods you like which are healthy and cheap to buy.
6 What sort of foods should we eat more of?

Enjoy your food and eat a variety

It is important that we enjoy our food, and it is good to eat a variety of different foods, rather than the same foods all the time. It is not only more interesting, it also means we are more likely to get the many different vitamins and minerals that different foods provide us with.

No individual food is 'good' or 'bad', it is the overall balance of foods over a period of time that matters. Some knowledge and understanding of what a healthy diet is helps us to make sensible choices from the huge variety of foods that are available.

Why do we choose as we do?

Even though we may have some knowledge of what makes up a healthy diet, we don't always choose as we know we should. There are many different reasons why people make the choices they do, including:

● taste
● price
● time and effort involved in preparation and cooking
● religion and tradition
● the influence of other people and of advertising
● conscience

Taste

This is always important, because no-one chooses food they don't like. Even so, we don't choose our favourite food all the time. It may cost too much, or we may think it's not 'good' for us, or it may take too long to prepare and cook. Some tastes, such as sugar and salt, can be a matter of habit. We may think we want 3 teaspoons of sugar in our tea, but if we wanted to (for the sake of our figure or our teeth) we could quite easily cut it down gradually to half a teaspoon or none at all.

Price

The cost of food is a major influence on our choice (see p. 76). Few people have unlimited money to spend, and many families have times when they have to manage on a low income. It becomes a big responsibility to try to provide cheap healthy food and to please everyone in a family. Not only is there the cost of buying the food, but there is the cost of gas or electricity for cooking.

Time and effort

When we are short of time, ready-made or take-away meals make life simpler, although they cost a lot more. Some people may also use ready-made meals because they lack confidence in their ability or skill at cooking. Most of the recipes in this book are quick and easy to prepare.

Religion and tradition

Most religions have rules about foods which may not be eaten or which must be prepared in a certain way (see p. 47). For example, Muslims may not eat pork, and Hindus may not eat beef. Different countries have different staple foods: Italians eat a lot of pasta, the British eat bread and potatoes, the Chinese eat rice. In homes where the male partner dominates, meals tend to be planned around his wishes and the female and children have to fit in.

Many people stick to the traditional pattern of foods which they know and are used to. Older people can be particularly unwilling to try anything new.

The influence of other people and advertising

Most people, especially younger people, are influenced by their peers, that is, people of their own age group, and want to be like them. There are fashions in foods and eating as in everything else, whether it is burgers or pizzas, cola or milk shakes.

Advertising is a multi-million pound business which successfully persuades us, in ways that we hardly know are happening, to buy one product rather than another. Many food and drink adverts are aimed at young people. They try to convince you that if you want to be seen to be in fashion, you must buy their particular product. You will be able to think of adverts like this. Their purpose is to make us buy the goods so that the producers make a profit.

Conscience

People's choice of food may be affected by their conscience. They may prefer not to eat meat (vegetarians) or not to eat any animal products at all (vegans). Animal welfare concerns make some people avoid eating meat from animals which have been intensively raised or cruelly treated. They may choose to pay a little more for eggs from free range chickens, or for meat from animals that have lived in good conditions. Some people are concerned about wasted resources in a world where many people go hungry (see p. 48).

QUESTIONS

1 What are the advantages of eating a wide variety of different foods?
2 Why do people choose certain foods? List all the reasons you can think of.
3 List some of the reasons why people do not eat their favourite foods all the time.
4 Make a list of some of the foods *you* eat. Choose ten of them and say why *you* eat them.
5 Talk to someone older than you. List ten of the foods they often eat, and say why they choose them.

Eat the right amount to be a healthy weight

Many people in the UK are overweight. Some are very overweight, or *obese*. Obese people are more likely than others to suffer from certain health disorders, such as heart disease, high blood pressure, diabetes, and some cancers.

Exercise

Very occasionally, people put on a lot of weight because of a medical condition. But most people put on weight simply because they continually take in more energy in food than they use up in their daily lives. People who lead very active lives and take a lot of exercise can eat more food without becoming overweight.

It is important to have exercise in your daily life at all ages. You will not only stay slimmer but usually you will feel fitter and have more energy and find life more enjoyable. Try taking part in sports and games, dancing, swimming, keep-fit, aerobics, and walking instead of catching a bus or going by car.

Foods to avoid

Foods high in fat are high in energy. Energy is measured in kilocalories (kcal) or kilojoules (kJ) (see next page). One gram of fat provides 9 kcal, whereas one gram of carbohydrate or protein provides about 4 kcal. This means that you can eat more than twice as much carbohydrate as fat for the same intake of kilocalories. So, a thin slice of bread thickly spread with butter could have twice as many kilocalories as a thick slice of bread with a thin scraping of butter. Pages 20–21 suggest ways you could reduce the amount of fatty foods you eat.

Foods to eat

Plenty of starchy carbohydrate foods are good for weight control. They are high in NSP (dietary fibre) and usually take some time to chew and digest, so they help you to feel full and avoid the hunger pangs that make it difficult to resist food. Bread, potatoes, cereals, pasta, rice, vegetables, fruit, semi-skimmed milk, cottage cheese, lean meat, and fish are all good choices. They provide nutrients but are low in fat and calories. Avoid adding too much butter, sugar, or rich sauce. It is not bread, potatoes, or pasta which are fattening but what you put on them.

Low calorie 'healthy choice' ready-meals can be expensive and are not very filling, but some people find them helpful when they are trying to lose weight. It can also help to join a support group for slimmers. Most food labels now show the energy content, and many foods have 'low fat' or 'low sugar' versions. You should aim to develop a healthy pattern of everyday eating balanced with enjoyable exercise. This is easier than continually eating too many of the wrong foods and then trying to stick to a very low-calorie diet.

Eating disorders

Anorexia nervosa and bulimia nervosa are serious psychological disorders which can sometimes lead to death. They are most often found in teenage girls, but also in boys and adults. People with these conditions behave in an extreme way, either avoiding food altogether, or alternately eating excessively (bingeing) and then making themselves vomit. Both conditions require medical treatment.

Energy

We need the energy that the body makes from the food we eat for three purposes: to stay alive, for the different activities we carry out, and to grow. If we take in more energy in food than we use up in these ways, the extra is converted to fat and is stored in our bodies, and we become overweight.

How much energy do we need?

Energy is measured in kilocalories or kilojoules (see below). These are the *estimated average requirements (EARs)* for young people 11–18 years old, that is, the average amount needed per day for people in that age group.

	Males		*Females*	
Age/years	11–14	15–18	11–14	15–18
Energy/kcal	2220	2755	1845	2110

Staying alive

We use energy even if we are doing nothing. We need it to breathe, for the heart to beat and blood to circulate, to digest food, to keep up our temperature, and for our brains to work. This basic rate at which we use energy just to stay alive is the *basal metabolic rate* (BMR). It is different for different people.

Different activities

Every time you move, you use energy. The heavier you are, the more energy you use up just to move. The more strenuous activity you carry out, the more energy you use. An average 25 year old woman might use up the following amounts of energy in kcal per minute:

sitting or eating	1.1	dancing	4.5
walking slowly	2.6	walking up and down stairs	6.5

People in different occupations use different amounts of energy. For example, 8 hours sitting at a desk might use 900 kcal; 8 hours of active outdoor work might use 1800 kcal. So adults need very different amounts of food if they are to stay at the right weight but still have enough energy for their everyday lives.

Measuring energy

Energy can be measured in different units. These are:

kcal	kilocalorie	=	1000 calories	=	1 Calorie	=	4184 kJ
kJ	kilojoule	=	1000 joules				

QUESTIONS

1 What is the single main reason why people become overweight?
2 Suggest 3 kinds of exercise that would suit you.
3 List ten filling foods suitable for anyone trying to stay at the right weight.
4 What are the two main types of food to cut down on if you want to lose weight?

Eat plenty of foods rich in starch and fibre

Carbohydrates

This is the group of foods which contains starch, NSP (dietary fibre), and sugar. The carbohydrate foods supply energy for all the activities of the body.

Starch

We should eat plenty of the starchy cereal foods which have been the basic diet of most people of the world for thousands of years. They include wheat, rice, oats, maize, barley, and rye, and starchy vegetables like potatoes, sweetcorn, beans, and sweet potatoes.

Some starchy foods made from cereals

Wheat is used for flour for different breads (wholemeal, brown, white, pitta, naan, chapattis), for breakfast cereals (e.g. Weetabix, Shredded Wheat), for pasta (e.g. spaghetti, lasagne), and for semolina.
Rice is used as it is, or ground to make ground rice for puddings and baking. It can be made into rice cakes or breakfast cereals like Rice Krispies.
Oats are used for porridge, muesli, oatcakes, and in baking.
Maize, often called corn, can be boiled as a vegetable (corn on the cob or sweetcorn) or ground to make maize flour for Mexican tortillas, corn chips, and tacos. Cornflakes and cornflour are made from corn.
Barley is added to soups and stews, and used in making beer and whisky.
Rye is used to make rye-bread and crispbread.

These cereal foods and potatoes should provide us with about half of the energy we get from food. As well as starch they provide other nutrients, depending on the individual food, including protein, iron, and B vitamins.

NSP (dietary fibre)

The term non-starch polysaccharides (NSP) is now used rather than 'dietary fibre' because it has a more exact meaning and is a part of food which can be measured accurately. Starchy foods like wheat, rice, and other cereals are usually 'wrapped' in fibrous cell walls made up of NSP in the form of cellulose.

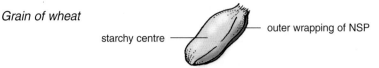

Grain of wheat

starchy centre ——

—— outer wrapping of NSP

NSP also includes pectin and gums which can help reduce cholesterol in the blood.

The starchy part of the food is absorbed and used by the body for energy, but the NSP outer layers are passed out as waste. Even though it is waste it has an important function. NSP is bulky and very absorbent. It holds a lot of water. This means that the contents of the bowel (the faeces) remain soft and are easily passed out of the body. This prevents constipation and other disorders. NSP may also 'mop up' poisonous substances from the bowel which may be harmful if left.

Fibre acts like a sponge, mopping up water and other substances.

People who do not eat enough NSP-rich foods are more likely to suffer from constipation, diverticular disease, cancer of the large bowel, and haemorrhoids.

Whole grains

When cereal foods are processed and refined, most of the outer fibrous layers are removed and thrown away. When grains of wheat are milled to make white flour the grain is broken open and the outer layer of NSP is discarded so that the flour is smooth and white. Wholemeal flour has more NSP as it is made from the whole grain. Brown pasta (from brown flour) has more NSP than white. Brown rice has the outer husky layer left on.

Foods rich in NSP (dietary fibre)

Bread, especially wholemeal and brown; wholemeal flour; wholegrain cereals
 including whole wheat breakfast cereals; brown pasta; brown rice; oats; barley.
Peas, beans, and lentils.
Root vegetables such as potatoes (especially in their skins), carrots, turnips.
Dried fruit such as figs, sultanas, dates.
Other fruit and vegetables.
The average daily intake of NSP for an adult should be about 18 g per day.

Including NSP in your diet

Eat plenty of the foods above. You can adapt recipes when you are cooking, using all wholemeal flour or half wholemeal and half white flour instead of all white. Add peas, beans, and lentils to soups and stews. Choose breakfast cereals made from 'whole' grains. The NSP in our diet should come from a variety of foods which naturally contain it, rather than by adding it as a separate supplement such as unprocessed wheat bran. Phytate in wheat bran may 'bind' some minerals (including calcium and iron) so that the body cannot use them.

 The diet high in NSP and low in fat that is recommended for adults and young people is not suitable for children under two and may be harmful to them. They need more energy-rich foods if they are to grow properly.

QUESTIONS

1 What group of foods do starches, fibres, and sugars belong to?
2 How much of our energy should we get from starchy foods?
3 Name eight starchy foods that people often have in their cupboards at home.
4 Name three cereal crops that breakfast cereals are made from.
5 What other nutrients are often found in starchy foods?
6 Find out the cost of 500 g of ten different starchy foods and two kinds of meat.
7 What could you suffer from if you did not have enough NSP in your diet?
8 List five foods you like which are high in NSP.

Don't eat sugary foods too often

Sugars

Sugars are carbohydrates, but we should not get more than about 10% of our daily energy from sugars. Sugar is called an 'empty' food, because it provides us with energy but nothing else. Other foods, like bread and potatoes, provide us with energy and valuable nutrients (protein, vitamins, minerals), so it is better to get our energy from them. Brown and white sugar are both 'empty foods'; there is no nutritional advantage in using brown sugar.

We consume large quantities of sugar in the UK, on average about 95 g per person every day. It is recommended that we reduce this to no more than about 60 g per person daily. This would help us to avoid tooth decay and becoming overweight. In countries where people eat less sugar, decayed teeth are rare. In the UK we have sugar in tea and coffee, on breakfast cereals, in canned drinks, sweets, biscuits, honey, jam, cakes, and puddings. If you read the labels you will also see sugar in foods such as baked beans, canned soup, and vegetables.

Artificial sweeteners

Saccharin and aspartame are classed as food additives. They can be up to 500 times as sweet as sugar so are used in tiny amounts. They are widely used in the manufacture of soft drinks as they produce a drink much lower in calories and they are cheaper than sugar. They are also used in granules as sugar substitute, where they are mixed in tiny amounts with a carbohydrate filler. The substitute can be sprinkled on breakfast cereals. It is much lower in calories than sugar.

Follow the dental hygiene rules to keep your teeth healthy.

Sugar and tooth decay

Sugary foods are a major cause of decayed and painful teeth. When you eat sugar, acids are produced in your mouth. These acids attack the enamel surface of the tooth, gradually causing a hole. If the acids are allowed to stay in your mouth for long periods there is plenty of time for them to start the process of decay. The amount of sugar in a food is just one of the factors which affect your teeth. Others are:

How often you eat Each time you eat sugary foods, the teeth are covered in acid for about half an hour. This is why it is better to avoid sugary snacks and drinks between meals.

Mealtimes Eating sugary foods at mealtimes is less harmful than eating them on their own, as more saliva is produced which helps to wash food off the teeth and to neutralize the acids.

Foods which help Some foods, including cheese and peanuts, eaten as a snack or after a meal are thought to reduce the damaging effect of acid on the teeth. Chewing sugar-free gum helps as well, by increasing the flow of saliva.

Sticky foods like raisins or toffees are bad as they cling to teeth for a long time.

Dental hygiene

1   Brush with fluoride toothpaste at least twice a day, and ideally after evey meal or snack. This strengthens the enamel on the teeth.
2   Do not eat sugary snacks in between meals. If you are hungry try to go for savoury snacks, cheese, a sandwich, or fruit instead.
3   Visit your dentist for a check up every six months.
4   Try to reduce the number of times sugar goes into your mouth. This is known to be the biggest influence on tooth decay.
5   Try to cut out sugar in your tea and coffee a little at a time. You could use sweeteners but it would be even better to lose the taste for sweetness if you can.
6   Cans and bottles of drinks are very popular but are not good for your teeth. 'Sugar-free' drinks are a little better, but they are usually acidic so they too can cause decay. Water, milk, and unsweetened tea and coffee are the best choices.
7   Fluoride in the water supply has been shown to be very good for teeth.

The classification of sugars

Sugars can be classified as *intrinsic* and *extrinsic* sugars.

Intrinsic sugars are those that are naturally part of the cellular structure of foods, for example in fruit. Intrinsic sugars have no bad effects on health or teeth.

Extrinsic sugars are those that are not contained within cell walls. They may be natural and unprocessed (such as honey), or refined (such as ordinary granulated sugar). Milk contains the naturally occurring extrinsic sugar *lactose*. Of the extrinsic sugars, the *non-milk extrinsic sugars* are the major cause of dental caries. These are the sugars we should cut out.

Diabetes

Diabetes is a disorder where the body fails to control the amount of sugar in the blood. Diabetics have to avoid eating sugar, but they can eat normal amounts of starchy and NSP-rich foods. They must avoid becoming overweight as obesity makes the condition worse.

QUESTIONS

1   Name ten very sugary foods.
2   Why are we advised to eat fewer sugary foods?
3   People often give small children sweets because they like to be kind to them. Is this always a good idea?
4   Teenagers often drink many cans of sweet drinks. What effect might this have on their appearance?
5   List the five rules for dental hygiene which you consider the most important.
6   Explain the differences between intrinsic and extrinsic sugars.

Fat

Why we need fat in the diet

We are recommended in the UK to eat less fat, especially animal fat. However, we still need some fat for a healthy balanced diet. We should get our energy from fat, protein, and carbohydrate in the proportions shown in the pie chart.

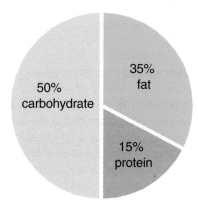

50% carbohydrate

35% fat

15% protein

We need fat for the following reasons:

Fat is a good source of energy

Although we can get energy from carbohydrates and proteins, fat is a very concentrated source (see p. 10). One gram of fat supplies 9 kilocalories, but one gram of carbohydrate or protein provides only 4 kilocalories.

Fat provides the fat-soluble vitamins A, D, E, and K

Some oils and fats are good dietary sources of these vitamins. For example, dairy foods high in fat (such as butter, margarine, cheese, full cream milk, and eggs) are good sources of vitamin A, and most vegetable oils are good sources of vitamin E.

Fat gives a good flavour to foods

It provides a taste and texture to food which we like and find satisfying to eat. It keeps us feeling 'full' for a long time after a meal.

Fat provides essential fatty acids

Essential fatty acids are nutrients which the body needs but cannot make. They must therefore come from the food we eat. The essential fatty acids provided by fat in the diet are linoleic acid and alpha-linolenic acid.

The role of body fat

Body fat, or 'adipose tissue', has several functions.

1   It provides a reserve of energy for the body.
2   It forms a layer around some of the body organs, such as the kidneys, cushioning and protecting them. Beef suet is the fat that encloses the kidneys of the cow.
3   Body fat in new born babies helps cut down loss of body heat.
4   In women, body fat has a role in fertility and reproduction, increasing the oestrogen produced by the ovaries.

evaporated milk, salad cream, yoghurt, mousse, cocoa, oven chips, crisps, burgers, sausages, ice cream. You can buy frozen yoghurt from supermarkets and from ice cream vans: it is very like ice cream but has much less fat. You can buy canned fish, e.g. tuna or mackerel, in brine rather than oil, and low fat canned ready-made meat dishes such as chicken in white sauce.

Many ready-made frozen meals are advertised as 'healthy choices' in supermarket freezer cabinets. They are very convenient and easy for one-person meals, and they do show you exactly how much fat they contain. But they may not be very filling as the portions are usually small, and they would be a very expensive way of feeding a large family.

11 *Do not use dripping or lard* for cooking. Use vegetable oil instead, and use as little as possible. All vegetable oils that are liquid at room temperature are suitable.

Chips

Potatoes themselves are low in fat, but they can absorb a lot of fat while they are being cooked. The amount of fat absorbed can vary a great deal depending on how you prepare and cook them. To cut down the amount of fat (especially saturated fat) in chips, follow these guidelines:

a Always use vegetable oil, not lard or dripping, in a chip pan or deep fryer.
b Cut chips *thickly* not thinly. Thick cut chips absorb much less fat (about 7–10% rather than 15%).
c Cook in very *hot* oil (preferably about 180°C), so the potatoes absorb less fat.
d Frozen chips absorb much more fat (up to 25%) because they lower the temperature of the cooking oil. You could avoid this by defrosting the chips, perhaps in the microwave, before cooking. This also helps them to cook more quickly and avoids spluttering.
e Home made chips fried in vegetable oil can contain as little as 7–8% fat if they are thickly cut and fried in very hot oil, and this can be reduced to about 5% by blotting them on kitchen paper.
f Crinkle cut chips absorb more fat as more surface area is exposed to absorb fat.
g Oven chips contain only about 5% fat. There are also lower fat versions, so read the label on the box or packet.
h Throw away the cooking oil from time to time as it gradually breaks down and does not give good results.

QUESTIONS

1 If someone wanted to reduce the fat in their diet, what would you suggest they spread on their bread?
2 How could you eat chips once a week but keep the fat to a minimum?
3 Name one recipe for a cake made with oil rather than animal fat, and two recipes for cakes using less than half the weight of fat compared to flour.
4 Lean meat can be expensive. How could you provide a hot main meal which is not high in fat and not too expensive?
5 In your local supermarket compare the prices of five ordinary foods with low-fat versions.
6 If you were on a low-fat diet and felt hungry, what sort of food could you fill up on?

Why should we eat less fat?

Coronary heart disease and fat

The death rate from coronary heart disease in the UK is among the highest in the world. It could be reduced to some extent by changes to the average national diet. Because heart disease can take many years to develop it is important that people have healthy eating habits from childhood onwards.

Several factors make coronary heart disease (CHD) more likely, including:

1 high blood cholesterol level;
2 high blood pressure;
3 smoking cigarettes;
4 heredity (a family history of heart disease);
5 obesity (being very overweight);
6 continual stress or tension;
7 lack of regular exercise.

Blood cholesterol, obesity, and high blood pressure are all directly affected by the food we eat, so we are advised to:

1 *Eat less fat.* No more than 35% of our daily kilocalories should come from fat, instead of the present average of 40%.
2 *Eat less saturated fat* (usually fat from animal rather than plant foods). No more than 10% of total energy should come from saturated fat, but the present level is 17%.
3 *Reduce obesity* (being very overweight). Diets high in fat tend to result in obesity as fat is such a concentrated source of calories.
4 *Reduce high blood pressure,* which is affected by obesity and by our sodium (salt) intake (see p. 34).

Links between CHD and diet

A diet high in saturated fats leads to a build up of fatty deposits on the inner walls of the arteries, restricting the flow of blood through them. This condition is called atherosclerosis. Most heart attacks occur when a blood clot blocks the flow of blood in an artery which is already narrowed by atherosclerosis.

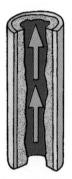

Normal artery: blood can flow through normally.   *Partly blocked artery: blood flow is restricted.*   *Badly blocked artery: blood cannot flow through.*

High rates of CHD are found in populations where the intake of saturated fatty acids averages between 15% and 25% of energy intake. That is why we are advised to reduce our intake to about 11% in the UK. A diet high in saturated fats (such as fatty meat and dairy products) can increase the risk of CHD in at least two ways. These are:

- an increase in the level of plasma cholesterol (high blood cholesterol level)
- an increased risk of formation of a blood clot or thrombus

The average blood cholesterol level of a population is the major risk factor for CHD. It is quite high in the UK, where the consumption of saturated fats is high. Eating foods which contain cholesterol, such as liver and eggs, has little effect on the level of cholesterol in the blood. It is the saturated fatty acids which raise it. Replacing saturated fats with either starchy carbohydrates or unsaturated fats can lower the blood cholesterol level. Obesity raises blood cholesterol.

Trans fatty acids may also increase the risk of CHD by increasing blood cholesterol levels. The average intake of trans fatty acids in the UK is about 5 g daily or 2% of food energy. Much of this is from hydrogenated fats in the margarine we eat and the cakes and other baked goods we buy (see pp. 18–19).

There is an increased risk of formation of a blood clot or thrombus in someone with a high dietary intake of fat. Some studies suggest that certain saturated fatty acids (particularly from beef and lamb fat, butter, and hydrogenated fats) are likely to cause blood clots to form, while some polyunsaturated fatty acids and some fish oils reduce the tendency of blood to clot.

Choosing healthy foods like these can help to protect against heart disease.

Cancer

It is thought that a diet high in fat may be associated with increased risk of cancer of the breast, colon, pancreas, and prostate. But this is not definite nor fully understood and so no specific dietary targets have been made in this area.

QUESTIONS

1. What factors make a person more likely to suffer from coronary heart disease?
2. Which of these are affected by the food we eat?
3. What recommendations are made to try to lower the risk of CHD?
4. Explain two ways in which a diet high in saturated fats is linked to a higher risk of CHD.
5. Suggest why oily fish is thought to be a useful part of a healthy diet.
6. Suggest six ways of including oily fish in your daily diet.

Butter, margarine, and low-fat spreads

There are dozens of butter and margarine spreads available in the shops, and it can be confusing to know how they differ from each other and which to buy. The reasons why we might choose one rather than another include:

Flavour. Most people think butter tastes best.
Ease of spreading. Soft margarine was always easiest to spread before soft butter became available.
Price. Margarine used to be cheaper, but can now be an expensive choice.
Health. We feel some choices may be 'healthier' than others.
Tubs. It can be convenient to have a tub rather than a packet.
Cooking. Some products can be used for baking or frying; some are not suitable.
Ingredients. Butter has only salt added. All margarines and low-fat spreads have many ingredients and additives listed on the label.
Slimming. Some spreads contain a lot of water, so are much lower in calories.
Vegetarians. Some margarine is suitable for vegans and vegetarians. Some strict vegetarians will not eat whey, which is made using rennet from calves' stomachs.

Butter

Butter is made from cream and is high in saturated fat. It must contain at least 80% fat, and the rest is water. The only additive allowed is salt. It has an excellent flavour which margarine manufacturers try to copy.

Margarine

Margarine must also contain at least 80% fat and so has the same energy content as butter. It is manufactured mainly from vegetable or fish oil, with vitamins A and D added, plus other ingredients for flavour and colour. Margarines vary a lot in flavour, price, and in the kind of fat they contain. Those labelled 'high in polyunsaturates' and 'low in saturates' are made from sunflower or soya bean oils. Some have butter added to improve the flavour.

Low-fat spreads

Low-fat spreads look like margarine, but contain less fat. The amount varies from about 60% to as low as 5%. The less fat, the lower the calorie content. In most low-fat spreads the fat is replaced by water, which gives a less satisfying taste. If you use an extra low-fat spread, you may use twice as much to get any flavour. Spreads containing less than 60% fat are too watery for baking or frying.

Comparing spreads

The choice of butters, margarines, and spreads can be very confusing. Compare labels and decide what your own priorities are in terms of price, flavour, convenience, polyunsaturated and saturated fat, ingredients, and additives.

Remember too that what we spread on our bread accounts for only about 14% of the fat we eat, and that other foods in combination contribute most fat. It is always the total balance of foods we eat that is most important, rather than any one food such as butter or margarine being 'good' or 'bad'.

Spread	Average cost per 250 g	Typical ingredients	kcal per 100 g	Fat in grams	of which saturates	of which poly-unsaturates
butter	85p	butter; salt	744	82	46.7	2.9
margarine	19–83p*	hydrogenated animal oil; vegetable oil; water; whey powder; salt; emulsifier (mono and diglycerides of fatty acids); colour (beta carotene); flavouring; vitamins A and D	730	80	30	10
margarine high in poly-unsaturates	49p	sunflower oil; vegetable oil; buttermilk; salt; gelatine; emulsifiers: lecithin, mono and diglycerides E471; preservatives: sorbic acid E200, lactic acid E270; vitamin E; flavourings; colour (beta carotene E160a); vitamins A and D	638	70	16.5	35
block margarine	26p	hydrogenated fish oils; vegetable oil; whey; water; salt; emulsifiers: mono and diglycerides E471, lecithin E322; vitamin E; flavourings; colour (beta carotene E160a); vitamins A and D	731	81	34	5
soya margarine	75p	soya bean oil; hydrogenated soya bean oil; water; salt; concentrated vegetable protein; emulsifier: lecithin; flavouring; colours: annatto, curcumin; vitamins A and D	736	82	15.4	36.8
low-fat spread	23–50p	sunflower oil; water; hydrogenated vegetable oil; vegetable oils; salt; whey powder; emulsifiers: lecithin, mono and diglycerides of fatty acids; preservative: potassium sorbate; colours: annatto, curcumin; flavouring; vitamins A and D	531	60	9	28

*varies a lot depending on flavour and packaging

QUESTIONS

1 Look at the chart above and say which (a) is lowest in fat and calories, (b) is cheapest, (c) is most expensive, (d) has the best flavour, (e) is easy to spread, (f) has fewest additives, (g) has most additives, (h) contains no hydrogenated oil, (i) is best for cakes, (j) is best for pastry, (k) is suitable for vegans, (l) contains least saturated fat, (m) contains most saturated fat, (n) is highest in polyunsaturates.
2 Which would you buy yourself, and why?
3 Ask six people what they spread on their bread, and why.

Protein

Protein is necessary for growth and repair of all the cells in the body. They all contain protein which has to be replaced at regular intervals. We get the protein we need from proteins in the plant and animal foods we eat.

In the UK, where most people have enough to eat, a shortage of protein in the diet is very unusual. We do not need large quantities of meat, eggs, milk, and another animal foods to supply us with enough protein, because nearly every food we eat contains some protein and so contributes to the total we need. Even in poorer countries, if people have enough to eat they have enough protein.

Both animal and plant foods are valuable sources of protein in our diet. Many people do not realise what a useful source of protein plant foods are, particularly bread, flour, beans, peas, and rice. Animal sources of protein include meat, fish, milk, eggs, cheese.

Good plant sources of protein

These include foods which are the seeds of plants, that is, beans of all kinds; peas and lentils; nuts; cereals including oats and wheat; and foods made from wheat such as bread, breakfast cereals, and pasta.

Soya beans are particularly high in protein, but are not often cooked at home as they take a very long time to cook and do not have much flavour. They are used to make *textured vegetable protein (TVP)*, which is shaped, flavoured, and coloured to look like meat. It is widely used by vegetarians as veggie mince or veggie burgers and sausages. The minerals and vitamins which meat provides, such as iron and vitamin B_{12}, are often added during production. When this is done we say these foods are 'fortified' by the minerals and vitamins.

Tofu is also made from soya beans. It is a soya bean curd, a little like cheese in texture. It has been used for hundreds of years in Far Eastern cooking and is now becoming more available in the UK.

Quorn is a newer product made from mycoprotein, which is a fungus grown commercially for food use. It is fermented with glucose syrup, with added minerals to encourage growth. Quorn is high in protein and low in fat, and has a good flavour and texture. It is used for burgers and sausages, and can also be bought as mince or chunks to use as a substitute for meat in many recipes.

Quorn and TVP are sometimes called 'novel' protein sources. They are good sources of protein and are low in fat, so are useful alternatives to meat both for vegetarians and for anyone wanting to reduce their fat intake for health reasons. A diet very high in animal proteins, such as meat and cheese, is often very high in fat and so has associated health risks.

The chemistry of protein

Proteins are made up of amino-acids. There are at least 22 different amino-acids, combined in a great variety of ways to make up the different proteins. They are essential for growth and repair of the body in children and adults. Some amino-acids cannot be made within the body so must be supplied in food. They are called *indispensable amino acids (IAAs)*.

Some proteins contain all the IAAs, and so are said to have a *high biological value* (HBV). These are found in animal foods (meat, eggs, milk) and in the soya bean. Other proteins are said to have a *low biological value* (LBV) as they do not contain all the IAAs. They are found in plant foods such as cereals, wheat, oats, rice, and pulses (peas, beans, and lentils).

As different plant foods supply different amino acids, eating a mixture of plant foods together can supply all the IAAs. A good example of this is eating beans on toast, or lentil soup and bread rolls. The IAAs are said to 'complement' each other and so provide as good and complete a source of protein as, for example, meat, which is much more expensive.

Animal foods are therefore not necessarily better sources of protein than plant foods. Their nutritional advantage lies in the micronutrients which they provide, including vitamin B_{12}, iron, and retinol (vitamin A).

Adverse reactions to protein

Proteins in kidney beans and soya beans are poisonous unless thoroughly boiled for at least 15 minutes before cooking.

Some people may suffer an adverse reaction to certain proteins. People with *coeliac disease* cannot cope with gluten in wheat flour and have to follow a gluten-free diet. Others have an allergic reaction to the protein in cows milk or in nuts. The reaction to peanuts can be very severe and can even cause death.

Average protein content of some everyday foods (g per 100 g)

White bread	8.4	Cheddar cheese	25.5	Quorn	11.8
Weetabix	11.0	Eggs	12.5	Tofu	8.1
Cornflakes	7.9	Baked beans	5.2	Boiled potatoes	3.9
Pasta, boiled	3.6	Roast chicken	22.6	Kidney beans, canned	6.9
Milk	3.3	Lentils, boiled	7.6		

An average 15 year old girl needs about 45 g of protein per day, and a 15 year old boy needs about 55 g. When you think about how much protein different foods contribute to your diet you have to consider how much of each one you are likely to eat in an average portion. The food tables on p. 44 show you what the average portion sizes are.

QUESTIONS

1   Why do we need protein?
2   Name three animal and three plant sources of protein.
3   Describe what is meant by novel sources of protein.
4   Why are we advised not to eat very large amounts of meat and cheese too often?
5   What nutrients, apart from protein, do animal foods provide?
6   Use the figures in the tables to show how a 14 year old boy who did not eat meat could have enough protein per day.

Look after the vitamins and minerals

The food we eat is mainly made up of proteins, carbohydrates, and fats, plus non-starch polysaccharides (NSP) and water. But it also contains thousands of other constituents in tiny amounts, including vitamins and minerals which are essential for many complex processes within the body.

Vitamins and minerals are sometimes called 'micro-nutrients' because they are needed in such small amounts. If we do not have enough of them over a long period of time, our health is affected. In countries where people have a good, varied diet, serious shortages are not very common, but they can occur.

Vitamins can be classified as fat-soluble or water-soluble depending on whether they are found dissolved in fatty foods or watery foods. Fat-soluble vitamins include vitamins A, D, E, and K.

Vitamin A

Vitamin A is needed for growth and for healthy development and function of skin and tissues. It can be obtained from the diet in two forms:

1 Retinol (pre-formed vitamin A)
2 Beta-carotene, which can be converted to retinol in the body.

The average teenager needs 600–700 micrograms of vitamin A each day.

Retinol is found only in animals and the richest sources are liver, fish liver oils, dairy foods, and margarine. Pregnant women, or those who hope to become pregnant, should not eat liver as there is thought to be a link between high levels of retinol in pregnancy and birth defects.

Beta-carotene is an orangey/yellow substance which gives the colour to carrots, apricots, peaches, and turnips. It is also present in green and red vegetables.

The effect of heat on vitamin A

Vitamin A is not easily destroyed by heat or light. Cooked or canned fruit, vegetables, and milk contain as much carotene or retinol after processing as before. We are not likely to be short of vitamin A in the UK if we have a good mixed diet.

Vitamin D

Vitamin D is essential for the formation of strong and healthy bones and teeth. Other nutrients such as calcium and phosphorus are also needed for vitamin D to work. A shortage of vitamin D in children causes rickets, where bones are deformed and not strong enough to support the weight of the growing child. The body obtains vitamin D from sunlight on the skin, and from food.

Sunlight

When you are exposed to sunlight, vitamin D is formed under the skin. The more time you spend in sunlight the more vitamin D will be formed, so we should all spend time out of doors. However, we should all limit our exposure to the sun, and use a suitable protective cream. Sunlight is a more important source of vitamin D in the UK than food.

Food

Few foods provide vitamin D. Oily fish such as tuna, sardines, salmon, mackerel, kippers, are a rich source, and should be eaten a couple of times a week (see p. 135). Margarine has vitamins A and D added by law, and they are usually added to low fat spreads too. Like vitamin A, vitamin D is quite stable.

The Asian community

A shortage of vitamin D occurs in some Asians in the UK. It seems to be caused by their type of vegetarian diet, a low calcium intake, and a limited time spent in sunlight. Their basic foods include ghee rather than margarine (which has vitamin D added) and chapattis rather than white bread (which has calcium added). This can result in a shortage of the basic nutrients needed to prevent rickets. Children thought to be at risk may be given a vitamin D supplement.

Vitamin D content of some foods (µg per 100 g)

Margarine	7.9	Sardines, canned	7.5
Butter	0.8	Salmon, canned	12.5
Low fat spread	8.0	Cornflakes (fortified)	2.1
Herring and kipper	25.0	Eggs, boiled	1.7

Reference nutrient intakes for vitamin D are not suggested as most people get enough from exposure of the skin to sunlight.

Vitamin E

Vitamin E is an antioxidant, of which there is rarely any shortage.

Vitamin K

Vitamin K is involved in the coagulation of blood, and a deficiency is rare.

Vitamins as antioxidants

Beta-carotene, vitamin C, and vitamin E are antioxidants. This means that they can reduce the harmful effects of oxygen species called 'free radicals' which the body normally produces. If free radicals accumulate, they can damage body cells, making them more prone to develop cancer. Free radicals also play a part in forming the 'plaque' which builds up on artery walls causing heart disease (see p. 22). People who eat large amounts of fruit and vegetables seem to be less likely to develop some forms of cancer. Research is currently going on to find out how antioxidants may help to prevent heart disease and cancer.

QUESTIONS

1 What do we mean by micro-nutrients?
2 Which vitamins are fat-soluble? What does this mean?
3 Name some cheap, easily available foods which help prevent rickets.
4 What is the connection between beta-carotene and vitamin A (retinol)?
5 Describe how antioxidants may help prevent heart disease and cancers.

Water-soluble vitamins B and C

The B group of vitamins

This group includes thiamin, riboflavin, niacin, tryptophan, pyridoxine, B_{12}, folate, pantothenic acid, and biotin. These substances are needed for many different body processes, including making use of the energy in foods and normal growth in children.

People in the UK are not very likely to suffer from a shortage of any of the B vitamins if they eat a varied diet. This is because these vitamins are found in small amounts in many different foods, particularly unprocessed whole foods. Wholemeal flour and cereals, potatoes, bread, yeast, yeast extract (Marmite), pork, bacon, liver, kidney, and nuts are good sources of many of the B vitamins. Dairy foods are good sources of riboflavin.

Most of the B vitamins except niacin are sensitive to heat so can be lost by cooking and processing. They can also be lost by dissolving into cooking water. Thiamin (B_1) and vitamin C are the most easily lost of all the vitamins.

Diet-related vitamin B_{12} deficiency has been observed in a few very strict vegetarians and vegans and so it is suggested that they consider B_{12} supplements or use foods with B_{12} added.

Folate and pregnancy It is thought that folate may reduce the possibility of neural tube defects such as spina bifida in babies. Pregnant women and those planning a pregnancy are therefore advised to take a folate supplement.

Vitamin C (ascorbic acid)

Vitamin C has several functions in the body. It:
● prevents scurvy
● helps with healing of wounds
● helps the body absorb iron
● is an important antioxidant (as are beta-carotene and vitamin E).

Soft drinks and squashes are low in vitamin C, unless it is added by the manufacturer. The five drinks on the left of the picture are low in vitamin C. The other foods and drinks are good sources of the vitamin.

Sources of vitamin C
Good sources of vitamin C include: citrus fruits such as oranges and grapefruit; soft fruits such as blackcurrants; tomatoes; red and green peppers; green vegetables such as cabbage, sprouts, and broccoli if they are cooked carefully; potatoes (especially new potatoes) as we usually eat a lot of them regularly (instant potato usually has vitamin C added). Fruit and vegetables which have been canned or frozen, and cartons of fruit juice, are still good sources of vitamin C.

Suggestions for including plenty of vitamin C in your diet

Eat plenty of fresh fruit and vegetables, including freshly boiled potatoes. Try to eat 5 portions of fruit or vegetables every day. Have a glass of orange or other juice for breakfast. Try adding blackcurrant syrup to ice cream or milk pudding (but don't have sweet sugary syrup too often). Try stir fry vegetables sometimes, and have plenty of salads (see recipe section).

Although vitamin C is found in many different fruits and vegetables, it is very easily destroyed by, for example, heat, light, or oxygen. Use fruit and vegetables uncooked when you can, and when you do cook them, follow these rules:

1   Use as soon as possible after they have been picked, and don't store them for a long time (unless you freeze them).
2   Cut with a sharp knife to reduce damage to cell walls.
3   Do not leave them to soak or the vitamin C will leach out into the water.
4   Put vegetables into a small amount of boiling water and cook with the lid on for as short a time as possible. Use the cooking water for gravy.
5   Do not keep vegetables hot for a long time, but eat as soon as possible after they are cooked.

Fruit drinks often have synthetic vitamin C added, as there may be very little real fruit juice in a drink. Look at the label to see how much vitamin C it contains, and also how much sugar is in it. Sweet, sugary drinks are very likely to make your teeth decay, and you should try to avoid drinking them too often.

Vitamin C content of some foods (mg per 100 g)

The amount of vitamin C varies a lot, depending on how fresh the fruit and vegetables are and how they have been stored and cooked.

Oranges	59	Green pepper, raw	120
Grapefruit	36	Cabbage, raw	49
Blackcurrant, stewed	115	Cabbage, cooked	20
Apples	6	Potatoes, baked	14
Kiwi fruit	59	Potatoes, old, boiled	6
Strawberries	77	Brussels sprouts	60

Reference nutrient intakes for ascorbic acid (vitamin C) (mg per day)

Males and females	11–14 years	35
Males and females	15–18 years	40

QUESTIONS

1   List the vitamins of the B group. Why are they necessary?
2   What sort of foods are good sources of many B vitamins?
3   List four functions and four sources of ascorbic acid.
4   How should you prepare and cook vegetables to keep their vitamin C content high?
5   Use the food table to show how you could have enough vitamin C in one day.

Minerals

Most of the known inorganic elements or minerals can be found in the human body. Only 15 are known to be essential, and must be supplied by food; these include iron, calcium, phosphorus, magnesium, sodium, chlorine, potassium, and zinc. Some are needed in very small amounts. They are called 'trace elements', and include iodine, copper, fluoride, and selenium.

Iron

Iron is needed to make haemoglobin, the substance in red blood cells which carries oxygen to parts of the body where it is needed. The oxygen is necessary for cells to work efficiently. Without enough oxygen, muscle cells do not work well and so we feel tired and lacking in energy. Brain cells do not work efficiently so we may be unable to concentrate and work well. Resistance to infection may be reduced. Shortage of iron is being seen increasingly in young children. Continued iron deficiency over a long time results in *anaemia*.

Some groups of people are more likely to suffer from a shortage of iron because:

1   they have a high requirement of iron for growing body tissue (small children, adolescents who are growing rapidly, pregnant women);
2   they lose blood (girls and women during menstruation);
3   they do not absorb the iron in food into their body efficiently (for example, the elderly).

The absorption of iron

Only a small amount of the iron in the food we eat is absorbed by the body (between 5% and 30%). The amount you absorb depends on:

1   how much you need;
2   the *kind* of iron in the food;
3   other foods which are eaten with the iron.

The different kinds of iron

Iron is found in foods in different chemical forms. Some of these are much more easily absorbed than others. *'Haem' iron* is like the iron in our blood, so it is easy to absorb. It is found in red meat, liver, liver pâté, corned beef, and black pudding. *'Non-haem' iron* is in a chemical form which the body can absorb less easily. It is found in cereals, including bread (which by law has iron added to it), pulses, vegetables, dried fruit, and eggs.

   The amount absorbed increases when stores in the body are low and when it is most needed, as for growing children, adolescents, and menstruating and pregnant women. It is also better absorbed in the presence of red meat and of vitamin C, but is less well absorbed in the presence of tannins in tea and some forms of NSP.

   Although pregnant women need good amounts of iron for the growth of the unborn baby, women who are or who might become pregnant are advised as a precaution not to eat liver or liver products. This is because liver contains very high levels of retinol (vitamin A) and it is thought that there may be a link between consuming high levels of retinol in pregnancy and some birth defects.

About half the iron in the UK diet comes from cereals (including breakfast cereals and bread) and about one fifth from meat. The foods in this picture are all rich in iron.

Iron content of some foods (mg per 100 g)

Stewing steak	3.0	Cornflakes	6.7
Roast chicken	0.8	Bran flakes	20.0
Lamb's liver, fried	10.0	Weetabix	7.4
Liver pâté	7.1	White bread	1.6
Corned beef	2.9	Wholemeal bread	2.7
Kidney beans, canned	2.0	Lentils, boiled	2.4
Dried apricots	3.4	Dried figs	3.9

Reference nutrient intakes for iron (mg per day)

Females	11–18 years	14.8 (more if heavy periods)
Males	11–18 years	11.3

Fluoride

Fluoride is a trace element needed for bones and teeth. It helps teeth to resist decay. Drinking water is a natural source of fluoride in some areas and people in those areas have less decay than others. Because of this, fluoride is added to some drinking water supplies in strictly controlled amounts (one part per million). Fluoride toothpaste also helps reduce tooth decay. It is important too to avoid eating a lot of sweet sticky foods, especially between meals.

QUESTIONS

1. What is meant by 'trace elements'? List some of them.
2. How does a shortage of iron over a long period affect your health?
3. What is the difference between 'haem' and 'non-haem' iron?
4. How can vegetarians have enough iron even though they do not eat meat?
5. Why are pregnant women advised not to eat liver?
6. List the amounts of foods from the table above that you could eat in one day to supply your daily requirement of iron.

Calcium and sodium

Calcium

There is about 1.2 kg of calcium in the body, which is more than any other mineral. Calcium is an essential part of the structure of bones and teeth and is involved in other complex body processes. Along with vitamin D, the minerals phosphorus and magnesium, and other nutrients, it is needed for the formation of strong, well-formed bones and teeth. It is also needed for normal blood clotting.

Good sources in the diet are milk, cheese, yoghurt, bread (calcium is added by law to white flour), and vegetables.

As people get older their bone density decreases through loss of all its different components, including calcium. Large losses of bone lead to *osteoporosis*, in which the bones become brittle and easily broken. Osteoporosis is common in elderly women and causes a lot of pain, disability, and need for health care. The cause of osteoporosis is not known and there is no proof that taking more calcium in the diet will prevent it. Several factors are thought to be involved, including oestrogen deficiency, body build, and exercise.

Average calcium content of some foods (mg per 100 g)

Milk, whole	115	Bread, white	110
Milk, semi skimmed	120	Bread, wholemeal	54
Cheese, Cheddar	720	Sardines, canned and drained	550
Cottage cheese	73	Okra, boiled	120
Yoghurt, low fat	150	Tofu	510

Reference nutrient intakes for calcium (mg per day)

Females	11–18 years	800
Males	11–18 years	1000

Sodium

Salt (sodium) is needed for maintaining the water balance of the body and for muscle and nerve activity. You will notice that eating a lot of salty food makes you thirsty. If you do not have enough salt you may have muscular cramps.

High blood pressure and salt

High intakes of sodium or salt over a long period can be associated with high blood pressure. High blood pressure is one of the factors which make coronary heart disease and stroke more likely; others include high blood cholesterol levels, obesity, smoking, and alcohol (see p. 22).

In order to lower the average blood pressure of the UK population it is recommended that adults consume no more than about 2300 mg sodium (6000 mg or 6 g salt) per day.

Very young children cannot cope with high salt intakes and salt should not be added to their food.

Good sources of sodium

Unprocessed food is fairly low in sodium, but salt is added to many foods during processing (for example, canning, smoking, curing pork to make bacon).

For example:

100 g of frozen peas boiled in unsalted water contain 3 mg sodium
100 g of canned processed peas contain 380 mg sodium
100 g of fresh haddock contains 120 mg sodium
100 g of smoked haddock contains 1220 mg sodium

Salt is added to canned vegetables, bread, cereals, meat products, butter, margarine, and many other foods. The nutritional labels on foods often tell you how much sodium there is in a product. Low salt substitutes are available in shops to use instead of table salt. To a large extent a taste for salt can be a matter of habit, like the taste for sugar, which you can gradually cut down. You could avoid cooking with salt, just adding it at the table if you need it.

Cured meat, smoked fish, yeast extract, and crisps are high in salt. The other foods are low in salt.

Average sodium content of some foods (mg per 100 g)

Bread, white	520	Boiled rice	1
Bread, wholemeal	550	Peas, frozen and boiled	3
Cornflakes	1110	Peas, processed, canned	380
Marmite	4550	Bacon	1500
Gravy instant granules	6330	Chicken	81

Reference nutrient intakes for sodium (mg per day)

Females and males	11–18 years	1600 (1.6 g)

QUESTIONS

1   What is calcium used for in the body?
2   Name three foods which are good sources of calcium and two further foods which would provide vegans with calcium.
3   List amounts of foods from the table opposite which could supply your daily requirement of calcium.
4   People with high blood pressure are advised to cut down on salt. Suggest some ways they could do this.

Summary of the main nutrients

Nutrients	Main functions in the body	Good sources in the diet
Protein	Growth and repair of body cells.	*Animal* – meat, milk, eggs, fish, cheese. *Plant* – soya and other beans, lentils, nuts, cereals (including bread and breakfast cereals). *TVP* – from soya beans. *Quorn* – from mycoprotein.
Carbohydrate	Main source of energy from food. NSP (non-starch polysaccharides) provides bulk to move food through the body though it is not a food.	*NSP* (dietary fibre) – whole cereals, vegetables, fruit *Intrinsic sugars* – in cell walls of fruit. *Milk sugar* – found naturally in milk (lactose). *Non-milk extrinsic sugars* – in granulated sugar, jam, honey. *Starch* – flour, other cereals, potatoes.
Fat	A concentrated source of energy. Insulates the body against heat loss. Protects organs, e.g. the kidneys. Provides fat-soluble vitamins A, D, E, and K. Provides essential fatty acids. Gives satisfying taste and texture to food.	*Animal* – milk, butter, cream, cheese, meat, cakes, pastries. *Plant* – margarines and oils.

Minerals	Main functions in the body	Good sources in the diet
Iron	Forms haemoglobin in red blood cells.	*Animal* – liver, red meat, pâté, corned beef. *Plant* – green vegetables, bread, dried fruit, breakfast cereals, nuts, black treacle.
Fluoride	Strong teeth and bones. Helps resist tooth decay.	Drinking water.

Calcium	Forms strong bones and teeth (together with vitamin D, magnesium, phosphorus, and other nutrients). Normal blood clotting.	Milk, cheese, yoghurt, bread, vegetables.
Sodium	Maintains water balance of the body. Too much is associated with high blood pressure.	High amounts in processed foods (e.g. canned, smoked); salt added to food.
Vitamins	**Main functions in the body**	**Good sources in the diet**
Vitamin A (fat soluble)	Growth of children. Healthy skin and tissues. Beta-carotene is an antioxidant.	As retinol in fish oil, liver, dairy foods, and margarine; as beta-carotene in orange-yellow fruit and vegetables, and green vegetables.
Vitamin D (fat soluble)	Works with calcium and other nutrients to form strong bones and teeth. Prevents rickets.	Main source in UK is sunlight on the skin. Foods – margarine, oily fish.
Vitamin B group (water soluble) (includes thiamin, riboflavin, niacin, tryptophan, pyridoxine, B_{12}, folate, pantothenic acid, biotin)	For growth of children and healthy working of many body processes, including the release of energy from foods.	Found in a wide variety of foods especially unprocessed foods: wholemeal cereals and flour, potatoes, bread, Marmite. Milk provides useful amounts of riboflavin.
Vitamin C (ascorbic acid) (water soluble)	Prevents scurvy. Heals wounds. Helps absorption of non-haem iron. Antioxidant.	Citrus fruits (oranges, lemons, grapefruit), blackcurrants, kiwi fruit, tomatoes, green peppers, potatoes, fresh green vegetables.

Food in pregnancy

When a woman is pregnant she should take extra care to eat well. A healthy, well-nourished mother is much more likely to have a healthy baby than a mother who has not taken much care of herself during pregnancy.

An expectant mother should:

1 visit the doctor as soon as she suspects that she is pregnant;
2 make sure she goes to the ante-natal clinic regularly and follows their advice;
3 try to give up smoking, or at least cut down;
4 cut down on drinking alcohol, especially spirits;
5 eat good meals, with plenty of variety and plenty of fresh foods.

Eating for two means that an expectant mother has two people to consider when she chooses what to eat. She is responsible for the baby's healthy growth and development now as well as her own. Eating for two does not mean that she should eat twice as much as she used to. If she did she would put on unnecessary weight which might be difficult to lose. She will only need to eat more food in about the last three months of pregnancy, and when breast-feeding the baby.

Foods to eat

It is especially important in pregnancy that a woman has a good, varied diet with plenty of fresh foods, like that recommended for all healthy adults. Foods like this will supply the nutrients needed for the healthy development of the baby. She needs enough energy, protein, iron, calcium, folate, and vitamins C and D. These are all essential for the baby to build up the necessary muscle, bone, teeth, and haemoglobin in the blood.

If enough of these are not provided in the diet then the baby will take what it needs from the mother's stores, and her health may suffer. For example, if the diet does not supply enough calcium, the baby will take what it needs from the mother and her teeth may be weakened and decay. If there is not enough iron in the diet the baby will take what it needs for its own growth and blood supplies and to build up its own store in the liver. This store lasts for the first few months of life when the baby lives only on milk and receives no iron in food. A healthy woman who has previously had a good diet will have a good store of iron in her liver which is available for the baby's needs. She will also absorb iron from foods more efficiently when she is pregnant.

Most of the extra nutrients a pregnant woman needs are easily obtained from a good, mixed diet which includes plenty of bread, cereals, vegetables, fruit, dairy foods, and meat or meat alternatives. Bread (especially wholemeal bread), whole breakfast cereals, vegetables, and fruit are also good sources of NSP (dietary fibre) which will prevent the constipation which is common in pregnancy.

Folate
Women who are planning a pregnancy or who are pregnant are advised to take a folate supplement (part of the vitamin B group) and to eat plenty of folate-rich foods. This reduces the risk of having a baby with a neural tube defect (such as

spina bifida). Good sources of folate include potatoes, fortified breakfast cereals, bread, and fresh vegetables.

Foods to avoid

Pregnant women should not take any pills or medicines, including vitamin and iron pills, unless advised to by their doctor. They are advised not to eat liver in pregnancy, as animal liver is very rich in retinol (vitamin A) and a high level of retinol in pregnancy may increase the risk of birth defects.

Like everyone else, an expectant mother should not eat too many sugary, fatty foods. If she suffers from sickness, indigestion, or heartburn then fried, greasy, or spicy foods may make it worse. Strong tea and coffee can also have this effect. If she is putting on too much weight she can safely cut out cakes and puddings and eat fresh fruit instead.

To avoid infection

Listeria Some foods have been found to have high levels of a type of bacteria called *listeria*. Listeria can cause miscarriage, still-birth (where the baby is born dead), or severe illness in the new born baby. Although this is rare, anyone who is pregnant should avoid the foods listeria is found in. These are:

● certain *ripened soft cheeses* such as Camembert, Brie, and blue cheeses. You can still have hard cheese, cottage cheese, processed cheese, and cheese spreads.

● *pâté*

● *cook–chill meals and ready-to-eat poultry* (chicken and turkey) which are ready cooked (not frozen) and kept in cold cabinets in the shops ready for the customer to eat cold or reheat. To be safe you should heat these foods until they are piping hot rather than eat them cold.

Salmonella This bacteria can make you feel very ill, even though it does not have a direct effect on the baby. It is often found in eggs and poultry, so these foods need special care. No one should eat uncooked eggs, and if you are pregnant you should only eat eggs where the yolk as well as the white is solid. Young children should not eat partly cooked eggs either. Poultry and raw meat should be thoroughly cooked to make sure any bacteria are destroyed.

Normal hygiene precautions are important (see pp. 88–89), especially remembering to wash your hands before preparing foods, and after handling cats and dogs or other animals, no matter how clean and healthy they are.

QUESTIONS

1   What is meant by the words 'eating for two'?
2   What sort of diet is suggested for a pregnant woman?
3   List some foods suitable for a pregnant woman.
4   How can the baby's need for iron be met?
5   Why is folate usually prescribed before or during early pregnancy?
6   Should an expectant mother take iron pills and eat liver?
7   What foods should expectant mothers avoid to reduce the risk of bacterial infection?

Babies and small children

The best source of nourishment for babies in the early months of their lives is breast-feeding. Breast milk is best for them for the following reasons.

1   It provides all the nutrients the baby needs, in exactly the right amounts, and in a form that the baby can easily digest and absorb.
2   It contains natural substances which protect the baby against harmful organisms.
3   It is clean, does not need to be mixed and prepared, and costs nothing.
4   It does not cause allergies such as asthma, eczema, or food allergies.

The benefits of breast-feeding carry on for some time even after breast-feeding stops, so it gives a baby the best start if a mother tries to breast-feed her baby for at least two weeks, and ideally for 4−6 months.

If a baby is not breast-fed, it is usually fed on an infant formula made from cows' milk. As cows' milk is produced for calves, which are very different from babies, the cows' milk is adapted to make it as much like human milk as possible. It is very important to make up the feed exactly according to instructions so that the baby's digestion can cope with it.

Solid foods should not be started before four months. The baby does not need them and it may encourage allergies and overweight. From about 4−6 months the baby may gradually start on solid foods with baby cereal foods, puréed fruit and vegetables, and egg yolk. He or she will start with sieved or finely mashed foods, and very gradually move on to minced and more solid foods. By about 12−18 months the baby can be eating most of the same foods as the rest of the family. Jars and cans of baby foods can be used when the family meal is not suitable, but they often contain a lot of sugar.

Drinks

Ordinary full cream pasteurized milk can be a main milk drink from one year onwards. It is an important part of a child's diet up to the age of two, after which semi-skimmed milk may be used. Children under five must not be given skimmed milk. Unlike adults, who need to limit the amount of fat in their diet, small children need the more concentrated energy and nutrients which the fat in the milk provides. The low-fat, high-fibre diets recommended for adults are harmful for babies and toddlers.

Sweetened drinks can do a lot of harm to children's developing teeth and can cause a lot of tooth decay. The best drinks for children are milk and plain tap water. There are special 'baby drinks' but although they have fewer additives than ordinary fruit squashes they still have added sugar. Children are sometimes given 'diet' drinks to avoid sugar but they may contain stimulants like caffeine and artificial sweeteners. Read the food labels for information. Tea, especially with sugar added, is not advised for young children as the tannin may stop the child absorbing iron from food, and many children of this age have low iron intakes.

If children are given sweet drinks, it is less harmful to teeth if they are given at the same time as other foods at mealtimes, and from a cup. It is very harmful to developing teeth if a baby or small child has a dummy dipped in syrup or is left with a sugary drink, as the child's mouth will then be coated in sugar for long periods.

Iron

Many young children have been found to have diets that are too low in iron, leading to listlessness, lack of energy, and lack of concentration. Because of this it is sensible for them to have plenty of iron-rich foods in their meals, and good amounts of foods rich in vitamin C to help them absorb it (see pp. 32–33).

Mealtimes

1 Young children often have small appetites and do not like large quantities. They like small portions of food neatly served.
2 Children need food which is easy to manage on a plate. They will not be very skilled with a knife and fork.
3 Young children usually enjoy eating from their own special dishes and using their own cutlery.
4 They may find large pieces of meat difficult to chew and swallow.
5 Do not give them a lot of greasy, fried, rich, or spicy foods, which can be difficult to digest.
6 Encourage them to enjoy a variety of foods. Sometimes they will refuse to eat certain foods, often vegetables. This will not do them any harm if they eat fruit and cereal foods instead.
7 Do not encourage them to want a lot of sugar. There is no need to add sugar to drinks, breakfast cereals, and fruit. Children do not need it and it will spoil their teeth. Do not give them sweets between meals.
8 Train them from an early age to have good table manners, setting them a good example yourself.

QUESTIONS

1 What advantages do breast-fed babies have over bottle-fed babies?
2 Is it worth breast-feeding a baby just for a couple of weeks?
3 When should a baby start solid foods? Why is it better not to give solid foods before then? Why do you think some mothers are tempted to try them?
4 Why are low-fat and high-fibre diets completely unsuitable for babies and toddlers?
5 What sort of drinks would you give a two year old? Explain your answer.

School children and adolescents

Children are growing quickly and are usually very active and energetic. They often have large appetites for their size compared with adults. Because they also have smaller stomachs, they need food which is not too bulky. Like everyone else, children and adolescents should try not to eat too many sweet, sticky foods and drinks, in order to avoid tooth decay. Pages 14–15 tell you how to take care of your teeth.

Too much 'junk' food, like sweets, biscuits, and sugary drinks, will also spoil your appetite for foods which are better for your health, your figure, your skin, your teeth, and your looks. Some children in the UK are now suffering from malnutrition. They are not going hungry, but they eat so much 'junk' food that they have no appetite left for more nutritious food. It is not that junk food is cheaper; in fact, it is easy to spend more on canned drinks, crisps, biscuits, and snacks than on good food. Foods like bread, potatoes, cereals, milk, beans, pasta, rice, meat, cheese, fruit, and vegetables will provide all the nutrients you need.

Meal patterns

Most people's eating patterns are changing away from conventional meal times where everyone sits down together to eat. People now tend to eat more 'snacks' and fewer large meals. They are also willing to try new foods. When children reach adolescence and become involved in leisure activities away from home, members of the same family may well eat at different times. As more households have microwave ovens and freezers, many teenagers make their own food, often with easy-to-prepare convenience foods bought from the supermarket.

Teenagers are increasingly in control of their food choices away from home too. Many now eat out of school at midday, often at one of the 'fast food' chains. More young people are becoming vegetarians, which also affects their eating patterns.

Anorexia nervosa and bulimia nervosa can begin in adolescence. Page 10 tells you about these disorders.

Energy balance

Adolescents between about 15 and 18 years old normally need more food than at any other time in their lives and can have very large appetites. As always, the amount of food you eat must be balanced with the energy you use up if you are to avoid becoming overweight. Exercise is really important to keep your weight in balance and to make you feel and look good. It is good to get involved in exercise you enjoy, whether it is sports, games, dancing, aerobics, or keep-fit. The requirements for energy will vary a lot from one person to another. If you are involved in a lot of sport or exercise you can eat a lot more food without becoming overweight than if you do not take part in much physical activity.

Some suggestions for meals

Breakfast Some young people go to school without having eaten anything at all for breakfast. This is not a good idea as your blood sugar will drop to a low level and you will be unable to concentrate. If you get very hungry you will probably fill up on sweets or biscuits to keep you going until lunchtime. It is better to have breakfast and it need not take any time to prepare. Try breakfast cereal and milk; porridge; yoghurt; a banana or other fruit; toast or bread with butter, peanut butter, or Marmite; milk, water, fruit juice, or tea to drink.

Packed lunch Sandwiches with a savoury filling; tomato or celery; low fat crisps or savoury biscuits. Instead of chocolate or sweets, try yoghurt, scone, teacake, or an apple.

Other meals Include meat or a meat-free alternative such as fish, cheese, or beans; have potatoes baked or boiled most days, with chips or other fried potatoes only once or twice a week; include bread of all kinds including pizza, chappatis, pitta, and naan; eat plenty of vegetables and fruit.

Estimated average requirements (EARs) of adolescents for different nutrients (per day)

	Males		Females	
Age/years	11–14	15–18	11–14	15–18
Energy /kcal	2220	2755	1845	2110
/kJ	9270	11510	7920	8830
Protein/g	42.1	55.2	41.2	45
Thiamin/mg	0.9	1.1	0.7	0.8
Riboflavin/mg	1.2	1.3	1.1	1.1
Niacin/mg	15	18	12	14
B_6/mg	1.2	1.5	1.0	1.2
B_{12}/µg	1.2	1.5	1.2	1.5
Folate/µg	200	200	200	200
Vitamin C/µg	35	40	35	40
Vitamin A/µg	600	700	600	600
Calcium/mg	1000	1000	800	800
Phosphorus/mg	775	775	625	625
Sodium/mg	1600	1600	1600	1600
Iron/mg	11.3	11.3	14.8	14.8

No figures are given for vitamin D as enough is formed from sunlight on the skin.

QUESTIONS

1 What is meant by 'junk food'?
2 Why should we avoid eating too much 'junk food'?
3 What changes in meal patterns often occur as children become adolescents?
4 Why is it important to balance the food you eat with the exercise you take?
5 Why should you always have at least a small breakfast before you go to school?
6 Suggest a healthy packed lunch for yourself which you would enjoy.
7 What is your own EAR for: energy, protein, vitamin C, and iron?

Food tables

Nutrients per 100 g of some everyday foods

	Energy	Protein	Fat	Saturated fatty acids	Calcium	Iron	Sodium	Vitamin A	Thia-min	Vitamin C
	kcal	g	g	g	mg	mg	mg	μg	mg	mg
White bread	235	8.4	1.9	0.4	110	1.6	520	0	0.21	0
Boiled rice (white)	138	2.6	1.3	0.3	18	0.2	1	0	0.01	0
Spaghetti	104	3.6	0.7	0.1	7	0.5	0	0	0.01	0
Cornflakes	360	7.9	0.7	0.1	15	6.7	1110	0	1.0	0
Weetabix	352	11.0	2.7	0.4	35	7.4	270	0	0.9	0
Milk, semi-skimmed	46	3.3	1.6	1.0	120	0.05	55	23	0.04	1
Low fat fruit yoghurt	90	4.1	0.7	0.4	150	0.1	64	11	0.05	1
Fruit pie	260	3.0	13.3	4.8	59	0.8	200	74	0.08	3
Cheddar cheese	412	25.5	34.4	21.7	720	0.3	670	363	0.03	0
Boiled egg	147	12.5	10.8	3.1	57	1.9	140	190	0.07	0
Butter	737	0.5	81.7	54.0	15	0.2	750	887	0	0
Low fat spread	390	5.8	40.5	11.2	39	0	650	501	0	0
Sunflower seed oil	899	0	99.9	11.9	0	0	0	0	0	0
Minced beef	229	23.1	15.2	6.5	18	3.1	320	0	0.05	0
Fried beefburgers	264	20.4	17.3	8.0	33	3.1	880	0	0.02	0
Roast chicken	216	22.6	14.0	4.2	9	0.8	72	0	N	0
Fried lambs liver	232	22.9	14.0	4.0	12	10.0	190	57300	0.26	12
Grilled pork sausages	318	13.3	24.6	9.5	53	1.5	1000	0	0.02	N
Fried cod in batter	199	19.6	10.3	0.9	80	0.5	100	N	0.20	0
Chips, fried in oil	189	3.9	6.7	0.6	11	0.8	12	0	0.24	9
Crisps	546	5.6	37.6	9.2	37	1.8	1070	0	0.11	27
Boiled potatoes	72	1.8	0.1	0	5	0.4	7	0	0.18	6
Boiled carrots	24	0.6	0.4	0.1	24	0.4	50	1260	0.09	2
Boiled lentils	100	7.6	0.4	0	16	2.4	12	3	0.11	0
Frozen peas	69	6.0	0.9	0.2	35	1.6	2	67	0.26	12
Apples	47	0.4	0.1	0	4	0.1	3	3	0.03	6
Chocolate	529	8.4	30.3	17.8	220	1.6	120	7	0.1	0

N = Not known

Average portions of some everyday foods

		Weight in grams
Bread	medium slice from large loaf	35
Rice	boiled, medium portion	180
Pasta	cooked, medium portion	230
Cornflakes	medium helping	30
Weetabix	2	40
Milk	enough for 1 cup of tea or coffee	25
Milk	1 glass	200
Cheddar cheese	1 matchbox sized piece	30
Egg	medium	55

Weight in grams

Butter	(or margarine or low fat spread) for 1 slice	7–10
Peanut butter	thickly spread on 1 slice	20
Jam or marmalade	average for 1 slice	15
Bacon	average rasher, cooked	40
Minced beef	average portion, cooked	140
Beefburger	cooked, 1	35
Roast chicken	medium portion	100
Liver	medium portion	100
Pork sausage	1 large, cooked	40
Chips	medium portion	165
Potatoes	boiled, medium portion	175
Peas	medium portion	70
Apple	medium, eating	115
Sugar	1 level teaspoon	5

Dietary reference values

The Committee on Medical Aspects of Food Policy (COMA) has defined the terms to be used when talking about the varying amounts of energy and nutrients that people need for a healthy life.

EAR is the *estimated average requirement* for a *group* of people for energy, protein, or a vitamin or mineral each day. About half will usually need more than the EAR and half will need less.

RNI is the *reference nutrient intake:* an amount of the nutrient that is enough, or more than enough, for about 97% of people in a group. If average intake of a group is at RNI, the risk of deficiency in the group is very small.

DRVs are *dietary reference values.* This term includes EARs and RNIs. Sometimes when you read the nutritional information on food packets or cans you will read that the food provides a percentage of RDA or *recommended daily amount.* The RDA is defined by EU labelling laws and is not the same as the RNI. It is considered to be enough for the needs of the population as a whole.

QUESTIONS

1 Choosing foods from the tables above, list the foods you are likely to eat in one day for your meals and snacks, with approximate amounts.
2 Use the food tables to show how your meals and snacks could provide you with enough energy.
3 Work out how much of the following nutrients your food might supply: protein, vitamin C, thiamin, and iron. Compare these figures with your EAR.
4 How much fat would your food provide?
5 How much of this would be saturated fat?
6 What meat would be a good choice for someone trying to lose weight? Why?
7 Use the food tables to explain why it is sometimes suggested that we have fruit or yoghurt through the week and a pudding only at the weekend.
8 Write a summary of your findings about your daily diet, noting what you consider is good or not so good about it and any changes you could make.

Food for elderly people

It is sometimes difficult for older people to feed themselves well, and over a period of time this can affect their health. As for everyone else, a good varied diet will help them to feel as fit as possible, and so to enjoy life. They should also be encouraged to have plenty of gentle exercise, and to spend some time in the sunlight where possible.

There can be several reasons why it is difficult for the elderly to feed themselves well, including some of the following.

1   Problems with teeth and gums which make it difficult to chew and swallow.
2   Problems with digestion. They may find that certain foods no longer 'agree' with them and cause indigestion.
3   Shopping can be difficult if they live some distance from the shops, or if the weather is bad.
4   Shortage of money. If they are living on a small pension, they may have to budget very carefully and consider the cost of fuel for cooking as well as the cost of food.
5   Buying amounts small enough for one can be difficult, especially without a fridge or freezer to keep food fresh.
6   Many elderly people live alone and may feel it is too much bother to shop, cook, and wash up just for one. This can lead them to eat too many cakes and biscuits just because they are easy to prepare and keep, rather than have a more varied diet which they need to keep in good health.

Foods to choose

Older people should be encouraged to prepare themselves at least one nutritionally well-balanced meal every day. This does not necessarily have to be a hot meal. Then they could try to include in their other meals foods that are good for health and easy to prepare, such as milk, yoghurt, cheese, eggs, bread, cereals, and fruit or fruit juice.

Like other adults, they should avoid eating too much saturated fat. This will help moderate their blood cholesterol level and reduce the risk of heart disease. They should try to eat oily fish once or twice a week, as this may help to avoid a blood clot (see p. 22). Easy to prepare meals with oily fish include sardines on toast, tuna sandwiches, and boil-in-the-bag kippers. All of these are also good sources of vitamin D.

They should avoid too many sugary foods, which may be eaten at the expense of more nourishing foods. This will also reduce dental decay and help them keep their own teeth. Fruit and vegetables will provide vitamin C and NSP (fibre). Bread (especially wholemeal) and cereals will also add NSP and reduce the need for laxatives to avoid constipation.

It is useful for the elderly to keep a store of 'stand-by' foods in the cupboard for days when they are unable to go out. If they have a freezer they can also store bread, semi-skimmed milk, and vegetables. Frozen ready meals are useful, for example, 'boil in the bag' liver in gravy, or fish in white sauce. With a boiled potato and a few frozen vegetables it is easy to prepare a hot nourishing meal, which can be made in one pan, so making very little washing up and using very little fuel.

Ethnic and religious groups

Different ethnic and religious groups practise various restrictions on the foods they eat and on the way foods are prepared.

Hindus eat no beef. They are mostly vegetarians, do not often eat fish, and often fast for certain periods (to fast means to go without food or to have very limited amounts of food).

Muslims do not eat pork or shellfish. They eat only *halal* meat. This meat is dedicated to God by a Muslim when the animal is killed. Muslims practise regular fasting, and at Ramadan they fast for one month.

Sikhs do not eat beef. Meat must be from animals killed in a certain way, with one blow to the head.

Rastafarians do not eat any animal foods except milk. Foods must be *I-tal* or alive, so canned and processed foods are not eaten. No salt or coffee is taken.

Hindus, Muslims, Sikhs, and Rastafarians do not drink alcohol.

Jews do not eat pork. Meat must be *kosher*, which means that the animal must be killed by a Rabbinical licensed person, then the meat must be soaked and salted. The only kind of fish eaten is that which has scales and fins. Meat must be prepared and eaten separately from dairy foods.

Ethnic communities eating their traditional foods usually have healthy diets. Some Asian vegetarians in the UK may have problems as they have very low intakes of vitamin D in their traditional food. If they do not have enough exposure to sunlight for vitamin D to be formed in the skin (see p. 28) they may develop rickets and osteomalacia (bone deformities). This most often occurs in women and children who spend little time out of doors. Vitamin D and calcium should be included in the diet (for example, with white bread and margarine). Sometimes vitamin D supplements may be needed.

Anaemia is also found sometimes in Asian women and children, since there may be little iron in their traditional diets.

QUESTIONS

1   What difficulties can old people experience which make it hard for them to have a good diet?
2   Is it necessary to cook every day to have nourishing meals? Explain your answer.
3   Suggest two main meals which would be easy to prepare and cook using fresh foods and two using some ready-prepared or convenience foods.
4   Describe some of the dietary restrictions that different religions practise.
5   Why are some Asian women and children in the UK at risk of rickets or osteomalacia? How can this be overcome?

Vegetarians

The term 'vegetarian' refers to all people who do not eat meat. Within this group are many different kinds of vegetarians: some will eat animal foods such as milk, eggs, and fish, and some will not.

Lacto-vegetarians will eat milk, butter, cheese, and other dairy foods.

Lacto-ovo-vegetarians will eat dairy foods, and eggs as well.

Vegans do not eat any foods from animal sources at all, including dairy foods.

Some religious groups have vegetarian diets, including *Rastafarians, Buddhists* and *Seventh Day Adventists.*

Why do people become vegetarians?

There are several reasons, apart from religious convictions. Some people feel that animals should not be killed for food, and find the thought of eating animal flesh distasteful. Many people feel there is unnecessary cruelty involved in intensive farming methods, in the transporting of animals (especially over long distances), and in the process of slaughter. Others are concerned about the doses of hormones and antibiotics given to animals which people are going to eat as meat. Other people feel that a vegetarian diet is healthier, as it is in line with the government's recommendations for less fat (especially animal fat) and more NSP (dietary fibre). Research has shown that vegetarians are usually leaner and have lower blood pressure, less coronary heart disease, and less risk of some cancers. Some people think that in a world where many people go hungry, it is wasteful of the world's resources to use land to rear animals for meat, when growing food crops could feed many more people.

There have been millions of healthy vegetarians throughout history. Human fossil discoveries in East Africa suggest that early humans lived entirely on a diet of nuts, grains, and vegetables. There is archaeological evidence of a vegetarian community in the Hebrides in Scotland 8,000 years ago.

Nutrition for vegetarians

Like everyone else, vegetarians need a balanced diet with a variety of foods, and preferably plenty of fresh, unprocessed foods.

Protein is needed for growth and repair of the body. A variety of plant foods can supply all the protein you need, so it is a mistake to think that animal foods are essential for protein. Good sources include bread, cereals, beans of all kinds (particularly soya beans and foods made from them, such as TVP, tofu, and soya milk), nuts, seeds, and potatoes. Dairy sources include cheese, milk, and eggs.

Carbohydrate for energy is easily provided by bread, potatoes, rice, cereals, and grains. These foods also provide plenty of NSP (dietary fibre).

Fat for energy comes from vegetable oils, nuts, seeds, olives, and dairy products.

Minerals A varied vegetarian diet can supply all the necessary minerals. Mineral deficiencies are not seen in vegetarian populations.

Iron Only about one-fifth of the iron in the average British diet comes from meat. The rest comes from eggs, cereal foods (including bread), potatoes, green vegetables, nuts, and pulses. Vegetarians and vegans are not usually deficient in iron because they eat large amounts of these foods. The absorption of iron is helped by vitamin C, of which there is usually a good amount in a vegetarian diet. NSP, soya, tea, and coffee can all reduce absorption of non-haem iron (see p. 32).

Calcium Dairy foods supply plenty of calcium. Vegans have low intakes but there is no evidence to suggest that they suffer from a deficiency. Good plant sources include bread, leafy green vegetables, dried fruit, tofu, nuts, and seeds.

Vitamins can all be supplied by plant foods, except B_{12}, which only occurs in animal foods. Fortified foods like soya milk, breakfast cereals, and yeast extract will supply enough B_{12}.

Adapting recipes

Many traditional recipes can easily be adapted for vegetarians. You can buy 'vegi-mince' or chunks, burgers, and sausages made of soya or Quorn to use instead of meat. You could try tofu or nut roast.

Food manufacturers now produce a wide range of vegetarian products.

Dairy products You can buy soya milk and margarine, or ordinary margarine (made from vegetable oil rather than fish oil), and vegetarian cheese (made without rennet, which comes from the stomach of calves after they have been killed). Instead of dripping, lard, or suet, use vegetable oil or vegetable suet for dumplings and Christmas pudding.

Other Look for biscuits and other foods without animal fat. Use vegetable stock cubes instead of meat. Health foods shops sell many foods with the Vegetarian Society 'V' symbol.

Read the ingredients lists on food packets to see what they contain. You could join the Vegetarian Society, whose address is on p. 234.

QUESTIONS

1 Explain the reasons why some people become vegetarian.
2 Suggest food for a vegetarian for one day which would provide a healthy, balanced diet. Explain why your choice provides a healthy diet.
3 Select two recipes containing meat or fish and show how they could be adapted for vegetarians.

Animal welfare

Freedom foods

The RSPCA (Royal Society for the Prevention of Cruelty to Animals) has set up a welfare scheme for farm animals, to promote the humane treatment of animals which are to be reared and slaughtered for human consumption. It is based on five basic freedoms which they believe all farm animals should enjoy.

freedom from fear and distress

freedom from pain, injury, and disease

freedom from hunger and thirst

freedom from discomfort

freedom to express normal behaviour

Farmers who take part in the scheme are inspected regularly to make sure that their animals are kept in accordance with these strict regulations. Food produced from animals kept in this way may carry the 'Freedom Food' label. For example, Freedom Food *pigs* must have room to follow their instinct to root about, and must not be tied to one spot. Freedom Food *chickens* must have space to move around. Freedom Food animals on their way to market are not subjected to journeys over 8 hours long.

If you read the labels on meat or eggs you will be able to look for the Freedom Food mark. The food may cost a little more but you may feel it is worth paying.

Chicken and egg production

Illustrations in children's story books usually show hens and chickens wandering around outside in a farmyard, foraging on the ground for food, with a clean straw nest to lay their eggs in. But hens are only rarely kept in such ideal conditions. The reality of hen and egg production is very different.

Most eggs in the UK are produced by 'intensive systems'. This includes eggs sold at market stalls and farm shops as well as in supermarkets. Intensive systems produce eggs cheaply, so that they can be sold at the lowest possible price.

Battery hens

A lot of people are concerned about the conditions that battery hens are kept in. They live in battery cages, usually with four hens per cage. Each hen has an area about the size of this page. Although they must be properly fed, watered, and protected from injury, they are kept in artificial light, never go outside, and cannot forage or move around.

In spite of this they are often sold in boxes with labels such as 'Country Farm Eggs' or 'Fresh Farm Eggs', which give us the false impression that they have come from the story book farm.

Colony systems: barn eggs and free range eggs

In these commercial ways of producing eggs, the hens are not kept in cages but in colonies in large barns. The eggs cost a little more to allow for the better conditions the hens live in. In both barn and free range systems the birds spend most of their time in barns, but free range hens have access to the outside

during the daytime. The space outside must be covered with vegetation, be actively managed, and have no more than 1,000 birds per hectare. Though still not like the old fashioned farm yard, these conditions are better for the hens.

Freedom Food labelled eggs come from producers who keep their hens in conditions above the minimum standards set by the UK and the EU. The RSPCA ensures that the hens are looked after by knowledgeable farmers; that their barns are kept ventilated and at the right temperature; and that they have constant fresh food, water, and access to perches and quiet nest boxes. They must be able to follow their natural behaviour which is to forage, peck and scratch the ground, preen and stretch their wings, and bathe in the dust. They also have more space than the minimum. You will see Freedom Food eggs in supermarkets.

Organic foods

Organic foods are those which have been grown without artificial fertilizers or pesticides and in a way which reduces damage to the environment and to wildlife. Some people prefer to eat only organic foods as far as possible even though they cost more.

The use of the word 'organic' to describe foods is strictly controlled to ensure that standards are kept and that false claims are not made. The principles which must be followed include:

● working with natural systems rather than trying to control them artificially;
● encouraging the natural biological cycles of micro-organisms, soil flora and fauna, plants, and animals;
● keeping existing features of the landscape such as woodlands, hedges, ponds, and habitats for wildlife, especially endangered species;
● keeping animals for meat in a way which reduces their need for medicines and other chemical treatments and which carefully considers their welfare;
● avoiding pollution;
● considering the wider social and ecological effects of farming methods.

QUESTIONS

1 What are the five basic freedoms for animals which the RSPCA encourages?
2 How do the lives of battery hens and free range hens compare?
3 What do we mean by 'organic foods'?
4 Would you be prepared to pay the extra cost for Freedom Foods and organic foods? Why do some people prefer them?

Using the oven

To achieve good results when you are cooking it is important to know how to use the oven properly. Many people spoil the dishes they have prepared by not cooking them correctly. If, when you are baking, the oven is too hot or too cold, or the shelf is too high or too low, or the baking tray is too big, then the results can be very disappointing. All of the following points are important if you are to use the oven successfully.

Pre-heating the oven

Pre-heating the oven means bringing it up to the right temperature before you put the dish into the oven. To pre-heat a gas oven you light it about ten minutes before you want to use it. To pre-heat an electric oven you switch it on about fifteen minutes before you want to use it, or about five minutes if you have an electric fan oven. Many electric ovens have a small light on the control panel which comes on when you switch the oven on. When the oven has reached the temperature you have set, the light goes off. You should check to see whether the electric oven you use works like this.

    The oven does not need to be pre-heated for dishes like casseroles, stews, or milk puddings. But for good results with most cakes, pastry, and yeast recipes, you should pre-heat the oven.

The position of the shelf in the oven

You should always put the shelf in the right position for the dish you are making *before* you switch on the oven. It is much easier and safer to move the shelves when they are cold.

    In an electric oven the temperature is fairly even. But in a gas oven the top is hotter and the bottom is cooler than the centre. So if you set the oven to gas mark 5, you will find that the temperature on the top shelf is equal to about gas mark 6 and the temperature on the lower shelf is equal to about gas mark 4.

    Sometimes this can be useful as it means you can cook dishes needing different oven temperatures at the same time. On the other hand if you were cooking, for example, three pies, the one on the top shelf would be cooked before the one in the centre, and the one on the lower shelf would take longer.

Baking trays

The size of the baking tray you use can also affect your cooking. You should never use a baking tray larger than the one which was provided with the cooker. If you do, you will find that dishes bake unevenly. For example, scones and biscuits on the edges of the tray may burn quickly, before those in the centre are even cooked. You must never let baking trays touch the sides of the oven. There should be a space of about 5 cm all round the edge of the tray, so that the heat can circulate and the food can be evenly browned.

The trays or tins should be placed in the centre of the shelf. Their exact position will depend on the shape of the shelf and the position of the heating elements or gas burners.

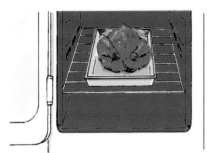
Electric oven

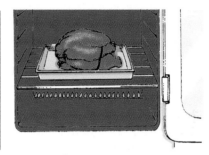
Gas oven

Varying temperatures in different ovens

When you are using different ovens for baking in school, you may find that the oven temperatures seem to vary, even though they are set at the same gas mark or temperature. Some ovens can be 'hot' and will brown food too quickly before it is cooked. Other ovens are 'slow' and can take too long to cook, resulting in spoiled food. So it is a good idea to become familiar with the oven you use most of the time at school. Then if you know that your oven tends to be hot (usually gas ovens), you could cook certain items on a lower shelf than the recipe says. If you know that the oven is 'slow', you could set the temperature higher than the recipe says. You may well find that this produces much better results when you are cooking.

QUESTIONS

1 How can careless use of the oven spoil a dish that you are making?
2 Name three recipes in this book for which (a) it is necessary to pre-heat the oven, (b) pre-heating the oven is not essential.
3 When is the best time to put the oven shelf in the correct position? Why?
4 Which part of a gas oven is hottest?
5 You want to cook these dishes in the oven at the same time: Swiss roll (Gas 6), ginger biscuits (Gas 4), and apple crumble (Gas 5). What gas mark would you turn the oven to and how would you arrange the dishes on the shelves?
6 Describe what might happen if you use a baking tray which is too large for your oven.

Cooking with a microwave oven

Microwave ovens are becoming more widely used all the time. In most homes they are used as much for defrosting and heating already cooked frozen dishes as for actually cooking foods. They are very quick; you can thaw frozen food and heat it through in minutes instead of hours. For example, a frozen bread bun may be thawed and ready to eat in less than a minute. A frozen cooked casserole may be defrosted and heated through in perhaps 10 or 15 minutes. Because a microwave oven is so quick, it is much cheaper on fuel than a gas or electric oven, which needs to be put on for 30 minutes to heat a dish through.

A microwave oven is ideal if you have a freezer. It means you can keep a store of food in the freezer and have it hot and ready to eat quickly when you want it.

It is useful where members of the household come home for meals at different times of day. It is also useful in households of only one or two people. You can cook a meal following the usual size recipe, which is normally for about three or four people. Then you can eat one portion, divide the rest into separate portions, cover and freeze them, and they are ready to defrost and eat another day.

A microwave oven stays much cleaner in use than an ordinary gas or electric oven. Food does not burn on or stick to the oven surfaces, which are easily kept clean by wiping with a damp cloth. Also, the dishes are easier to wash than saucepans used on top of a cooker or in an ordinary oven, as food does not dry out or stick to the dish.

Suitable containers

You must not use metal dishes, foil, or foil dishes in a microwave oven as this may damage the cooker. Apart from these, use any dishes: pottery, china, polythene, or just stand the food on kitchen paper. You can buy special plastic microwave dishes which are cheap and versatile as the food may be cooked and frozen in the same container. Some kinds can also be used in an ordinary gas or electric oven up to a certain temperature. If you are making cakes in the microwave oven, these dishes are especially useful as they are available in the shape of traditional cake tins, which of course *must not* be used in the microwave oven.

Microwave cooking dishes

kitchen paper

Pyrex measuring jug

casserole

clay flower pot

microwave-suitable spoon

plastic ring mould

Foods which are being heated or cooked should usually be covered during cooking. You can use a plate, kitchen paper, or cling film for this. Always use 'food safe' cling film when heating food. It is thought that the chemicals which give ordinary cling film its clinging qualities may be absorbed by the food when it is closely wrapped and heated in the film.

Uses for the microwave oven

Heating pre-cooked food from frozen or cold.
Baking a potato for a quick snack.
Cooking frozen vegetables in a little water, saving flavour and vitamins.
Making white sauce and custard.
Cooking sponge puddings and dark coloured cakes like chocolate cake or
   gingerbread.
Softening butter.
Melting jelly cubes or ingredients for cakes made by the melting method.
Stewing fruit.

Browning food

Food does not become brown and crisp in a microwave oven so some foods such as bacon, chicken, and sausages can look pale and unappetizing. This can be overcome by using a browning dish (quite expensive to buy). The dish is pre-heated in the microwave oven and food that is cooked on it becomes golden brown. Some more expensive models have a built in browning device similar to a grill. Cakes baked in a microwave oven do not become golden brown so recipes which include some dark ingredients such as cocoa, brown sugar, or ginger look the most appetizing.

Choosing a microwave oven

Compare the cost and features of different models. More expensive models may have electronic controls, a temperature probe to see if meat is thoroughly cooked, automatic timers to start cooking if you are out, memory banks to store programs for recipes you use regularly. If you are unlikely to use these features often it may not be worth paying extra for them. Read *Which?* magazine at your library (see p. 62) to help you choose.

QUESTIONS

1   How can a microwave oven be used to save fuel when cooking?
2   How could a microwave oven be useful to a single person out at work all day?
3   Describe three ways in which a family could find a microwave oven useful.
4   Describe two ways in which you could overcome the problem of the microwave cooker not browning food.
5   What sort of dishes (a) are safe to use (b) should never be used in the microwave oven?
6   What features could you expect to find on the most expensive models?

Weighing and measuring

For good results in most recipes, accurate weighing and measuring is essential. It does not make much difference whether you put two onions into a stew instead of one, or whether you put an extra apple into an apple pie. But when you are baking with flour, sugar, and liquids, making cakes, pastry, and so on, you must measure carefully or your cooking will be spoiled. For example, if you do not add enough flour to a cake, or if you add too much sugar or baking powder, the results can be disastrous.

All the recipes in this book give quantities in metric weights (grams). Some recipe books give both metric weights and imperial weights (pounds and ounces). You must stick to *either* metric *or* imperial. For example, if a bread recipe says 250 g/½ lb flour, 125 ml/¼ pt water, you should not weigh out 250 g of flour and then measure a quarter of a pint of water to mix with it, or your dough will be too dry and the bread could be spoiled. So always use either all metric or all imperial measurements and never mix the two.

Kitchen scales

This is the usual type of scales. They can weigh up to 5 kg. In practice, however, it is more useful to have scales which help you weigh smaller quantities more easily.

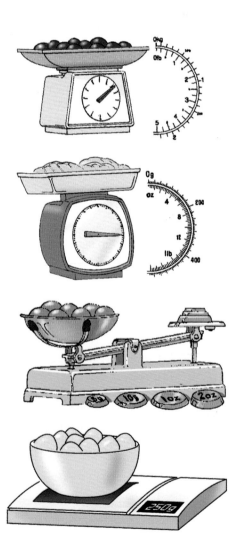

These scales will weigh small quantities, such as 5 g, accurately. It is much easier to be accurate with these scales than with the more usual kind shown above, as there is much more room on the face to show the marking. They are often called 'diet' scales.

These scales are reliable and accurate, once you know how to use them. If you have both a metric and an imperial set of weights then it is easy to use either kind of recipe.

Electronic scales are very accurate. They are often used in shops, where they are set to work out prices as well as weigh goods.

Measuring cups and jugs

Measuring cups are very useful. They are much cheaper than scales and less easily damaged. The quantities corresponding to the weights of most everyday ingredients, such as flour, sugar, currants, and rice, are marked on the inside. These cups are very easy to use. They cannot be used to weigh lard or margarine, but it is quite easy to divide blocks or tubs of these into 50 g portions.

A measuring jug is needed for liquids. A jug which is marked in ml (millilitres) on one side and pints and fluid ounces on the other, is the most useful kind to have.

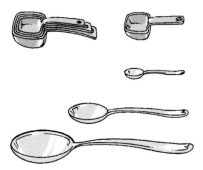

You can also buy metric measuring spoons quite cheaply.

A level teaspoon holds 5 ml.

A level dessertspoon holds 10 ml.

A level tablespoon holds 15 ml.

QUESTIONS

1   Why is it important to measure very accurately when you are baking?
2   Explain why imperial and metric quantities should never be mixed when following recipes.
3   What basic equipment is essential before you can cook using metric weights and measurements?
4   Describe and draw (a) the kind of weighing scales you would like to have at home, and (b) a measuring cup.
5   How much would you expect a level teaspoon, dessertspoon, and tablespoon to hold?

Basic kitchen equipment 1

Cook's knife – a large knife for cutting and chopping meat, vegetables, etc.

Vegetable knife – a small knife for preparing fruit and vegetables.

Palette knife – used for lifting biscuits, scones, and so on from a baking tray.

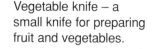

Whisks of different types.

Pastry brush – for brushing pastry with egg and milk before baking, or for greasing tins.

Spatula – for scraping all the mixture from a bowl.

Fish slice – for lifting larger items from a frying pan or baking tray.

Sieve – can be made of nylon, or metal, which is stronger. Clean with a brush.

Colander – for draining vegetables or pasta.

Grater – with different sized cutting surfaces. Metal is best as it is sharpest. Clean with a brush and dry well to avoid rusting.

Flour dredger – for dusting the work surface with a little flour when rolling out pastry, biscuits, and so on.

Pastry cutters – can be plain or fluted. You can also get fancy shapes like gingerbread men, animals, or stars.

Mixing bowl – for all general mixing jobs.

Pudding basins – are available in different sizes. They are used for steaming puddings, etc.

Wire cooling tray – for cooling cakes, bread, biscuits, scones, and so on.

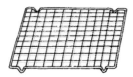

Cake tins and baking tins

Many tins can now be bought with a non-stick finish, but they are more expensive. Non-stick cake tins still have to be greased before they are used. It is usually better to line them with greaseproof paper too, to ensure that the cakes come out of the tin easily. Non-stick tins are easy to wash and dry and they do not go rusty. They must be washed carefully with a soft cloth and must never be scratched with any metal spoon or utensil. Never use a harsh pan cleaner on them, or the non-stick coating will be spoiled.

Cake tins may be round or square. Some have a loose bottom for easy removal of the cake.

Sandwich cake tins are shallower, for cakes which are to be sandwiched together.

Loaf tins are usually made in two sizes, large and small.

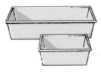

Bun tin, or patty tin, for small cakes and tarts.

Swiss roll tin, for Swiss roll or general use.

Baking tray or sheet for general use.

Roasting tin, for roasting meat.

Yorkshire pudding tins.

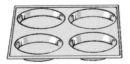

Pie plates. Metal plates give the crispest pastry.

Sponge flan tins. They need to be very carefully greased before use.

Flan rings, plain for savoury flans, fluted for sweet flans.

Deep pie dish, for meat or fruit pies with a pastry lid.

QUESTIONS

1 Name and draw three pieces of kitchen equipment which would be useful when you are preparing, cooking, or serving (a) vegetables, (b) scones, (c) cakes, and (d) meat.
2 How would you clean (a) a grater that has been used for cheese, (b) a sieve that has been used for flour, (c) a pastry brush that has been used to grease a tin?
3 What are the advantages and disadvantages of non-stick tins?
4 Name the type of tin you would use to cook each of the following:
a fruit loaf, some cheese scones, a Christmas cake, a Victoria sandwich cake, an apple pie, some roast potatoes, some sweet mince tarts.

Basic kitchen equipment 2

Different types of pans

When you are choosing pans, remember that they get a lot of heavy use. You would expect them to last for many years, so choose carefully. Remember:

1 Heavier pans will last longer and spread heat more evenly, but they should not be too heavy to lift easily.
2 Handles should be heat-resistant and firmly fixed.
3 Lids should fit well.
4 Pans for electric cookers should have a heavy base.

Aluminium pans are very widely used and available in different thicknesses. If they are fairly heavy, they will be strong and hard-wearing. They are easy to clean and reasonably priced.

Vitreous enamel on steel pans often have very attractive patterns and are made in different colours, but they need more care in use than aluminium pans. You cannot use metal utensils in them, nor can you use scouring powder or steel wool to clean them, or they may become scratched.

Stainless steel is very expensive, but it is hard and strong. Stainless steel pans are not really stainless, as if they are not carefully dried after use they will become marked. These pans tend to be thin because of the high cost of stainless steel, so they often have a heavy base added, to spread heat evenly.

A non-stick finish is available on many pans. It makes them easier to clean, but you must be very careful to avoid scratching. Never use metal utensils or pan cleaners in them. They should just be washed in hot, soapy water.

Saucepans, in different sizes. They should have well-fitting lids.

Milk pans have slanted sides or a lip for easy pouring.

Frying pans should be fairly heavy, so that food does not stick easily.

Deep fat pan. This has a basket so that food can be easily removed.

Omelette pan. This has curved edges.

Pancake pan. This is about 15 cm in diameter.

Double pan, for cooking food gently over water, e.g. lemon curd, porridge, egg custard.

Steamer. This has a lid and will fit over most sizes of pan for steaming puddings or other food.

Jam pan. This is heavy, large, and wide, ideal for jam, marmalade, and chutney.

Disposable paper and plastic products

Kitchen paper, usually sold on a roll. It can be used for many different purposes, such as mopping up spills, wiping fat from greasy pans before washing them, and draining fried foods.

Greaseproof paper, for lining cake tins. When you are cutting paper to shape to line a tin, it is useful to cut several layers at the same time, so that you have a ready supply for the next time you bake.

Kitchen foil is used for wrapping meat before roasting it, to keep the meat moist and to avoid splashing the oven. Foil is also used for wrapping food to keep it fresh, or before freezing it. It can be used to cover food when you reheat it in the oven, to prevent it from drying out.

Cling film or wrap is used to cover food to prevent it from drying out. It will stick to most dishes, and can also be used to wrap packed meals. Some cling films must not be used to wrap fatty foods (e.g. cheese, meat) as they contain harmful chemicals which are absorbed into the fat. For the same reason, most cling films must not be used to cover foods in a microwave oven, as chemicals may pass in to the hot food. Cover food with a plate or lid instead. If you do use cling film, read the directions carefully to make sure you use the right kind.

Polythene bags can be bought in different sizes and thicknesses. They are useful for wrapping food to keep it fresh, and for keeping bread dough moist while it rises. Thicker polythene bags can be used for wrapping food before it is frozen; thinner bags are not suitable.

QUESTIONS

1   What points must you consider when choosing saucepans?
2   Give the advantages and disadvantages of (a) aluminium pans, (b) vitreous enamel on steel pans, (c) stainless steel pans, (d) non-stick pans.
3   Arrange the nine types of pan named opposite in the order in which you think they would be most useful in a kitchen.
4   If you could afford to use only three of the paper or plastic products on this page, which would you choose and why?

Choosing equipment

Choosing equipment

When you are thinking of buying any equipment, you need to consider several points if you are to end up with something that suits your needs at a price you can afford. The most expensive is not necessarily the best: it may cost more because it has features you would not use. If you are going to use something often it needs to be strong and well made, and must not be too difficult to clean or too complicated to use easily. It must be the right size for your needs and must fit into the space you have available.

The Consumers' Association

This independent association provides consumers with information and advice, so that they can make informed decisions when it comes to choosing what to buy. The organization publishes a magazine called *Which?*, which you can read in your local library or by taking out a subscription.

If you decide you want to buy, for example, a food processor, they give detailed information on the models available in the shops, and their good and bad points. They get this information by buying them in the usual way and testing them carefully. They usually recommend 'best buys' and can save you from making expensive mistakes. They test for value for money, safety, durability, reliability, ease of use, and after sales service.

They report not only on household equipment but on such varied issues as cars, saving schemes, washing powders, and funeral services. The example opposite comes from their report on microwave ovens. Look at the report and answer the questions below.

QUESTIONS

1 Is the Best Buy the cheapest of the microwave ovens?
2 Which will take up least space on a kitchen worktop?
3 Which is the least powerful oven?
4 Which has the most usable room inside?
5 Which model can a child not switch on accidentally?
6 What does this symbol ☆ mean?
7 Which model reheats most evenly?
8 Which models have most drawbacks?
9 Which model has the best view of the inside of the oven?
10 Explain exactly why the Matsui M162 TC is the best buy.
11 How do the test scores on the other models compare with the Matsui?
12 Is the Matsui widely available in different stores?

Microwave ovens without grill		Daewoo New Cooking KOR-6105	Goldstar MS-1715E	Hinari Lifestyle MX416TC	Matsui M162 TC	Panasonic NN-3454
Specification						
Price (£)	1▷	90	100	87	90	*130*
Country of origin		France	UK	France	UK	UK
Dimensions (hxwxd) cm	2▷	28x47x36	26x47x34	26x47x36	25x48x34	30x46x33
Usable volume (litres)	3▷	12	10	13	11	12
Stated power (watts)		800	800	750	800	800
Features						
Digital timer	4▷			✓	✓	✓
Automatic programs	5▷			✓	✓	✓
Boost/quick power function	6▷				✓	
Programming in stages	7▷			✓	✓	✓
Child lock	8▷				✓	
Grill-only option						
Grill/microwave						
Performance						
Manual defrosting	9▷	☆	○		○	
Automatic defrosting	9▷			○	☆	○
Evenness of reheating	10▷	○	○	○	☆	○
Grill area						
Grill evenness						
Drawbacks						
No 'start' control	11▷	✗	✗			
Cleaning awkward				✗	✗	
Rotary controls awkward	12▷		✗			
Touchpads need firm pressure	13▷			✗		✗
Labels/controls hard to read	14▷	✗	✗	✗	✗	✗
Not easy to see inside oven		✗	✗	✗	✗	
Turntable difficult to handle						
Total test score		6	6	6	7	6
Info Additional notes/update since our tests		Similar model: KOR-610P with electronic controls £100	Similar model: MS-1705 with cosmetic differences £100	Similar model: MX707 with manual controls £69	Exclusive to Currys	

Total test score

This score, out of ten, takes into account all our test results. It ignores price and reliability, and gives more weight to the more important tests. These are:
Reheating: 40 per cent
Convenience: 30 per cent (20 per cent for those ovens with a grill)
Defrosting: 25 per cent
Grilling (where appropriate): 10 per cent
Ovens which had unacceptable reheating performance were further penalised, and have lower overall scores.

Key

★ = best
☆
○
◑ ↕
● = worst

✓ = Has this feature
✗ = Has this drawback

Notes

Microwave ovens highlighted in red appear in the Best Buy Guide, p. 13.

Specification

1 This is the price you should expect to pay by shopping around. For less widely-available models, we give manufacturers' guide prices in *italics*.

2 Figures are rounded up to the nearest centimetre. You need to leave a few extra centimetres air clearance all round.

3 Our measurements are usually smaller than those claimed by manufacturers, as they're based on the maximum size of plate or container that will rotate inside the oven, rather than the total interior volume.

Features

4 Digital timers can be set more accurately than manual rotary timers.

5 Automatic programs – like options to defrost or reheat particular types of food –

may look useful, but our tests show they don't always work properly. See 'Too much automation', p12, for more details.

6 A short blast of high power suitable for heating liquids.

7 This allows you to defrost something and cook it without having to reset the oven.

8 This prevents a child being able to operate the oven in your absence.

Performance

9 We defrosted a 500g block of minced beef to see how evenly manual and automatic programs defrosted, without starting to cook the food. Where there is no rating, the function was not possible.
★ = all parts of food less than 5°C
◑ = some parts more than 20°C
● = some parts more than 30°C

10 Our tests simulated reheating a typical ready-meal, like lasagne. No oven excelled but those with a ☆ rating were the most even. The ovens which scored a ◑ or ●

had temperature differences between the warmest and coldest parts of the food of at least 32°C.

Drawbacks

11 These ovens start operating as soon as the door is shut, even if you take food out before the time is up. This is not only annoying, but you could accidently leave it running with nothing inside.

12 For people with poor dexterity or grip problems, rotary controls need to be easy to grip. They should feel positive, without being stiff.

13 Small touchpads, or closely laid-out control panels can be a problem for those with dexterity problems, particularly if the switch underlying the fascia is hard to operate.

14 We checked whether the controls, labelling or digital read-outs are easily distinguishable to people with poor eyesight.

Pressure cookers and deep fat fryers

Pressure cookers

The pressure cooker works on the principle that when the pressure inside the pan is increased by preventing the escape of steam, a higher temperature is produced which cooks food in a shorter time.

Advantages of having a pressure cooker

1 Food can be cooked very quickly, in one-quarter to one-third of the usual cooking time. For example, a stew which would normally take hours can be cooked in about twenty-five minutes, and potatoes can be cooked in six minutes.
2 Fuel can be saved, because food takes less time to cook and several foods can be cooked in the pan at the same time (for example, meat, potatoes, and other vegetables).
3 It is particularly useful for foods which would normally take a long time to cook, for example, soups or stews containing dried pulses (peas, beans, lentils); cheaper, tougher, cuts of meat; joints of bacon or ham; steamed puddings.
4 The nutritive value of food is high. Vegetables are cooked in steam rather than water, so there is a smaller loss of vitamins into the water.
5 The cooker can be used for different jobs, like bottling fruit and vegetables to preserve them, sterilizing babies' bottles, making jam and marmalade, and making baby foods.

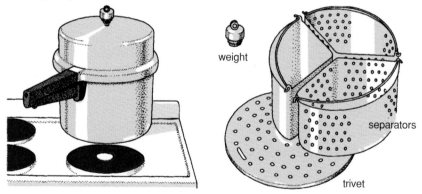

weight

separators

trivet

How to use a pressure cooker

1 Study and follow the instruction book carefully.
2 Do not overfill. The pressure cooker should be no more than half-full for liquids, two-thirds for solids.
3 Put the food in the cooker, put the lid on, and add the weight (the weight you use will vary according to the recipe you are using). Place the cooker over a high heat until it hisses loudly. Start to time the food. Turn the heat down so that the cooker just keeps up a steady hiss.
4 Time the food carefully. Do not overcook it.
5 Cool the cooker either by leaving it for five to ten minutes or by running cold water from the tap over the cooker. The method you choose depends on the food in the cooker (see the recipes).
6 When the hissing stops, remove the weight and the lid.

Suitable recipes

There are many suggestions for recipes in the instruction booklet which comes with the pressure cooker. Here are a few suggestions:

Soups

The cooker is ideal for making soups. If you thicken the soup with blended flour and milk or water, add it after the soup is cooked.

Meat

Suitable for cooking beef or chicken casserole, minced beef, chilli con carne, chicken or beef curry, or the meat for mince pie. Always thicken the gravy with blended flour and water after the meat is cooked rather than before.

Vegetables

Timing is very important. As they cook so quickly, vegetables can easily become overcooked. Follow the instructions carefully.

Puddings

The pressure cooker is very useful for reducing the cooking time of steamed puddings, especially Christmas puddings. See the recipes for steamed sponge puddings for instructions. Rice pudding is delicious when cooked in a pressure cooker, and cooks much more quickly than usual (see recipe).

Jam and marmalade

The pressure cooker will cook the fruit quickly before the sugar is added (see the recipes). Once the sugar has been added the jam is boiled without the lid on. As the pressure cooker is thick and heavy, it is ideal for making jam.

Deep fat fryers

There are many different models of electric deep fat fryer. They are safer than traditional 'chip pans', and have these advantages.

1 They have thermostatic control so do not overheat.
2 They are less likely to spill or get knocked over.
3 They often have 'coolwalls' so are not hot to touch.
4 When used with the lid closed they reduce the spread of cooking smells. Some have lids which lock during cooking.
5 You can set the temperature control on most models to get the best cooking results for different foods.

Some disadvantages

1 They may encourage you to eat fried foods too often which is bad for health.
2 They take up space on your kitchen bench.
3 Like traditional chip pans, they can become messy, and the oil needs to be changed at intervals, which is a messy job to carry out.
4 The filters have to be changed at intervals.

For more on deep fat fryers, see pp. 74–75.

Mixers and blenders

Mixers

Mixers can be bought in different sizes, ranging from a small, hand-held mixer to a large, powerful model with its own bowl and stand and a range of attachments.

Hand-held mixer   *Larger mixer with bowl and stand*

A small model is sufficient for most cookery jobs. It can be attached to the wall in a convenient place in the kitchen so that it is always ready for use. It can be used directly in a pan to mix a sauce or to cream boiled potatoes. It is the best kind for whipping small amounts of cream or egg whites.

The largest models are very powerful. They should be kept out on the kitchen work bench so that they do not have to be lifted in and out of a cupboard before they can be used. These large mixers are very useful if you do a lot of cooking for a large family or if you cook in large quantities for a freezer. The wide range of attachments you can buy as extras include:

Dough hook Extremely useful for taking the heavy work out of yeast cookery. They knead dough efficiently and thoroughly, giving very good results.

Slicer and shredder This will slice and shred vegetables for soups, salads, coleslaw, and potato crisps, or oranges for marmalade. It will shred cheese, nuts, or chocolate finely and quickly.

You can also buy mincers for meat or marmalade, juice extractors, bean slicers, coffee-grinders, and tin-openers. Whether or not these are useful depends on how often you use them. You have to be prepared to spend time putting them together, taking them to pieces, washing and drying them, and putting them away.

Jobs that can be done with a mixer include:

1 creaming fat and sugar,
2 whisking eggs and sugar for sponges,
3 whipping cream,
4 whisking egg whites,
5 mixing a sauce or batter,
6 rubbing fat into flour. (Some mixers do this more efficiently than others. It is often simpler and better to rub in by hand.)

Recipes made with the help of a mixer

Creaming – cakes, biscuits, puddings. Whisking – Swiss roll, whisked sponge cake and other sponge mixtures, jelly whip. Rubbing-in – (only if your mixer will do this satisfactorily) shortcrust pastry, crumble, rock cakes, fruit cakes, scones.

Blenders or liquidizers

Blenders are very useful. You can buy one as a separate piece of equipment or as an attachment to a mixer.

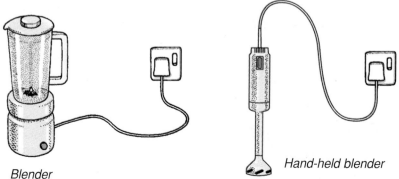

Blender

Hand-held blender

Hand-held blenders are very good for making a purée from soup. You simply hold the blender in the pan, so you do not have to pour the soup from the pan into the blender, which can be messy. They are easy to use and to clean. You can use them to whip cream and egg whites as well, but they are not very good for this.

Blenders can be used for many jobs, including:

1   making a smooth purée from fruit or vegetables, e.g. stewed apple,
2   making a purée from soup, instead of sieving it,
3   making a purée suitable for baby food,
4   blending cooked fruit and custard for a fruit fool,
5   making crumbs from fresh or dried bread, cake, or biscuits,
6   chopping nuts or chocolate,
7   making granulated sugar finer, like caster sugar,
8   making pâté,
9   making batter for Yorkshire pudding or pancakes,
10 making mayonnaise.

Blenders vary according to their size and the power of the motor. When using a blender follow these guidelines:

1   Always follow the manufacturer's instructions for your particular model.
2   Do not run for longer than recommended, or the motor may burn out.
3   Run at the correct speed.
4   Small blenders may not chop dry food very well.
5   Wash by filling with hot, soapy water, run for a few seconds, rinse and dry.
6   Do not overfill.
7   When blending large amounts of a thick mixture like pâté, you may need to switch off a couple of times while blending, to push the mixture down on to the blades.

Recipes made with the help of a blender

Soups, toad in the hole, mayonnaise, fruit fool. Breadcrumbs for stuffed tomatoes, burgers, apple charlotte, stuffing, cheese and lentil bake. Biscuit crumbs for lemon cheesecake.

Food processors and slow cookers

Food processors

A food processor can be used to carry out a wide range of food preparation tasks. It will beat, cream, rub fat into flour, knead, purée, chop, slice, mince, grate, extract juice, or liquidize, using one bowl and a metal or plastic blade, or a slicing or grating disc.

It does any of these jobs in seconds, a fraction of the time it takes to do them by hand. A food processor gives good results and is quicker to assemble and easier to clean than many of the attachments which are available for electric mixers to do these tasks. As it does a similar range of jobs to a large electric food mixer with a few attachments, it is probably a matter of personal choice as to which you would choose; one is not necessarily better than the other. A large mixer will generally hold more ingredients than a processor. For example, a large mixer with a dough hook will knead a full 2½ kg bag of flour, where a food processor may only knead up to 500 g of flour. If you do a lot of yeast cookery or if you often batch bake large quantities, this should be taken into consideration. If, however, you chop and slice a lot of vegetables, or prepare fruit for marmalade, then a food processor is probably simpler to use and clean than a mixer with an attachment.

Uses for the food processor

You can use it to help make many recipes. Here are some suggestions:

Batters for making Yorkshire pudding, pancakes, dropped scones, or any other kind of batter.

Biscuits Most biscuit mixtures, including shortbread, are easily and quickly mixed.

Bread dough and all other yeast mixtures, e.g. pizza, can be mixed and kneaded.

Breadcrumbs Use the metal disc to make fresh crumbs from brown or white bread. You can make a lot when you have left-over bread and store them in a polythene bag in the freezer, taking out the amount you want and leaving the rest frozen. It is useful to have crumbs ready for recipes such as cheese and lentil bake, apple charlotte, and fried fillets of fish. You can also use the processor to make crisp golden crumbs: bake bread or crusts in a low oven until golden brown, then process to fine crumbs. Cool, then keep in an airtight jar.

Cakes A food processor makes light cakes quickly and easily either by creaming fat and sugar or by rubbing fat into flour.

Cheese can be grated or processed with the metal blade until it is as fine as breadcrumbs.

Cream It is not recommended that you use a food processor to whip double cream as it can easily be overwhipped and spoiled. The same applies to whisking egg whites. Some manufacturers of food processors say that their machine can be used for these tasks. If this is the case, follow any instructions very carefully.

Flans You can make the pastry and chop, slice, or mix the filling.

Fruit You can purée raw or cooked fruit, e.g. for fruit fool.

Marmalade The metal blade is ideal for chopping oranges or lemons for marmalade, which is otherwise very time consuming.

Meat Fresh or cooked meat can be chopped or finely minced.

Nuts can be chopped or sliced.

Parsley, mint, or other herbs can be finely chopped. Make sure the bowl and blade are very dry. You can chop quite a lot of parsley and freeze some for use another time. Put the parsley into ice cube trays, add a small amount of water, and freeze. Store the ice cubes in a polythene bag and use them as you want them.

Pastry Use to rub the fat into the flour, then add liquid to make light, smooth pastry.

Pâté Mackerel pâté or meat pâtés are easy and quick to make in the processor.

Pizza Use to mix and knead the dough and to prepare and mix the fillings.

Sauces Use to mix sauces or to make a smooth creamy sauce from one which has gone lumpy.

Soup Chop, grate, or purée vegetables for soup, either before or after cooking.

Vegetables can be chopped or sliced in the processor, e.g. potatoes, carrots, or courgettes can be sliced, and cabbage, onion, and carrots grated for coleslaw.

Slow cookers

These are large, well-insulated pans which can be plugged in, switched on, and left to cook slowly all day. You could start a stew cooking in the morning, go out, and return to a hot, well-cooked meal. The cooker is well sealed to keep in moisture and flavour and is ideal for the long, slow cooking of inexpensive, tougher cuts of meat. It is quite economical, using only about the same amount of electricity as a light bulb.

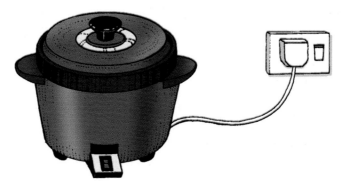

Cooking methods 1

Although many foods, particularly fruit and vegetables, are good to eat raw, most of the food we eat is cooked. We cook it for several reasons.

1   The heat during cooking kills any bacteria which may be harmful to us.
2   Cooking makes food easier to digest. We could not eat raw flour, rice, or potatoes.
3   Food often looks and tastes more pleasant when it is cooked.
4   Cooked meals can be more varied and appetizing than raw foods, especially in cold weather.
5   Sometimes we cook food to preserve it, that is, to make it keep longer. For example, we preserve fruit when we cook it with sugar to make jam or marmalade.

We use several different methods for cooking food. They include stewing, boiling, steaming, roasting, baking, grilling, and frying. The method we choose depends on the kind of food we are cooking and on the kind of results we want.

Stewing

Stewing is a moist method of cooking, which means that the food is cooked in liquid. It is mainly used for meat and vegetables. They can be stewed either in a saucepan with a close-fitting lid on top of the cooker, or in a covered casserole in the oven.

Because it is a long, slow process, stewing is suitable for tougher, cheaper cuts of meat, which can be made tender and appetizing. During the long, slow cooking the juices and flavour from the meat and vegetables enter the liquid, so producing a very well-flavoured gravy.

   Stewing is quite an economical way of cooking, for several reasons. You can use cheaper cuts of meat and can add plenty of vegetables or pulses to make the meat go further. The food is cooked on a very low heat so that it is just simmering. Stews are easy to prepare and the food will 'look after itself' once it is cooking.

   A slow cooker (see p. 69) is ideal for making well-flavoured stews and casseroles.

the inside is cooked. The most reliable way of checking that the fat is at the right heat is to use a special thermometer. But as a rough guide, a small piece of bread dropped into the fat should turn a pale golden brown in about 30 seconds. Sometimes a faint haze over the fat shows it is ready. But as some modern fats do not haze, this is not always a reliable guide.

Take care when frying

Be extremely careful when using a deep-fat fryer or chip pan. The fat can become very hot and dangerous. If it is heated to a very high temperature it will burst into flames. Many fires in homes have been started by chip pans. You should never go away and leave the pan unattended. If the door bell or the phone rings, turn the heat off under the pan before you answer it. It is easy to forget about the pan once you start to talk to someone, and this is how fires start.

If the pan does catch fire, cover it with the pan lid, a baking sheet, or a thick towel which is very slightly damp. *Never* throw water on to it and *never* try to move a burning pan.

Ideally, you should keep a small fire extinguisher or fire-blanket in the kitchen. They are not very expensive and will put out a fire quickly and efficiently.

Rules for frying successfully

1 Never fill the pan more than two-thirds full. Lower food into it very gently.
2 Keep water away from hot fat or it may spit and burn you.
3 Do not try to cook large amounts of fried food at once. The fat will become too cool for good results and the pan may become dangerously full.
4 Use clean oil. Do not let it overheat and burn.
5 Drain fried food on absorbent kitchen paper before serving it, to remove any excess fat.
6 Strain the oil after use, using muslin or a fine metal strainer. This will remove crumbs and particles of food which could otherwise cause the fat to decompose.

Suitable foods for frying include the more expensive, tender cuts of meat: beef – rump, fillet, or sirloin steak; pork and lamb – chops or cutlets. Tougher meat can never be made tender by frying. Sausages, bacon, fish, liver, and chicken portions can all be fried.

Recipes which involve frying include fish cakes, burgers, chilladas, samosas, chapattis, and pancakes. In many stews and casseroles, too, the meat and vegetables are lightly fried before cooking in order to develop the flavour.

QUESTIONS

1 Why is frying a popular method of cooking?
2 Give an alternative method of cooking these foods instead of frying them: eggs, bacon, fish fingers, sausages, chops.
3 Why do most foods except potatoes have a coating added before being deep-fried?
4 How would you know when oil was hot enough for frying?
5 Chip pans which overheat are a frequent cause of fires in kitchens. What precautions would you always take when using a chip pan?
6 If the fat you used for frying chips was rather burnt and full of particles of food, what results do you think you would have?

The cost of food

The price of food is one of the main factors which affects the food we choose. Buying food can be one of the highest expenses in a family budget, and where money is limited it can take a lot of skill and careful shopping to get the best value.

Shopping

If you are fortunate enough to have enough money, a car to carry your shopping home, and a fridge and freezer to store food in, it is quite easy to buy food cheaply. If you have a limited income, have to carry all your food home (perhaps with a couple of small children and a pushchair), and have no freezer and a small fridge, it is not so easy to shop cheaply.

Supermarkets

A large supermarket is often the cheapest place to shop, with the widest range of foods to choose from. The national chains such as Tesco, Asda, Sainsburys, and Morrisons compete with each other for customers all the time, which helps to improve the services they offer and to keep prices down.

They often have bulk packs and larger sizes which work out quite a lot cheaper, but you can only take advantage of these if you have plenty of cupboard

space for storage, a large fridge and freezer, and money to spare at the time you buy them. This can be particularly difficult for a single person, and so buying food for a single person nearly always costs more weight for weight. About 26% of British households have only one person in them.

Some supermarkets put a label with the price per 100 g next to the price of the packet or can, so you can see at a glance which size works out cheapest. Without this information it would be hard to work out which is the best buy without a calculator.

They sell their 'own label' brands, and often an even cheaper range of everyday foods (such as 'Safeway Savers' or Tesco 'Basics'). It is often hard to tell the difference between these and the well known names which are a lot more expensive. The largest stores may have a café, crèche, public toilets, bank, dry cleaners, easy parking, and cheap petrol, as well as the usual range of goods.

Other supermarkets such as Netto, Kwik-Save, and Aldi try to provide food at the very lowest price possible. They do not have such a wide choice, are not so carefully laid out, and do not have as many trained staff to help the customers. However, they are hard to beat for low prices on a wide range of basic foods.

Markets

Markets are another source of cheap, fresh foods, especially fruit, vegetables, and meat. Prices are good and food usually fresh, though with fruit and vegetables you may have to check that the fruit and vegetables you get are as good as those on display.

Dry foods stores

These sell a variety of dry foods such as cornflakes, dried fruit, nuts, and coffee. The foods are displayed in large tubs and you serve yourself with a scoop to just as much as you want. Because money is not spent on packaging materials (boxes, packets, and jars) nor on advertising the brand name, food bought like this costs less, and you can buy just the amount you need.

Smaller shops

Smaller shops have a difficult time competing with supermarkets, and many have closed down in recent years. They cannot often compete on price, but they are still used because they are near where people live so you do not need a car or bus trip to get there. They are often 'open all hours', although supermarkets too are extending their opening hours. You can go in and out of a small shop quickly, and don't have to walk all the way round and then queue at a checkout if you are in a hurry.

Many small independent shops have joined a group such as *Spar* or *VG* which helps them buy and therefore sell goods more cheaply than they otherwise could. Other small food shops which survive and do well are those which specialize in one kind of food, for example greengrocers, bakers, specialist cheese shops.

Take-away food shops

These include Indian and Chinese take-aways, and kebab, pizza, fish and chip, and sandwich shops. Take-away meals can be convenient and appetizing. Although they are not cheap, they take no time to prepare and cook, and cost you nothing in fuel.

QUESTIONS

1 It is easier to buy food cheaply if you have more money. Explain why this is.
2 Suggest five ways of buying food more cheaply.
3 Why are corner shops still popular even though they cost more?
4 Name three kinds of specialist food shops in the area where you usually shop.
5 Why are dry foods stores able to sell foods more cheaply than some other shops? Why could you not do all your shopping at a dry foods store?
6 Select five everyday foods which are available in a supermarket's economy range and as brand named goods. Set up a taste panel (see p. 96) to compare the cheaper and more expensive brands. Record the information and opinions you obtain, and evaluate the findings of your research.

Saving money on shopping

Money spent on good food is money well spent. There are many ways you can save money if you are a careful shopper, to make the most of what you have available.

1 Plan a week's meals ahead and make a shopping list. You will then be able to work out exactly how much you need to buy.
2 Look out for special offers on foods you normally buy. If you know the usual prices of foods you will know whether offers are really much cheaper or not.
3 If you can afford them at the time, large packs usually work out cheaper than small ones.
4 Supermarket own brands and basic packs with plain labels are much cheaper than famous brand names and are often just as good.
5 If you have time and energy you can shop around in different stores to get the best buys. But try not to go shopping too often or you may be tempted to buy things you don't really need.
6 Fruit and vegetables can be much cheaper in markets and greengrocers than in supermarkets. Look out for the ones in season, which are much cheaper because they are plentiful. If you have a freezer you could freeze vegetables when they are in season. Jam and marmalade can be really cheap to make and home-made versions taste much better than cheap, bought jam. Those that don't cost much to make include plum jam, and marmalade made from canned, ready-chopped oranges.

7 Home-made bread, scones, and cakes can be cheaper than bought ones and usually taste much better. When you have the oven on, it is more economical with fuel to bake several things at once.
8 Look out for cheaper meat and fish. Try eating meat just four times a week instead of seven. The cheapest meats are usually mince, burgers, and sausages, and the cheapest of these are often very fatty. A healthy choice would be to have a smaller portion of leaner meat and more potatoes and vegetables to go with it. Make meat go further by adding plenty of vegetables, rice, pasta, dumplings, stuffing, or Yorkshire pudding. Try vegetarian alternatives to meat (which are usually cheaper) and try vegetarian and fish dishes sometimes. There are plenty of recipes in this book.

Some of the cheapest sources of energy and nutrients

Energy	Margarine, bread, oats, rice, pasta, potatoes, breakfast cereals, peas, beans, lentils.
Protein	Bread, liver, pasta, beans, eggs, herrings, chicken, milk, mince, cheese, potatoes, frozen peas, rice, lentils.
Vitamin C	Frozen fruit, instant potato (most have vitamin C added), oranges, canned tomatoes, turnips, swedes, green vegetables, potatoes, frozen peas.
Vitamin D	Margarine and low fat spreads, canned fish (tuna, mackerel, sardines, salmon), dried milk, eggs, liver.
NSP (dietary fibre)	Bread, wholegrain breakfast cereals, beans, canned or frozen peas, potatoes, apples, vegetables, lentils.
B group vitamins	Breakfast cereals, bread, liver, yeast extract (Marmite), potatoes, peas, beans, lentils.
Calcium	Milk, bread, cheese, eggs, ice cream.
Iron	Beans, liver, oatmeal, breakfast cereals, bread, canned or frozen peas, potatoes, eggs, lentils.

QUESTIONS

1 What are the advantages and disadvantages of sticking to your shopping list?
2 Does it save you money if you shop every day?
3 How could you save money on fruit and vegetables?
4 Is it always cheaper to make your own bread, cakes, and jams?
5 How can you cut down on the money spent on meat?
6 Why is buying cheap burgers or sausages not a very healthy option?
7 How many times do the following foods appear on the list of cheap sources of nutrients: bread, potatoes, beans, lentils, breakfast cereals, frozen peas. What conclusion do you draw from this?
8 Name 3 foods which are good, cheap sources of both protein and iron.
9 Name 3 foods which are good, cheap sources of energy, protein, NSP, and B vitamins.

Saving fuel

Fuels used for cooking and heating include gas, electricity, and solid fuel. The cost of fuel is continually rising, and there are a number of ways in which you can save fuel when you are cooking. Careful planning can save money, and avoid wasting valuable fuel resources.

1   Plan your meals carefully. If you do you will find that you can cook complete meals using the cooker top only, without having to light the oven as well. Or you can make a complete meal in the oven without using the rings.
2   Some electric cookers have two ovens, one small and one large. You can save fuel by using only the small one if you are not cooking much food.
3   Some electric cookers have grills or boiling rings where you only need to switch on half of the grill or ring. This is useful if you are only grilling a small amount of food or using a small saucepan.
4   If your cooker is electric, it is much more economical to use an electric toaster and kettle than to use the cooker for making toast and boiling water.
5   When you put the kettle on, don't overfill it. Only boil as much water as you need, but always make sure that the element in an electric kettle is covered.
6   When you are baking, fill the oven. You could try to bake all you need for the week at once. If you have a freezer you can freeze bread, cakes, casseroles, and other food for use later in the week.
7   A pressure cooker is very economical with fuel. It cooks very quickly and will cook several items together (meat, potatoes, and vegetables, for example), using only one boiling ring on a low heat. It also saves money as you can use it to make cheap, tougher cuts of meat more tender (see p. 64).

8   You can buy divided pans with three compartments which fit together so that you can cook foods separately, still using only one ring.
9   You can try cooking vegetables together in the same pan, for example, potatoes and carrots, or carrots and peas.
10 When cooking vegetables, cut them fairly small and all to the same size, so that they cook quickly and evenly. Use just a little water and simmer gently. Don't have the heat too high. As well as saving fuel, you will get better-tasting vegetables.

Microwave cooking is quick and economical with fuel. See p. 54 for more information.

Meals made using the cooker top only

Chilladas, tomato sauce Boiled potatoes Fresh fruit salad	Sweet and sour pork Rice Steamed chocolate pudding Chocolate sauce

Other suitable dishes

Soups and cold starters.

Minced beef, cooked on the hob instead of in the oven. Ratatouille pasta, chilli con carne, chilli bean casserole, pork and apricots, spaghetti bolognese, fish cakes, fish with cheese sauce.

Most vegetables and salads.

Fruit fool, dried fruit salad, lemon cheesecake, rice pudding made in the pressure cooker.

Meals made using the oven only

Baked chicken Tomato salad Cucumber salad Fruit crumble	Cheese-filled baked potatoes Lettuce and cucumber salad Apple charlotte

Other suitable dishes

Most cold starters.

Liver casserole, fish and tomato casserole, toad in the hole, baked chicken joints. Roast potatoes, savoury cheese potatoes, pizza.

Pineapple upside-down pudding, sponge flan or gateau, rice pudding.

QUESTIONS

1 Describe how planning meals ahead can save money in a family budget.
2 Some gas and electric cookers have economy features. List as many as you can think of.
3 What kitchen equipment can be bought which saves money on fuel?
4 Suggest a three course meal which could be made using only the cooker top and one using the oven only.
5 Many domestic appliances have energy saving features. Find out what energy saving features are available on appliances of all kinds; ask people who own or use the appliances how useful the features are; and compare the costs of buying appliances with and without energy saving features. Design and use a questionnaire to record and collate your information. Evaluate your research and your findings.

Ready-made foods

At one time most people ate most of their meals at home, eating at the table at the same time as the rest of the family. Meals were cooked at home, from fresh ingredients. Now patterns of living are changing, so patterns of eating are changing too. More and more ready-prepared or *convenience* foods are available in supermarkets, and there are many different kinds of take-away outlets (including sandwich shops and burger bars), cafés, and restaurants.

Lifestyles

When most mothers worked at home, they had time to shop, prepare, and cook meals. Now many go out to work, and have less time to shop and cook. Many people now have a fridge and a freezer, so most shopping can be done on one day a week and it is convenient to buy a lot of ready-prepared frozen food.

Single households

About one quarter of households in the UK have just one person living in them. These people may not want to cook meals starting with fresh ingredients every day, and convenience foods may suit their lifestyle, especially if they have a freezer and microwave.

Cooking skills

Some people think they can't cook, or they don't want to cook, and convenience foods make their lives easier. People who dislike cooking can use some convenience foods to mix with fresh foods to add some variety.

Adolescents

Adolescents often spend leisure time outside the home and may want to eat at different times to the rest of the family. They may have large appetites and with a store of ready-prepared foods in the house they can make themselves meals and snacks.

Storage

It is always useful to have a store of stand-by foods for times when you can't go shopping or have unexpected visitors. Convenience foods in packets, cans, jars, and in the freezer are always useful.

Different kinds of ready-prepared or convenience foods

Cook–chill foods are cooked in factories, chilled, and then sold from refrigerated cabinets in supermarkets. They are not frozen. Meat pies and pasties have been available for a long time, but you can now buy flans, ready-to-cook filled pasta, curries, samosas and other Indian foods, pizzas, fresh soup in cartons, trifle, salads. These foods taste good but can be quite expensive.

Frozen food Most people use their freezers mainly to store ready-frozen foods rather than their own home-frozen foods. You can buy most foods frozen, from complete roast dinners to vegetables, chips, pizza, fish, meat, and puddings.

Cans are useful for foods that would take a long time to cook from fresh ingredients, like kidney beans, baked beans, chick peas, or rice pudding.

A useful store of foods in the freezer

As well as buying ready-frozen foods to keep in store, you can use the freezer to store other foods and ingredients.

Bread If you keep a loaf sliced in the freezer you can take out a couple of slices for toast or a sandwich. Bread rolls can be defrosted in seconds in a microwave.

Breadcrumbs can be made using a food processor or blender, and kept for later use. Store in polythene bags.

Pastry or crumble or biscuit mix You can rub-in more mix than you need and keep it ready for use. This is especially useful if you have a food processor.

Cheese can be kept ready grated in the freezer to use for sandwiches or to top cooked dishes. Freeze it loosely rather than in a lump, so it is easier to use the amount you want.

Lemon You could store slices of lemon for drinks or a garnish.

Beans Cook a large amount of kidney or other beans, and store what you do not want in useful sized packs in the freezer. This is cheaper than buying cans.

Herbs Chop fresh herbs and freeze in ice cube trays with a little water. Drop the cubes into soups or stews still frozen.

Milk Semi-skimmed or skimmed milk can be frozen in a plastic bottle or carton (not in a glass bottle).

Tomato purée If you do not use all the can at once you can put some into a polythene bag and freeze for later use.

Fruit Store fruit as a purée or stewed. Cook the fruit according to the kind it is and store in polythene bags or tubs. It is then ready to use as it is or in a recipe. You can add sugar before or after freezing.

Some fruit freezes well dry, such as raspberries, rhubarb (cut into 2 cm lengths), blackcurrants, or gooseberries. It is then ready to use in a pie or crumble. You can add sugar when you come to use it.

Baked goods Cakes, pies, pizza, puddings, scones, and biscuits all freeze well. They may need to be carefully wrapped to avoid being damaged. Some icings and creams do not freeze well, so it is safer to freeze cakes undecorated. Biscuits are improved by reheating for 5 minutes in the oven after thawing.

QUESTIONS

1 Describe the three different kinds of freezers, with the advantages and disadvantages of each. Which would be useful in your own home? Why?
2 Name six foods which it would be useful to have in store in your freezer. How would you pack and label each one?
3 What precautions would you take when cooking a curry dish for the freezer?
4 Suggest at least five foods suitable for a party for some friends. Explain fully why each food would be suitable for a 'help-yourself' party. You want to prepare as much in advance as you can and plan to use the freezer for this. Suggest how the freezer could be used at different stages of preparation and cooking, and say exactly how you would wrap, store, and use each item you freeze.

Food safety and hygiene

Food poisoning

It is essential that standards of care and hygiene are high at every stage of handling food, otherwise there is a danger of food poisoning. This can cause anything from a mild headache to death. The most common symptoms of food poisoning are stomach ache, diarrhoea, and vomiting. It can start within an hour of eating unfit food or may take up to five days to develop. If you think your food poisoning was a result of food from a particular shop or eating place you should contact the Environmental Health Officer at your local council so that they can look into hygiene practices at the place concerned.

Food poisoning is caused by harmful bacteria in large numbers in the food we eat. These include *salmonella*, *streptococcus*, *listeria*, and *clostridium botulinum*. For the bacteria to increase to large numbers they have to have conditions that suit them. They like:

● warmth (a temperature about that of the human body), but not too hot or cold
● moisture
● food

If we want to stop bacteria multiplying and causing us food poisoning we have to avoid keeping our food in the warm, moist conditions which suit them.

Temperatures for storing food

Bacteria grow most quickly between 10°C and 65°C. A safe temperature for a fridge is therefore between 0 and 5°C in the coldest part. This will slow the increase of most bacteria. A safe temperature for a freezer is below –18°C. This will stop the increase of bacteria (although it will not kill them). You can buy a fridge or freezer thermometer to check the temperature. Bacteria are killed by high temperatures: heating for two minutes at 70°C will kill most harmful bacteria.

Food hygiene

We need to be aware of food hygiene at every stage of buying, storing, preparing, and cooking food.

Buying food Perishable foods (the foods that 'go off' most easily) have a 'use by' date. They include cook–chill foods (the kind that is chilled and ready to eat but not frozen, like meat pies and flans), cream, and pre-packed meat. It is illegal to sell foods after their 'use-by' date, and if you have them at home unused it is better to throw them away. ('Best before' dates are different, see p. 116.) You must follow storage instructions on foods with 'use-by' dates or you cannot expect them to keep. For example, if you kept a packet of sausages on a warm kitchen bench instead of in a fridge it could go off well before its 'use-by' date.

Do your shopping in shops which are clean, where refrigerated and frozen food is really cold. Don't shop where cooked and raw meats are kept together as bacteria will be transferred from raw to cooked meat. Assistants should not touch raw meat then cooked meat without washing their hands in between.

Taking your shopping home Do not buy frozen food then leave it for a long time in a warm car. Try to get it into a fridge or freezer as soon as possible. Keep a cold-box in the boot of the car if you have one.

Storing foods at home Keep your fridge and freezer at the right temperature and keep the most perishable foods in the coldest parts. Do not put warm food into the fridge as it will raise the fridge temperature and spoil the food already in there. Do not let raw meat drip down onto other foods. Keep eggs in the fridge, rather than in a warm kitchen. Follow storage instructions on food.

Hygiene in the kitchen Wash hands with soap and warm water before handling food. Always wash them after going to the lavatory, touching pets or dirty washing, or blowing your nose. Dry your hands on a clean towel, *not* the tea towel.

Keep kitchen cloths, dish cloths, and tea towels clean, and change them often. Wear a clean overall or apron. Use very hot soapy water for washing up and cleaning worktops, and change it often. Rinsing in hot water and leaving to drain is better than drying with a tea towel that is not scrupulously clean. Keep your pets away from food and worktops. If you cut up raw meat on a board, wash the knife and board before using it again for other food.

Do not leave scraps of food and open packets lying around, because they will attract mice and flies.

Cooking food Make sure that food is thoroughly cooked especially if it has been frozen. Defrost frozen foods thoroughly so that they will be cooked in the centre. The temperature in the centre must reach 70°C for at least two minutes to kill bacteria. This is especially important with chicken and turkey.

Eggs may contain *salmonella*. Pregnant women, small children, and elderly or unwell people should only eat eggs which have been thoroughly cooked until both yolk and white are solid.

Sometimes we cook food to eat later. Once it is cooked, cool it down as quickly as you can in a cool place (not the fridge as this would raise the fridge temperature). Then put it in the fridge or freezer. Your aim should always be to avoid the warm and lukewarm temperatures at which bacteria grow most quickly.

When re-heating any previously cooked food, re-heat until piping hot. Do not re-heat more than once.

QUESTIONS

1 Why do we have to bother following food hygiene rules?
2 What are some common symptoms of food poisoning?
3 Name three kinds of harmful bacteria.
4 What conditions do bacteria need to increase rapidly?
5 What temperatures are safest for (a) a fridge (b) a freezer?
6 What precautions should you follow when buying and storing perishable foods?
7 What do you consider the six most important rules for kitchen hygiene?
8 Why should frozen food be thoroughly defrosted before it is cooked?
9 Why must re-heated food be warmed until 'piping hot'? What temperature is this?

Safety in the kitchen

The kitchen is usually the most dangerous room in the house. Accidents can happen easily if people are careless, so always follow these safety rules.

1 Never allow pan handles to stick out over the edge of the cooker. Pans can easily be knocked over and can cause serious burns and scalds. You can buy a special guard for the cooker top if there are small children around.
2 Do not let small children play with the cooker controls in case they accidentally turn on the gas without lighting it.
3 Make sure you turn hobs off after using them, especially electric ones where it may not be obvious they are still on.
4 Mop up any spills straight away so that no one will slip and fall.
5 Do not have any curtains where they can blow onto a cooker and catch fire.
6 Do not put oven gloves or tea towels on the cooker where they can catch fire.
7 In most homes, bleach and household cleaners are kept under the sink. This is dangerous if there are small children around, so they should be kept out of reach.
8 Keep aspirin and other pills and medicines out of reach of children, and remember that they can climb up on chairs and tables. Pills can look like sweets to young children. 'Child proof' bottle tops are much safer than ordinary tops.
9 Suffocation and choking are the commonest accidents among children under four. Do not leave them on their own with a bottle or food. Cut food into small pieces and look out for bones, eggshell, tough meat, and stringy vegetables.
10 Do not leave matches within reach of children.
11 Use proper thick oven gloves or a cloth to lift hot dishes from the oven.
12 Do not let tablecloths hang down over the edge of the table where they could be pulled. Keep tea pots and hot drinks and dishes away from children.
13 Keep sharp knives and utensils away from children. Do not put sharp knives to soak in washing-up water as you may pick them up by the blade.
14 Leaving metal spoons in hot pans will cause burns. Always use wooden spoons.
15 One of the most common causes of fire at home is chip pans. Never leave them unattended if you leave the room, but always switch them off. Do not turn the heat up too high or fill the pan more than two thirds full. Lower food in very gently. Electric deep-fat fryers are much safer.

First aid box

Every home should have a box of basic first aid equipment. It must be easily available when needed, but out of reach of children. It should contain:

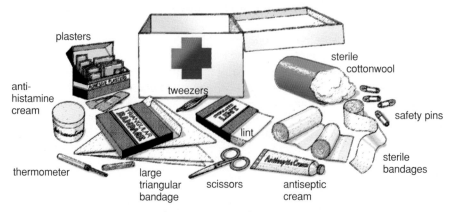

plasters · anti-histamine cream · tweezers · sterile cottonwool · safety pins · lint · thermometer · large triangular bandage · scissors · antiseptic cream · sterile bandages

Simple treatments

1 *Small cuts* Clean the wound with cool, running water, dry the skin with cotton wool, and cover with a clean dressing.
2 *Minor burns and scalds* Put under cool running water to reduce the heat and relieve the pain. Dry carefully and cover loosely with a clean, dry dressing. Never cover with fat, ointments, or creams.
3 *Extensive burns and scalds* Place gently in cool running water and keep immersed for at least ten minutes. Cover loosely with a clean, dry cloth and send for medical help at once.
4 *Fainting* If someone feels faint, get them near fresh air and give a drink of water. Put their head between their knees so that blood can reach the brain. If someone faints, keep them lying flat. Raise the legs slightly above the level of the head. Do not make them sit up or move too soon. Loosen any clothing which is tight round the neck, chest, or waist.
5 *Poisoning* Get medical help as soon as possible. Keep the poison so that it can be identified and keep any vomit. Treatment varies with the type of poison: if there are red marks around the mouth and lips (which suggests a strong corrosive poison) do *not* try to make the patient sick but give large amounts of milk to drink (or water if milk is not available).

QUESTIONS

1 What sort of kitchen accidents are most likely to involve small children?
2 How would you reduce the likelihood of cuts in the kitchen?
3 List the hazards shown in the kitchen above and explain why each is dangerous.
4 You burn your hands on an oven shelf because you are not using thick oven gloves. What would you do?
5 What would you do if a child in your care swallowed some pills? How should this have been prevented?

The design process

The first part of any design process is to think carefully about your *design brief*. The design brief is the task that you have been asked to carry out. You will often be asked to design and make a food product suitable for a particular purpose. To carry out the brief successfully, you have to work through the steps involved in a sensible order. You have to:

1 Define your objectives, that is, define exactly what you want to achieve.
2 Research and investigate to find information.
3 Draw up a *product specification* (a precise description of your product) based on that information.
4 Plan how you will produce the product, and work out the cost.
5 Produce the product.
6 Evaluate your results and your method of working.

1 *Define your objectives.* Read the design brief carefully and decide exactly what is being asked for. What must you do to achieve these objectives?

Example design brief: Design a new filling for a savoury snack made with ready-made pastry.
Your objectives: the filling must be new (not already available); savoury (not sweet); a snack (not too filling).

2 *Research and investigate.* First you need to find out what products are already available, what is in them, and what people think of them. There are many ways of collecting this information. You could ask people you know, or produce a questionnaire (see p. 95). You could study some existing products to see what is in them (see p. 98), and set up a taste panel (see p. 96) to get opinions on them. You could look in recipe books for ideas.

Example: Go to a supermarket and see what savoury snacks are available. Produce a questionnaire to find out what sort of savoury snacks people would like to buy. Set up a taste panel to see what people like about existing snacks and how you could improve on them.

3 *Draw up a product specification:* what must the product do to fulfil the design brief successfully?

Example: The snack must be nutritious, appetizing, fairly cheap to produce, and not too fragile. You find from your research that many people would like a vegetarian pastry snack, and that although there are several available they are too fatty, too expensive, or do not have much flavour. You might conclude that a firm-textured, cheese-based snack with herbs is likely to be most popular.

4   *Plan exactly what you are going to produce, and how.*

Example: You decide on a filling containing grated cheese, egg, breadcrumbs, and herbs. Work out how much you will need to buy, and calculate the cost. Work out the energy content and food value of each individual snack item. Plan how you will make your product efficiently, safely, and with regard to food hygiene. Plan the time needed for preparation and cooking.

5   *Produce your product* according to your plan, working efficiently and safely within the time available. If you have to make any changes to your plan while you are working, make a note of them.

Example: You make the snack item using the recipe you have selected. When you have mixed your filling, you find that it is too sloppy to spread on the pastry, so you add more breadcrumbs – make a note of this.

6   *Evaluate your results and your method of working.* Does your finished product meet your objectives? Is the flavour good? (You could use a taste panel.) Would you work in a different way next time? Would you change the ingredients? Could you vary some of the ingredients for an alternative flavour? See p. 102 for more on evaluation.

Example: Your snack food had a good flavour when warm but not when cold. It was too expensive – so you decide to use less cheese or cheaper cheese next time. The oven was too hot, which meant that the food was crisp on the outside before the inside was cooked – so you decide to reduce the temperature slightly next time.

DESIGN BRIEF

1   (a) Design a soup which fulfils all the following criteria
        ● it uses at least three root vegetables
        ● it is inexpensive
        ● it is easy to make
    (b) Produce the soup and evaluate your results. Show how your product has met the given criteria. (c) How could you make this soup a main meal? (d) What variation to your product could you suggest for a change? (e) What practical skills would you use when you prepare the soup? (f) What electrical equipment could you use to save time or energy in producing this soup?

Researching and investigating

When we are deciding what to buy, we often compare different brands of the same product. So when you are designing a food product – whether at home, at school, or in the food industry – you should do the same. You should look at existing products, and compare their good and bad points. This will help you to see how you could make a better product.

If you are designing a new product, you need to:

1 Find out what similar products are available.
2 Evaluate the products – find out how good they are and what people think of them.

With that information you can start to design a product that fulfils your design brief.

Finding out what is available

There are several ways of doing this:
● Look at the products available in your local shops. Check the prices and look at the packet labels. The labels will give you a lot of information about the product, including the ingredients, calorie content, and nutritional value. Sometimes there is an address you can write to for further information.
● Ask people you know: friends, family.
● Use books, leaflets, and magazines. You may find advertisements for products that aren't in your local shops. Look at *Which?* magazine, which carries out comparisons of food products. Page 234 has addresses of several organizations that might be able to provide you with information.

Evaluating existing products

There are lots of ways you can evaluate products to find out what they are made of, how good they are, and how you could make a product which is as good or better. You can:
● Ask people their opinions, perhaps using a questionnaire.
● Get people to taste products and describe in detail what they think of them. This is done using a *taste panel* (see p. 96).
● Look closely at the ingredients, either by reading the labels or by actually taking the product apart. For example, if you bought a ready-made tuna, pepper, and pasta salad, you could drain off the dressing and separate out the other ingredients, to see how much of each there was. This is called *disassembly* (see p. 98).

Compiling a questionnaire

The purpose of a questionnaire is to get the information needed to help you design and produce a product which people will like. With this in mind you could ask people to evaluate an existing product, using questions like these:

```
                                    Questionnaire

                                                          Yes    No
  Does it taste good?
  Is the portion size right?                               ✓
  Is it filling?                                           ✓
  Does it fit in with your ideas on healthy eating?              ✓
  Will you find it easy to prepare?                              ✓
  Will it take too long to cook?                           ✓
  Would you like an alternative flavour?
  If so, what? ..................................................
  Would you like a vegetarian option?
  Would you pay this price?
  Is it well packaged so that you can carry it home easily?
  Will you find it easy to store until you are ready to eat it?
  Would you like
```

Using your questionnaire you can get a lot of information about the sort of food products people like, and what is important to them. But if you wanted people to give you more detailed information about the taste of the products, you'd set up a taste panel, as you'll see on the next page.

QUESTIONS

1   There are many different breakfast cereals. (a) How do *you* choose a cereal? List all the factors that influence *your* choice. (b) List any extra factors that might be important to other people. (c) Compile a questionnaire to find out which cereals people prefer, and how you could improve any of them.
2   You are set the task of designing and producing a new snack bar to sell at morning break. What would you need to find out about the snack bars that are already available before you start? List as many points as you can.
3   Supermarkets often sell many brands of the same product. (a) Plan a visit to a supermarket to do some research into: cans of cola, sliced white bread, Cornish pasties, baked beans. Your research should answer the questions: i) How many brands of each product are sold? ii) What is the highest and lowest price for each? iii) What differences are there in the packaging? Plan how you will record your findings. (b) Carry out your research and write up your findings.

Analysing food products: taste panels

When you are testing and comparing similar products, or developing a new food product, it is useful to get people to taste the products and give their opinions. To do this, you set up a *taste panel*. Each member of a taste panel tries the food product, describes its taste, and says whether or not they like it.

Describing food

We react to food through our senses of taste, touch, smell, and sight. There are many ways of describing food so it is useful to have a *word bank* – a list of words to choose from. The word bank gives you the necessary vocabulary to describe the ways your senses react. For example:

Taste – sweet, sour, spicy, bland, tangy, savoury, salty, creamy, bitter
Touch – the feel of food in our mouth – crumbly, chewy, tough, melting, soggy, greasy, crisp, heavy, light, lumpy, smooth, tender, firm, soft, crunchy, hot, cold, juicy, dry
Smell – appetizing, savoury, fruity, meaty, 'off', strong, burnt, rancid
Sight – colourful, golden, well-shaped, fresh, crisp, smooth, creamy, moist, dry, lumpy, separated, grey, soggy

Star diagrams

You can use a *star diagram* to summarize the description of your food product. Star diagrams work like this.

First you choose six important features of your food product from the word bank. For example, for a fruit flapjack you might choose: sweet, fruity, chewy, moist, golden, crunchy. Then you draw six 'spokes' of a wheel, and write each description at the point of the spoke. Then you think about each word in turn and how well it describes your food product. You mark this on to the spoke – make a mark near to the point of the spoke if the word is a good description and near to the centre of the wheel if the word is a poor description. Then you join up the marks on the spokes.

Here are two examples.

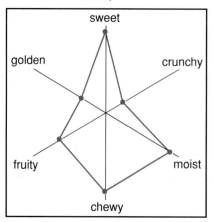

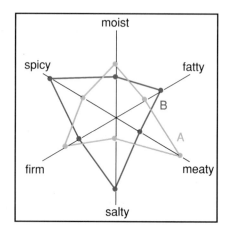

The first star diagram describes a fruit flapjack which was:

- very sweet, moist, and chewy
- quite fruity
- not very golden or crunchy

Star diagrams can be used for your own descriptions, or to summarize the results of your taste panel. You can also use a star diagram to compare two products.

The second star diagram is for two different types of burger. The different shapes of the stars show how different the two burgers were.

Likes and dislikes

Many of us find it hard to describe a food exactly, but we all know whether we like it or not. So it is easy to ask your taste panel this sort of question about a food:

	Very good	Good	Not good
Does it taste good?			
Is the texture good?			
Does it look good?			
Is it good served warm?			
Is it good served cold?			
Is it good value for money?			
Is it a good product overall?			

You could use the opinion of a taste panel to compare, for example:

- a jacket potato cooked in the microwave with one baked in the oven
- a home-made cake with a 'bought' one or a packet cake mix
- a can of fruit salad with home-made fruit salad
- pastry made entirely with margarine with pastry using half lard/half margarine
- bread spread with butter or with low fat spread
- home-made pizza with 'bought' or take-away pizza

To make full use of a taste panel you must plan your questions carefully and record all the information you gather so that you can analyse it accurately. Then you can get proper comparisons with existing food products, and evaluate whether or not your product is likely to be successful.

When a food manufacturing company is developing a new product they use specialists trained in *sensory analysis* to taste the product and describe its qualities very precisely. This helps them to produce something that people really like and will buy (see p. 106).

QUESTIONS

1 Look at the star diagram for the burgers (opposite). (a) Which burger tastes the most meaty? (b) Which is the most spicy? (c) Describe the two burgers.
2 (a) Copy the star diagram for the flapjack on the opposite page. Add to this a star for a flapjack which contains no fruit but is very golden and crunchy, quite sweet, quite moist, and not very chewy. (b) Which flapjack would you prefer?
3 Next time you eat a meal, describe the main dish with words from the word bank.

Analysing food products: disassembly

When you want to analyse a product more carefully you can disassemble it. When you assemble a product you put the bits together. When you disassemble it you take it apart to see what it's made of. You can see what's in a food product by reading the ingredients list on the label. In some cases you can see what's in a food product by literally taking it apart.

Some food products are much easier to disassemble then others. A fruit salad is easy to disassemble because you can drain off the liquid and separate out the different pieces of fruit. A biscuit is harder to disassemble because you can't separate out the ingredients once the biscuit has been baked.

Muesli is easy to disassemble because you can separate the bits. The basic (and cheapest) ingredients of muesli are rolled oats (porridge oats) and wheat flakes. Manufacturers may add raisins, sultanas, other dried fruits, nuts of different kinds, and sugar to this. By varying the ingredients, and by adding more of some or less of others, they make a slightly different product.

Where there are more of the expensive ingredients, the product will probably cost more. But just because a product is expensive doesn't mean it contains a lot of expensive ingredients. Some products are much better value then others in terms of what you get for your money.

Different brands of muesli

Look at the labels for the four different types of muesli, and at the table below. You can start to disassemble the mueslis by listing the ingredients each one contains. Remember that the ingredients on the packet label are listed in order of how much the packet contains: the ingredient there is most of comes first.
If you had samples of the mueslis, you could disassemble them by hand, by splitting them up into their separate ingredients. This would give you a very good idea of exactly how each muesli is made up.

	Packet size and cost	Cost per 100 g	kcal per 100 g
Safeway Savers	79p for 750 g	10.5p	358
Jordan's Natural Country Muesli (no sugar)	£1.65 for 1 kg	16.5p	350
Safeway Luxury Fruit and Nut	£1.25 for 500 g	25.0p	373
Alpen (no added sugar)	£1.49 for 500 g	29.8p	357

Disassembly tells you what ingredients a product contains, and sometimes it tells you how much of each ingredient a product contains. So it is helpful to you if you are planning to make a similar product yourself. It gives you some useful information about what is in a product. But, of course, it doesn't tell you anything about the taste of the product, and that is important too.

QUESTIONS

1 List all the ingredients in each of the mueslis.
2 What are the basic ingredients which all the mueslis contain?
3 What are the special 'added extras' found in some mueslis but not in others?
4 Here are descriptions of two of the mueslis, written by looking at the information on the packet.
   Savers 'A basic muesli without many added nuts or much dried fruit, but quite a good, plain product offering very good value for money at 10.53p per 100 g.'
   Jordan's 'A very good product with a wide variety and good amount of added dried fruit, dates, and nuts. There is no added sugar. At 16.5p per 100 g it is definitely the best buy.'
   Try writing descriptions of the other two mueslis, using the information on the packet.
5 Suggest a recipe for your own muesli. Give reasons for your choice of ingredients and the proportions you use.

Working out the cost of your product

The cost of a product is very important to people when they are deciding whether to buy it. So you need to know how much your product will cost to make, and how much other products cost, so that you can compare value for money.

Some supermarkets display the cost of 100 g of a food product, so that you can compare prices easily. Without that it would be very difficult to work out what offers the best value for money without using a calculator. For example, it would be difficult to work out which of the mueslis on p. 98 was the most expensive as the packets contain different amounts. But remember, the most expensive product is not necessarily the best, and cheaper products can offer good value for money.

How much will my product cost?

When you are working out the cost of a food product or recipe you are making yourself, a calculator is very useful. You need to know:

● the price of a packet of the food – you need to keep till receipts for this as most products do not now have a stick-on price label.
● the weight of the packet – this is printed on the packet.

Then you work out the cost like this:

Food item	Packet price in pence	÷	Weight of packet in grams	×	Amount used in recipe in grams	=	Cost in pence
Butter	89	÷	250	×	100	=	33.6
Margarine, block	26	÷	250	×	100	=	10.4
Plain flour	80	÷	1500	×	75	=	4.0
Dried yeast	76	÷	35	×	7	=	15.2
Noodles	59	÷	250	×	75	=	17.7
Milk	102	÷	2000 ml	×	500 ml	=	25.5

Some items are sold and costed individually, such as:

1 lemon	22p
1 x 400 g can of tomatoes	20p
1 x 420 g can of chick peas	40p

Some recipes might state '1 onion' or '2 carrots' where the exact weight is not important. You have to use your own judgement here to work out an approximate cost.

It is useful to keep a list for quick reference of approximate prices of foods you often use, for example:

25 g flour	1p	1 average onion	6p
25 g margarine	2.5p	1 cooking apple	16p
25 g Cheddar cheese	10p	1 large egg	11p

This enables you to quickly work out an approximate price for many everyday food products.

To work out the exact cost of a food product and of one portion

Here is an example calculation for the recipe for *mushroom risotto*, on p. 153.

Ingredient	Packet price in pence	÷	Weight of packet in grams	x	Amount used in recipe in grams	=	Cost in pence
4 tablespoons oil (60 ml)	65	÷	1000 ml	x	60 ml	=	3.9
250 g mushrooms	129	÷	500	x	250	=	64.5
2 cloves garlic, per bulb	20					=	4.0
1 onion	65	÷	1000	x	100	=	6.5
175 g rice	80	÷	500	x	175	=	28.0
1 stock cube	88	÷	8 in pkt.	x	1 cube	=	11.0
50 g cheese	220	÷	500	x	50	=	22.0
1 teaspoon mace (5 g)	102	÷	25	x	5	=	20.4

Total cost of recipe	160.3p
No. of portions	3
Cost per portion	53.43p

QUESTIONS

1   Make a list of 20 food items you would often use for everyday cooking and work out the cost of a useful amount (e.g. 50 g) of each.

2   Select a recipe for any food product. Work out the cost per dish and the cost per portion or (in the case of small cakes or biscuits) the cost per item.

3   Calculate the cost of any cake recipe which is made with margarine and granulated sugar. Work out the cost of the same cake made with butter and caster sugar. Make the two cakes and taste them. What differences do you notice when preparing the two cakes? Record any differences between the two in cost, taste, appearance, and texture.

4   (a) It is the end of the week and you do not have much money left. You decide to make the Mushroom Risotto. How could you adapt this recipe to make it as cheap as possible but still enjoyable to eat? (b) Select another recipe from this book and show how you could adapt it to reduce its cost.

5   (a) Look at the muesli packets and prices on p. 98. Make a list of some of the basic ingredients such as fruit and nuts. Find out the cost of 100 g of each of these. (b) Design and produce your own muesli, adding what you think is the right amount of 'extra' ingredients to make a really good product. Work out the cost of 100 g of your muesli and compare this with the other mueslis.

Evaluation

When you have made your product, it is important to evaluate it. Your design task is not complete until you have done this. You need to ask yourself: was my product so good that I would produce it in exactly the same way next time, or could it be improved in any way?

In practice we evaluate all the time, though we may not call it that. For example, you might decide to make a fruit cake for your family to eat for tea on a Sunday afternoon and select a certain recipe. When it is made and eaten you may think that it took far too long to cook: you wanted to eat at 5 pm and it wasn't ready until 5.50 pm. So you might decide to cook the cake in a large shallow tin rather than a loaf tin next time, so that it would not take 1½ hours to cook through to the middle. You might decide to use margarine instead of butter next time to save money, and that having the oven on for one cake for 1½ hours was not economical with fuel. You might think that if you had used a food processor it would have taken much less time to prepare. And you might decide to add cherries and nuts next time, instead of currants and sultanas. But overall you might think that your cake had a good taste and texture and it could become a favourite you would produce often again in the future. You have been evaluating the success of your product while you have been thinking about it.

Evaluating your product

When you are evaluating your product, there are two things to consider:

- the quality of the design – is it well designed?
- the quality of manufacture – is it well made?

For example, a food processor might have good design features (high speed, easy to clean and use) but be badly made of poor plastic that is liable to crack. Or you may have designed a tasty, moist sandwich filling, but cut the bread too thick so that the sandwich was bulky and had thick, chewy crusts.
So when evaluating your design, you need to look both at the finished product and at how you produced it.

What sort of questions should I ask?

These are the sort of things you should consider.

- Were my results satisfactory, or could I improve them? If so, what changes in method or materials can I suggest to improve my product? For example:
  Flavour Could this be improved with different or extra ingredients, or more salt or spices?
  Colour Could this be improved by longer cooking or cooking at a higher temperature for a more golden finish? Or adding more colourful ingredients like tomatoes, or a colourful garnish?
  Shape Would a cake have been a better shape if cooked at a lower temperature for a longer period?
  Volume Would my ingredients have produced a larger cake if I had used a food mixer to beat more air into the mixture?
  Texture Would my sauce have been smoother and free of lumps if I had made it more carefully?
  Calories Could I have produced a version which was lower in fat or sugar for a calorie-conscious person?
- How would any improvements affect the cost? Is cost an important factor in this design brief?
- Is the product fit for the purpose I intended it for? For example, if you had designed a product to carry to school in a lunch box, would it keep its shape without breaking up?
- Was my pre-planning satisfactory?
- Could I have worked more efficiently to save time, energy, or money?
- Was the equipment I used suitable? Would other equipment have helped me? For example, could you have used a food processor instead of chopping by hand? Or a microwave oven instead of a conventional oven? And how would these changes have affected your results?
- Can I suggest any variations or alternatives to my finished product?
- What did I learn as a result of carrying out my brief?

DESIGN BRIEFS

1 (a) Design a main meal dish containing meat for yourself and a friend, that meets the following criteria:
   - it can be prepared and cooked in no more than 40 minutes
   - it costs no more than £1 per head
   - it is low in fat and provides plenty of starchy carbohydrates

   (b) Produce the meal and evaluate your results.
   (c) Suggest variations you might make if:
   i   your friend was a vegetarian
   ii you wanted to cut the cost
   iii a third friend turned up hungry 15 minutes before you were going to eat.

2 (a) Design a product suitable for selling on a cake stall at a school fund-raising day in summer. (b) Calculate the cost of producing the item and the price you think you could sell it for. (c) What factors would you have to consider when designing wrapping and packaging? (d) Produce and wrap the item ready for sale, and evaluate the success of your project.

Developing a new food product

We do not actually *need* new food products but food companies are always working to produce them. If they can persuade us to try a new product, we might like it. If we like it and the price is right, we will continue to buy it. If a company can continually produce products that consumers want to buy, it will make money and stay in business.

There are many stages between the first 'good idea' for a new food product and its appearance on the supermarket shelf. The flow chart shows these stages.

Step 1	**Concept generation** Development of ideas from market analysis, consumer research, and brainstorming.
Step 2	**Concept screening** Some product ideas are eliminated due to lack of market opportunity, problems in obtaining ingredients, or high cost of production.
Step 3	**Product development** A suitable product is developed, tested, and improved. This intense period of activity can last up to three months.
Step 4	**Product testing** Consumers around the country taste the product.
Step 5	**On-pack information and advertising material** Nutritional, legal, and recipe information is devised to go on the pack. The necessary photographs and artwork are produced.
Step 6	**First production run** The food technologist is present to ensure that large quantities of product can be produced to an approved standard.
Step 7	**Launch**

Step 2 → idea dropped

Step 3 → unsuitable idea dropped

Step 4 → fail means rejection

The initial idea – concept generation
Companies get ideas for new products in several ways. They will look at what sells well for them or for other companies, and think of products which are 'similar but different'. They will ask consumers about their likes and dislikes (consumer research), and will hold 'brainstorming' sessions. These are meetings designed to get people to think creatively and come up with lots of new ideas, without worrying about whether the ideas are good or bad.

Choosing the best idea – concept screening

Several ideas will be put forward, and many will be rejected. They may be too expensive, or they may not get the approval of consumers. A company must be very confident before it takes an idea any further. Developing the product, setting up the factory to produce it, and launching it all cost money. If the product does not sell well, the company won't get its money back. But perhaps one good idea will emerge which seems likely to develop into a successful product.

Putting the idea into practice – product development

Once research has shown that an idea is likely to be successful, home economists and food technologists try out recipes on a small scale to produce a suitable product. The taste is all important, so the product is tested in *sensory analysis* laboratories (see p. 106). But other factors are also important. How much does the product cost? Can it be mass produced easily? Can it be packed to travel well? Will it keep well? Can it easily be re-heated at home? Can the consumer prepare it easily?

Trying it out – product testing

At this stage, consumers taste the product. If it is not very popular, the company has to think again.

Telling consumers – on-pack information and advertising material

The company spends a lot of money getting these right so that consumers will buy the product. You can read more about labelling on pp. 116–119, and more about advertising on p. 107.

Making it – production

Once the company has decided to go ahead, it has to invest money in designing and setting up a production plant. Then they can start selling the product and if it is successful they will start to get their money back. You can read more about methods of production on pp. 108–109.

Selling it – the launch

The distribution network – from factory to wholesaler to retailer to customer – is set up, perhaps with refrigerated transport. At last the product appears in the shops.

Is it working? – evaluation

After the product has been on sale for a while the company will evaluate its success. Has it become popular enough? Are sales high enough to make it worth continuing production? Could it be produced more cheaply? Is the advertising directed at the right people?

QUESTIONS

1   Why do food companies continually have to look for new ideas for products?
2   Why do companies look closely at other companies' products?
3   What costs are involved in launching a new product?

Product development and marketing

Would you buy a food product that was good value, beautifully packaged, nutritious, and advertised by your favourite pop star if you couldn't stand the taste? Probably not! The taste of a food is all-important, so companies spend a lot of time and money getting the taste right. They use two groups of people for 'taste testing', as you can see in the pictures below. They use:

● trained experts, who do *sensory analysis* under laboratory conditions (left)
● consumers, who take part in *consumer testing* (right)

Sensory analysis

We all react to foods through our senses of sight, smell, touch, and taste. Trained tasters can analyse their response to a food very exactly: its appearance, its aroma (smell), the way it feels in their mouth (the 'mouthfeel'), and its taste. This is *sensory analysis*.

The trained tasters describe foods using the sorts of words in the word bank on p. 96. These are called 'sensory descriptors' because they describe how our senses react to the food. This analysis helps the food producer to define the product very exactly so that the best possible version of the product can be put into production. The product is then continually re-assessed and controlled to keep it at top quality.

Consumer testing

Once the company is confident that the best possible product has been defined by sensory analysis, it will invest money in *consumer testing*.

Consumer testing is carried out by untrained members of the public. The aim is to find out whether they enjoy the product enough to buy it if it is produced. Several hundred consumers may be involved at this stage, so that the manufacturer can get a wide range of opinions. The consumers do not have to describe the product very precisely because this can be difficult for an untrained person. But everyone knows whether they like a product or not, so consumers describe their likes and dislikes using words like: delicious, awful, enjoyable, appealing, acceptable, disgusting.

Marketing the product

A company must achieve good sales if it is to make a profit. To do this it must advertise and market the product successfully.

Product image

A company develops a food product with a particular set of customers in mind. For example, it might expect to sell a new soft drink to teenagers, a new brand of coffee to working adults, and a new low-fat cheese spread to slimmers. The group of people the product is aimed at is called the *target market*.

The name and image of the new product are carefully chosen to appeal to the target market, so that those customers will be willing to try it. The packaging, labelling, and advertising are all designed to promote the product image.

Advertising

The point of adverts is to make us buy things. We usually choose from a range of products (for example, different breakfast cereals, different soft drinks) so each advert has to convince us that one product is 'better' than another.

All advertising is carefully regulated, and food producers are not allowed to mislead consumers or make false claims about their products. So although a company might use an athlete to advertise a breakfast cereal, they cannot say that the cereal will improve our health or make us run faster.

TRY NEW COPELLA CHILLED

QUESTIONS

1 Look at the food advert above. (a) Who is this product aimed at? (b) What words does the manufacturer use to get people to buy the product? (c) How does the picture help to persuade you to buy the product?
2 Here is a list of target markets: slimmers; young children; teenagers; people with little time to prepare a main meal.
   Suggest one food product you have seen advertised or in the shops which is aimed at each of these markets.
3 Name ten everyday food products that have been around since the adults you know were children. Name ten that have appeared much more recently.

Food production

Food companies manufacture their products in many different ways. As you would expect, a small family bakery will organize things quite differently from a multi-national company.

But the general principles are the same – in big companies, small companies, and even at home. Food production involves the *input* of raw materials or ingredients, the *processing* of the raw materials, and the *output* of the finished product. For example, if you were making biscuits at home, you would input your raw materials of flour, fat, sugar, and flavourings; you would process them by mixing, beating, shaping, and baking; and you would achieve your output of biscuits which were crisp, golden brown, and a uniform size.

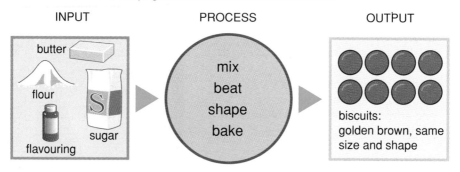

INPUT

butter
flour
sugar
flavouring

PROCESS

mix
beat
shape
bake

OUTPUT

biscuits:
golden brown, same
size and shape

There are four main ways of organizing food production, depending on the size of the operation.

One-off or hand-crafted productions

A specially made child's birthday cake or a wedding cake is a 'one-off' production. Items made this way are expensive because they take a long time to produce. But people will pay more because the product is special and unique.

Batch production

Batch production is used when more than one example of a product is required. For example, a baker might produce different shaped loaves, and a sweet maker might produce different flavoured fudges. In batch production, the different parts of the product are made separately and then assembled at the end of the process. The diagram below shows how the jobs might be divided in a pizza company:

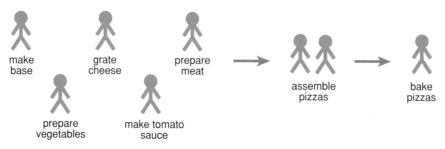

make base

grate cheese

prepare meat

prepare vegetables

make tomato sauce

assemble pizzas

bake pizzas

Each person in the production process has a particular job to do. The people who assemble the pizzas can vary the finished product by choosing to use some or all of the prepared toppings. They might make one batch of pizzas with just cheese and tomato sauce; a second batch with cheese, tomato sauce, and vegetables; and a third batch with meat as well. The different types of pizza will be bought by different customers, depending on what they prefer.

Batch production is generally used when quite a small number of products is being made, say in a family bakery business. It is often used for high-quality, specialist foods sold by delicatessens, such as game pies or hand-made chocolates. Foods produced in smaller batches are usually more expensive than those mass produced on an assembly line, but labour and fuel costs are less than in one-off production.

Repetitive flow or assembly line

Food manufacturing companies use assembly lines if they are producing very large numbers of products. Many production line workers are needed to put together and package the products, but some of the processes are automated and may be controlled by computer. Large-scale machinery is used for mixing and processing the foods. The system must be carefully organized, controlled, and maintained, because a breakdown in just one part of the assembly line could cause expensive delays and losses.

This kind of production method can be used for products like biscuits, cakes, frozen food, breakfast cereals, and chocolates. It produces a product which is uniform (the same every time), so manufacturers can easily check and maintain the quality.

Continuous flow or continuous production

Continuous production methods are highly automated at every stage: from the input of raw materials, through processing, to output and packaging. Most processes are computer controlled, so very few people are involved – only those needed to control and check machinery. Production often goes on 24 hours a day, seven days a week, with staff working in shift systems. It is more efficient to keep the plant and machinery in continuous production than to close down and set up again. So keeping the machinery in good working order is extremely important, because the manufacturer needs to keep the plant running all the time to be profitable.

Continuous production produces a uniform product of consistent quality. It is used, for example, in the manufacture of sugar and soft drinks. The cost of setting up the specialized plant and machinery is high, but once the plant is in full production it is relatively cheap to run.

QUESTIONS

1 Look at the recipe for onion soup on p. 133. Draw a diagram like the one opposite to show the input, the process, and the output for this recipe.
2 What production method is used in producing (a) pork pies in a large factory, (b) sandwiches in a local café, (c) a birthday cake at home, (d) a birthday cake in a family bakery?

Systems and control

Food manufacturers want their process to produce the same results every time – they want a *consistent outcome*. This is important to them because:
● Consumers expect to buy a product of consistent quality every time.
● If consumers trust the quality of one product produced by a company, they are more likely to buy other products from that company.
● It means that they can easily vary a product (by making it a different shape or adding a different flavour) and know what the result will be.
● It helps them ensure that their products always meet legally required standards.
● It helps them keep costs under control.
Manufacturers can ensure a consistent outcome in two ways. One way is to use standard components, such as stock cubes or ready-made pizza bases. The second way is to use control systems.

Control systems

Manufacturers need to control their processes carefully to get a consistent outcome. To do this they build checks and controls in to the production process. Control systems control the *process* so that manufacturers get the required *output* from what they *input*. They might need to control:

● size – for example of pastry cases
● thickness – for example of a biscuit mix being rolled out
● weight – the amount of product going into a packet
● temperature – for example of chocolate so that it will coat a product
● flow rate – for example of milk through a spray drying chamber so that all water is removed from the milk efficiently.

Controls may be:

● *human*, such as someone tasting samples of the finished product
● *mechanical*, such as checking the speed of a machine which chops up ingredients
● *electronic*, for example to control temperature, or the timing of a process.

Part of the bagel production process

Computer-aided manufacture

Computers can be used to control many parts of a manufacturing process. For example, a biscuit dough may need to be rolled out between two rollers. A sensor can measure the thickness of the dough as it leaves the rollers and before it is cut to shape. If the sensor finds that the dough is too thin, the computer responds automatically by increasing the space between the rollers. If the dough is too thick, the computer automatically reduces the space between the rollers.
Using a computer to control the process can have two advantages for the manufacturer. First, it means that the process is controlled very accurately because there is less scope for 'human error', that is, for someone to make a mistake. Second, it does not involve very many people (it is not 'labour intensive'), so the manufacturer can save on labour costs.

Controls also include safety and hygiene checks (see p. 114).

In this salmon processing factory in Ireland the fish is sliced by machine ...

... then weighed and packed ready for sale.

QUESTIONS

1   Why is a reputation for good quality products important to a company?
2   If you often made a favourite food product at home, how would you ensure a consistent outcome each time?
3   What parts of the production process must manufacturers control to ensure a consistent outcome?
4   Look at the first photograph above. (a) What is the computer being used for? (b) List the advantages of computer-aided manufacture.
5   Look at the second photograph above. (a) What items of protective clothing are the food packers wearing? (b) Why?
6   The photograph opposite shows part of the bagel production process. (a) What is the food production worker doing? (b) Draw a flow diagram of the steps in the process shown in the photograph. (c) What is the next stage in the process? (d) Suggest three controls that are built in to the bagel production process.

Manufacture of McVitie's Penguin biscuits

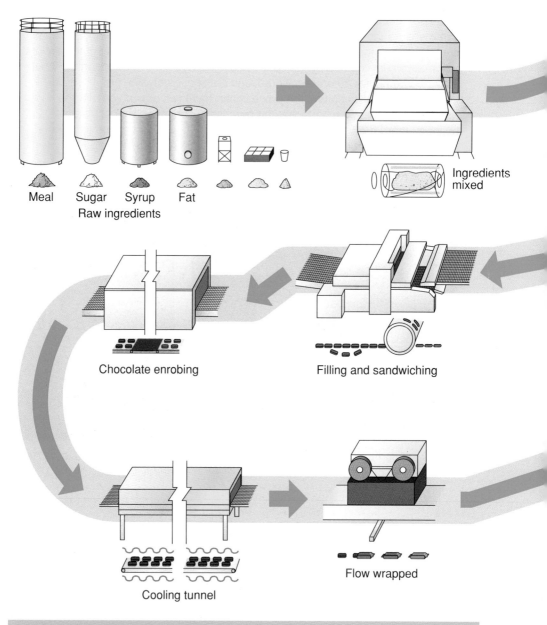

Meal   Sugar   Syrup   Fat
Raw ingredients

Ingredients mixed

Chocolate enrobing

Filling and sandwiching

Cooling tunnel

Flow wrapped

QUESTIONS

1 List the raw materials for Penguin biscuits.
2 Which parts of the process are carried out by hand?
3 Why is the cooling tunnel needed?
4 What does 'enrobing' mean?
5 Is the production of Penguin biscuits 'one-off', batch, assembly line, or continuous flow? Explain your answer.
6 Why are there two stages labelled 'flow wrapped'?

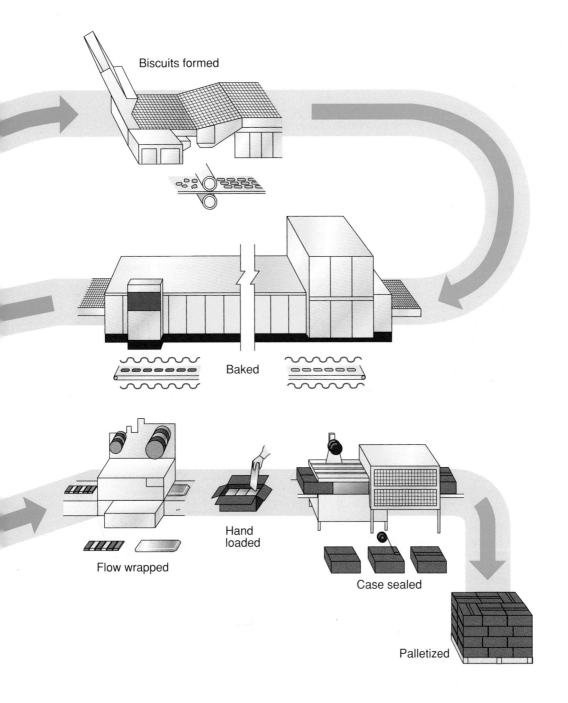

Biscuits formed

Baked

Flow wrapped

Hand loaded

Case sealed

Palletized

7 (a) What does 'palletized' mean? (b) What happens to the Penguins after they
    have been palletized?
8 One control point in this process will be checking that the biscuits are rolled out to
    a consistent thickness. Suggest six others.
9 Draw a flow chart to show the stages you would go through if you were making a
    batch of chocolate covered biscuits at home. How is your process different from
    the Penguin process?

Food safety and the law

The Food Safety Act 1990

This Act was passed to protect consumers from being sold food which:
1   is unsafe because it is injurious to health or is unfit or too contaminated for human consumption;
2   is not of the required nature, substance, or quality;
3   is labelled, advertised, or displayed in a way which falsely describes or misleads.

The Food Safety (General Food Hygiene) Regulations 1995

These regulations brought in the same food hygiene rules throughout the EU. They cover all aspects of food hygiene in every business which produces and sells food. The owners must identify and control potential hazards to food safety.

Commercial kitchens must be kept clean at all times.

HACCP and Food Safety

HACCP stands for *hazard analysis of critical control points*. It is a system of food safety used by the food industry to avoid food poisoning. The principles it uses can be just as useful when producing food for meals at home or school.

The person or company responsible for producing the food has to analyse any possible hazards to food hygiene and safety which might occur in producing the food item. These hazards might occur at any stage: bringing in and storing raw ingredients; preparing and cooking them; and cooling, packing, and storing the finished product.The critical control points are those points in producing the food where there is a high risk of possible hazard to food hygiene where control can be used to reduce that risk.

For example, if you were making sausage rolls at home, you could identify several areas in the process where there is a possible hazard of food poisoning.

When you bring the sausage meat into your home you must keep it stored in a cold place until you are ready to use it, and use it by the date given on the packet. When you are preparing the sausage rolls you must follow hygiene practices such as washing your hands before you start, and wearing a clean apron or overall. When you bake them you must make sure the meat is thoroughly cooked at the correct temperature. When cooked you must cool them quickly and not leave them lying around in a warm kitchen for a long time. Once cold, you should store them cold until you are ready to eat them. If re-heating, heat until piping hot.

With any food you are producing you can analyse the points at which food safety hazards might occur, and in this way reduce any risk of food poisoning.

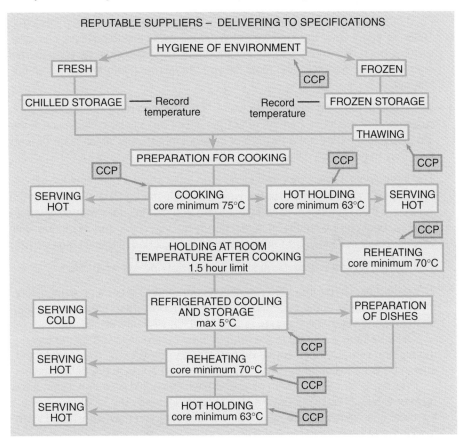

Flow chart showing how HACCP can be applied to a high-risk food such as poultry

QUESTIONS

1 How does the Food Safety Act protect consumers?
2 Suggest five types of business that have to abide by the 1995 Food Safety Regulations.
3 You plan to make a chicken casserole one morning to eat in the evening. What areas of food poisoning hazard can you identify? How would you control them?

Food packaging and labelling

Packaging

Food manufacturers have to take care to choose the right packaging for a food product, as the packaging has several important functions. It must:

- keep the product safe and prevent any damage
- keep the product clean and protect it from contamination
- attract the customer to the product
- convey the information required by food labelling regulations

Food labelling in the UK

Food labelling in the UK is controlled by EU regulations which came into effect in 1983. As so much of the food we eat is hidden away inside packets, tins, and cartons, good labelling is particularly important. The label must be easy to see, to read, and to understand, and must tell you the following information about the product.

1 *The name of the food* must be shown on the label and must not mislead the customer. For example, cartons of orange juice can only be called 'juice' if they are pure juice. If they are a mixture of different ingredients which taste of orange, then they may only be called 'orange drink'.

2 *The ingredients* Labels on pre-packed food must show a complete list of ingredients, in descending order of weight (heaviest first). That means that the ingredient there is most of is shown first. So you can tell, for instance, if what is called a 'beef curry with rice' is in fact nearly all rice, soya, and flavouring, with very little beef in it. Any food additives must be included in the list (see p. 126).

3 *The instructions for use* must be shown if it is not obvious what to do.

4 *The datemark* Under the 1983 regulations date-marking became compulsory for most foods. Some of the exceptions are frozen foods, fresh bread and cakes, fresh fruit and vegetables, sugar, and food which will last over 18 months.

   The datemark is usually in the form of 'best before' followed by the day, month, and year. Sometimes the day or year can be left out. The food should stay in peak condition of flavour, crispness, and so on up to the date shown.

   Perishable foods like cream or yoghurt, which should be eaten within a few days or weeks of packing, have a 'sell-by' date instead. The label also has a 'use by' date, after which it is illegal to sell it. It also tells you how you should store the food if it is to keep fresh for that time.

   Sometimes you will see food past its 'best before' date being sold cheaply in shops. This is not illegal provided the food is fit for consumption and the customer realizes what is being offered.

5 *Storage instructions* are important if the date marks are to apply. For example, if you keep a packet of butter in a warm kitchen when it should be stored in the fridge, you cannot expect it to keep fresh for the recommended time.

6 *Net quantity,* that is, the quantity without any packaging. This must be shown by wieght or by volume of the can or packet. Breakfast cereals, such as Weetabix and Shredded Wheat, need only state how many items are inside the packet.

7 *Name and address of the manufacturer or packer* of the food must be shown, because they are responsible for the original condition of the food.

8 *Place of origin* should be shown if it is not what the buyer might have expected.

9 *Special claims* Some foods claim to be suitable for slimmers, babies, or diabetics, or to contain extra amounts of vitamins or minerals. Any claims like this must be backed up with clear factual information on the label. (For nutritional information see p. 118.)

Some foods are exempt from these regulations and have their own rules, including milk, honey, hen's eggs, sugar, chocolate, and coffee.

Using food labels

Many people use food labels to help them follow the recommendations for a healthy diet or avoid food with a lot of additives. Because of this, manufacturers may advertise their products as 'low fat', 'sugar free', 'high fibre', or 'free from artificial colours and preservatives'. This is a useful guide, although you may find that foods which are 'good' in one way are not so good in another. For example, a bran breakfast cereal may be high in fibre, but may also contain a lot of sugar and salt. A 'sugar free' fruit drink may contain artificial colour and sweeteners. If you start to read food labels you will pick up a lot of information and will be able to make informed choices about what you eat.

(S) SAFEWAY CHICKEN JALFREZI WITH BASMATI RICE

Tender pieces of chicken breast in a medium spiced sauce with onion, tomatoes and peppers

INGREDIENTS
Cooked Basmati Rice, Water, Chicken, Onion,Tomato, Green Peppers, Vegetable Oil, Tomato Paste, Coriander Leaf, Unsalted Butter, Garlic, Flavouring, Salt, Ginger (contains Citric Acid), Modified Starch, Ground Cumin, Ground Coriander, Green Chilli, Isolated Soya Protein, Sugar, Ground Turmeric, Lactose, Pentasodium Triphosphate, Chilli Powder, Concentrated Lemon Juice, Cardamon Pods, Cloves

Minimum 17% meat

NUTRITION INFORMATION

Typical Values	Per 100 g	Per Pack
Energy	508 kJ (121 kcal)	1778 kJ (424 kcal)
Protein	5.8g	20.3g
Carbohydrate	12.3g	43.1g
of which sugars	1.1g	3.9g
starch	11.2g	39.2g
Fat	5.4g	18.9g
of which saturates	1.5g	5.3g
polyunsaturates	1.0g	3.5g
Fibre	0.3g	1.1g
Sodium	0.3g	1.1g

This pack provides 1 serving

STORAGE

Product stored in	Consume within
Main compartment of refrigerator or cool place	24 hours of purchase
★ Frozen food compartment (-6°C)	1 week of purchase
★★ Frozen food compartment (-12°C)	1 month of purchase
★★★ Frozen food compartment (-18°C)	until best before date
★★★ Food Freezer (-18°C)	until best before date

Do not refreeze after thawing

Produced in the UK for Safeway, 6 Millington Road Hayes, Middlesex UB3 4AY © Safeway 1994

REFUND & REPLACE Safeway brand products are double guaranteed. If you are not totally satisfied with any item, please return it to a Safeway store for a refund *and* a replacement. This does not affect your statutory rights.

COOKING GUIDELINES
For best results, cook from frozen.

OVEN Remove from outer packaging. Place on a baking tray in a preheated oven 200°C/400°F/Gas Mark 6 for 30-35 minutes, stirring half way through cooking and at the end of cooking time.

MICROWAVE Remove from outer packaging and pierce film lid. Stir half way through cooking.

MICROWAVE	ON FULL POWER	STANDING TIME
650W	9 minutes	1 minute
750 W	8½ minutes	1 minute
Category B	9 minutes	1 minute
Category D	8½ minutes	1 minute

Remove film lid, stir and serve.

CHECK FOOD IS PIPING HOT BEFORE SERVING
For ovens marked with a heating category, select appropriate times for your oven. For other ovens, refer to timings given of oven wattages. When using ovens of different power, heating times must be increased or decreased accordingly.

QUESTIONS

1 What basic information must be shown on all food packets?

2 If you saw a pizza for sale on its 'sell-by' date, marked at half price, would you think it was a good buy? Why?

3 Look at the information on the above pack and on pp. 11 and 27. What proportion of your requirement for (a) energy and (b) protein does this provide? (c) What two sources of protein are there in addition to the chicken? (d) What suggestions are made to make sure the food is kept free from bacterial infection?

Nutritional labelling

Many food manufacturers and retailers print information about the nutritional value of their products on the packet. They do not have to do this (unless a nutritional claim about the product is made, e.g. low fat, high fibre), but if they do it has to be in a certain format. This example is from a frozen vegetable lasagne for 1 person.

Eating well and keeping a healthy weight m.. .good sense fo. the whole family. That is why Weight Watchers from Heinz recipes have been carefully created with today's healthier eating guidelines in mind, with controlled levels of fat, sugar and salt, as well as calories. Plus all the taste to make healthy eating easy with Weight Watchers from Heinz.

NUTRITION INFORMATION		
Typical Values	Amount per 100g	Amount per Serving (320g)
Energy	339kJ/81kcal	1115kJ/265kcal
Protein	3.3g	10.9g
Carbohydrate	10.7g	35.1g
(of which sugars)	(3.7g)	(12.2g)
Fat	2.7g	9.0g
(of which saturates)	(1.5g)	(4.9g)
Fibre	0.9g	3.1g
Sodium	0.3g	1.0g

Additional information may be included such as the amount of:

- monounsaturates
- polyunsaturates
- trans fats
- vitamins

Nutritional claims

'Reduced fat' means that the product contains 25% less fat than the standard product. (Low fat spreads are an exception to this ruling.)

'Low fat' means that the product contains less than 5 g of fat per 100 g.

Some labels say that a product provides a % of RDA (recommended daily amount). To carry this claim, the product must contain at least 15% of the relevant RDA in 100 g (or in a packet if a single serving). The RDA in this case is defined by EU labelling legislation and is not the same as the RNI (see p. 45). It is a figure considered to be enough for the needs of the population as a whole.

Average portions

As labels all have to show food values per 100 g it is possible to compare one food with another. But for this information to be useful you have to think about how much of a food a person is likely to eat at any one time, and allow for very large and very small appetites. This is the average portion size or serving size. For example, which of the following could you easily eat as an average portion?

100 g baked potato	(1 medium)
100 g salt	(1 cupful)
100 g bread	(3 slices)
100 g boiled carrots	(2 medium)
100 g butter or margarine	(about half a tub or packet)
100 g egg	(2 eggs)

100 g crisps	(3 packets)
100 g cornflakes	(3 bowls)
100 g apple	(1 apple)

You will see that 100 g is a typical portion size for some foods, but not for others.

Bar coding

Many of the products we buy from supermarkets or large stores have a square of numbered black lines of varying thickness on the wrapping. The square is called a 'bar code' and is part of an electronic system increasingly used in shops.

Each group of lines of the bar code gives certain information. The first two reveal the country the product has come from, the next five reveal the manufacturer of the product, the next five identify the product itself. The thirteenth group is an accuracy check.

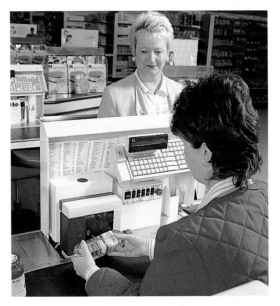

5 011415 000726

As you take your purchases out of your basket at the checkout the assistant passes the bar code on each product through a laser scanner. The laser unit is linked to a computer which holds the price of each item. The price is retrieved from the computer file, displayed on the till for the customer to see, and both the name of the product and its price are printed on the receipt. This means that it is easy to check exactly what you have bought and what it has cost when you get home. At the same time the computer records the sale of each item so that the shop knows at any time how much of any product has been sold and how much is in stock.

QUESTIONS

1. Is it compulsory for manufacturers to supply nutrition information?
2. Why could nutrition information be useful to someone on a weight-reducing diet?
3. Who might benefit from information on the amount of sodium or salt in a packet?
4. Why do you think cereal packets have information on vitamins?
5. Why do you need to remember average portion sizes (p. 44) when you compare nutrients per 100 g?
6. How does bar coding help managers of supermarkets? How can it help the shopper?

Preserving food 1

At one time, foods had to be preserved to make sure there was enough to eat in winter when the supply of fresh foods was very limited. Now we use preserved foods to give us variety and choice all year round. We do not have to shop every day, and because of refrigerated transport, bottling, canning, and drying we can have food from all parts of the world.

To preserve food means to treat it to prevent the natural process of decay. Food may be spoiled by oxidation, enzyme action, or micro-organisms.

Oxidation

Oxidation is the reaction of oxygen in the air with the chemicals which.make up food. Oxidation can cause fats to go rancid, which not only produces a bitter taste but can be harmful to health. If you look at food labels you will often see additives called antioxidants in fatty or oily foods. These are added to help stop oxidation reactions. For example, the antioxidants BHA (E320) and BHT (E321) are added to fats and oils, soup mixes, and cheese spreads.

Enzyme action

The enzymes naturally present in foods cause food to decay. For example, it is the action of enzymes which makes apples and potatoes go brown when they are cut or bruised. As soon as fruits are picked they start to dry out and to decay through enzyme action.

Micro-organisms

The micro-organisms which make food decay are bacteria, moulds, and yeasts.

Bacteria There are many different kinds of bacteria which can cause food spoilage and food poisoning. Not all bacteria are harmful but those that are include *Salmonella, Streptococcus, Bacillus cereus,* and *Clostridium welchii* (see p. 88). They can be seen under a microscope.

Moulds are tiny plants which you will probably have seen growing on cheese, fruit, or bread. They increase by means of spores which pass through the air and land on other food to create more mould. If a food is mouldy you should throw it away rather than just cut off the mould and eat the rest. The mould can send harmful substances into the food.

Yeasts are tiny single-celled fungi. They can spoil foods liked canned fruit and fruit juice by fermenting the sugar to produce alcohol and carbon dioxide. You may have noticed this 'fizzy' effect in fruit juice which has been kept too long. If you make bread with fresh yeast you will see bubbles of carbon dioxide produced when you add water and sugar to the yeast.

Not all bacteria, moulds, and yeasts have harmful effects. Many are deliberately used in the production of foods such as Danish blue and gorgonzola cheeses, yoghurt, and bread.

Conditions for growth

Most bacteria, moulds, and yeasts need food, moisture, warmth, and air in order to grow and increase. If we want to preserve food we have to keep it in ways which do not provide these conditions. For example, if food is *dried* there is no moisture; if food is *frozen* there is no warmth; if food is *vacuum-packed* there is no air. In these conditions bacteria, moulds, and yeasts cannot increase and cause food spoilage, so the food can be preserved.

Chemical preservatives

Chemical preservatives can be added to foods to keep them fresh. You will often see, for example, 'preservative E200, sulphur dioxide' on food ingredients lists. Other chemical preservatives include acids and sugar.

Acids

Acids such as ethanoic or acetic acid (vinegar) can be used for preserving, as bacteria, moulds, and yeasts do not grow and increase in acidic conditions. We use this method of preserving at home when we pickle vegetables or make vegetable chutney with vinegar. Acids can also help prevent enzyme reactions; for example, putting lemon juice on apple slices will stop them going brown.

Sugar

Bacteria do not grow in foods where there is a high concentration of sugar. We use this principle at home when making jam and marmalade.

QUESTIONS

1 What are the advantages of preserving food?
2 What are the three types of micro-organisms that cause food to decay?
3 You open a jar of home-made jam and there is mould on the top. Would you scrape off the mould and eat the rest? Why?
4 Look at the labels of some commercially made jams. What substances do they contain that stop mould growing?
5 Look at some food products at home or in a supermarket. List three chemical preservatives used in food.

Preserving food 2

Freezing

Bacteria do not reproduce at very low temperatures, so frozen food can be kept for long periods of time. Low temperatures also slow down oxidation and enzyme reactions.

Food can be frozen at home (see p. 84) or commercially. The commercial freezing process is very quick, and this keeps the food in better shape when it is thawed. Sometimes food is placed in or sprayed with liquid nitrogen, which is extremely cold and freezes the food extremely quickly. This is called cryogenic freezing and is often used for strawberries which would otherwise fall to a mush when thawed.

Peas are rapidly frozen in a freezing tunnel.

Freezing has little effect on the nutritional value of foods. The fruit and vegetables used are generally picked at their peak and frozen very quickly and their vitamin C content can be as good as or better than that of fresh vegetables or fruit which have been picked and stored for a time before cooking.

Canning and bottling

Food is put into the cans or bottles, sealed, then subjected to very high temperatures which kill most bacteria. The food can then be kept unopened for up to several years. Blown cans or dented cans should not be used as they may contain harmful bacteria. The high temperatures used will destroy some of the vitamin C and B vitamins in the food.

Drying

Micro-organisms need moisture to grow and reproduce. If moisture is removed by drying, food can be preserved for long periods of time. For example, peas, beans, lentils, and rice are all dried so that they keep well. At one time, the sun was used to dry foods such as grapes (to produce currants, raisins, and sultanas), leaves from the tea plant (to make tea leaves), and sun-dried tomatoes. Most drying is now carried out in factories, where food is dried on trays in hot air. Milk is dried by spraying liquid milk into hot air so that it dries out almost immediately to solid droplets. Instant coffee and instant potato are made by accelerated freeze drying. The food is quickly frozen and then the ice crystals removed by heating in a vacuum.

Drying foods has little effect on most nutrients but destroys about half the vitamin C. Dried (instant) potato usually has vitamin C added to it, so it is still a good source.

Vacuum packing and modified atmosphere packaging

These both work by removing the air from food. Removing the air helps prevent oxidation reactions and slows down the growth of micro-organisms which need air to grow.

In *vacuum packing*, the food is wrapped in plastic and the air is sucked out. Vacuum packing of bacon, cooked meats, and cheese extends their life for a short time, but they should still be stored in a cool place.

In *modified atmosphere packaging*, the air is replaced by an unreactive gas such as nitrogen. For example, some crisps are packed in a modified atmosphere, so that there is no air to oxidize the fat.

QUESTIONS

1. How does the vitamin C in frozen and canned food compare with that in fresh food?
2. You see a can of food with a dent for half price in your corner shop. Would you think it was a bargain?
3. How does drying food help to preserve it?
4. Look at the label of a packet of dried milk. What does it contain, apart from milk? Why?
5. Why does vacuum-packed bacon keep longer than bacon stored in a plastic bag? Why should vacuum-packed bacon be kept in the fridge?

Food additives

Food additives are substances added to food in small quantities while it is being prepared for sale. If you make a habit of reading the labels on food packets you will soon realize that they are very widely used. They are added for one of two main reasons:

1 to prevent food going 'off'
2 to try to improve its colour, texture, or flavour

Why are additives so widely used?

In its natural state, food decays and goes 'off' fairly quickly. In the UK most people live in towns and cities quite a long way from where food is grown or produced. To keep it fresh until we can eat it, much of it is preserved by chilling, freezing, canning, vacuum packing, or adding preservatives. The present vast range of reasonably priced foods on our supermarket shelves includes very many preserved and processed foods.

People now expect a lot of the food they eat to be prepared and cooked in the factory so that it is ready to eat when they buy it. On the whole they spend less time preparing fresh ingredients at home and buy more food in packets, jars, cans, or frozen. Nearly all foods are available like this: meat dishes, soups, vegetables, bread, cakes, biscuits, jams, sauces, and so on. For example, instead of spending time making soup by peeling, washing, cutting, and cooking fresh vegetables we may want to pour boiling water on to a packet mix and have the soup ready in minutes. Instead of making a cake with sugar, butter, eggs, and flour we may go to the supermarket for a cake in a packet that was made weeks ago and is kept fresh by additives.

When foods are cooked in the factory and put into jars, cartons, tins and so on, the natural colour, flavour, and texture is often altered, so additives are used to try to improve them in these respects. Look at the ingredients in the two packets shown below and opposite, and compare them with the home-made versions.

Cream of Chicken
SOUP

INGREDIENTS, WHEN RECONSTITUTED:
SKIMMED MILK, BUTTERMILK, WHEY, MODIFIED STARCH, ONION, POTATO STARCH, SALT, HYDROGENATED VEGETABLE OIL, MALTODEXTRIN, CHICKEN, FLAVOUR ENHANCERS (MONOSODIUM GLUTAMATE, SODIUM 5'-RIBONUCLEOTIDE, SODIUM GUANYLATE), YEAST EXTRACT, CASEINATES, SOY SAUCE, STABILISER (SODIUM TRIPOLYPHOSPHATE), HERBS, FLAVOURINGS, CITRIC ACID, SPICES, CELERY EXTRACT.

Chicken

Water

Milk

Flour

Salt and pepper

Ingredients for home-made cream of chicken soup (above)

Ingredients for packet chicken soup (left)

NO ADDED SUGAR

Chocolate flavour dessert mix

INGREDIENTS
Modified Starch, Vegetable Oil (Hydrogenated),
Whey powder, Fat Reduced Cocoa, Emulsifiers
(Propylene Glycol Monostearate, Soya Lecithin),
Gelling Agents (Disodium Phosphate, Sodium
Pyrophosphate), Milk Protein, Colour (Caramel),
Flavourings, Artificial Sweeteners (Aspartame,
Acesulfame K).

47 g e

Chocolate

Butter

Eggs

Cream

Ingredients for home-made chocolate mousse (above)

Ingredients for packet mix (left)

Some possible effects of food additives

Many people wonder whether additives are harmful or not. Their use is strictly controlled in the UK, and there are hundreds on the 'permitted' list. However, some countries do not allow some of the additives freely used in other countries. They all have to be tested to see what effects they may have, but it is not easy to know how much or how little of a substance may be considered 'safe' or 'harmful' over a long period of time. Some additives are widely used in many foods, some are used very little.

Many food manufacturers now advertise their products as 'free from artificial colours or preservatives'. Natural colours such as annatto, curcumin, or beta-carotene are often used now as yellow colouring, instead of E102 tartrazine which used to be widely used.

Reactions to food additives Many people blame food additives for unpleasant reactions to food but research has shown that reactions to food additives are rare, probably affecting only one in 10,000 people. Adverse reactions to 'ordinary' foods such as milk, egg, shellfish, nuts, soya, tea, coffee, and citrus fruits are much more common.

QUESTIONS

1 What are the two main reasons for using food additives?
2 What advantages are there in using preservatives?
3 How do processed foods compare with freshly made foods in terms of flavour?
4 Look at the butter, margarine, and spreads on p. 24. What would you choose to spread on your bread, and why?
5 Why do you think manufacturers of drinks often put 'free from artificial colours and preservatives' prominently on their labels?
6 Which cause more unpleasant reactions to foods, additives or 'natural' foods?
7 List the advantages and disadvantages of using food additives.
8 List the ingredients found in a packet of chicken soup that you would not use if you were making fresh chicken soup.

Control of additives

The use of additives is controlled by the Food Safety Act 1990 which forbids the addition to food or drink of any substance which may be harmful to health. Under EU food labelling regulations, food packets must give information about the purpose of the additive and its name or agreed number. An 'E' in front of a number means that the additive has been tested and is permitted for use throughout the EU. Additives without the 'E' in front have the approval of the British government but not the EU.

Types of additive

Additives may be grouped into four main types, according to their purpose.

Additives to preserve food or improve its keeping qualities

This group includes:

a   *Preservatives* (E200 numbers). These prevent food being spoiled by bacteria, mould, or yeasts, e.g. E202 potassium sorbate.

b   *Antioxidants* (E300 numbers). These prevent fats and oils from going rancid. You will often see them on snack foods like crisps which have been fried in oil, as well as on lard and margarine packets. Examples are E320 butylated hydroxyanisole (BHA), E321 butylated hydroxytoluene (BHT).

Additives to improve the texture and consistency of foods

This group includes:

a   *Emulsifiers, thickeners, and gelling agents* (E400 numbers). They may, for example, stop foods like salad cream or instant dessert whips from dividing into separate layers, or make sure that jam 'gels' or sets. This group also includes *humectants* to keep foods soft and prevent them going dry (often used in bought cakes). They include sorbitol (E420) and glycerol (E422) which is found in cake icing.

b   *Anti-caking agents* (E551 to E572). They prevent powders or salt from sticking or caking in the packet (e.g. calcium silicate (E552) is added to icing sugar to stop it going lumpy).

Additives used to alter the appearance or taste of food or drink

This group includes:

a   *Colours*

yellows	E100s and E110s
reds	E120s
blues	E130s
greens	E140s
browns and blacks	E150s

E160s are all natural colourants rather than artificial ones and include annatto, curcumin, and beetroot red. Most food manufacturers now use natural colours because some of the synthetic ones are suspected of having harmful effects. E170s are metal and mineral colourings.

Strawberry **Trifle**
FLAVOUR

INGREDIENTS **Strawberry Flavour Jelly Crystals:** Sugar, Gelling Agents (Carrageenan, Dipotassium Phosphate, Potassium Chloride), Adipic Acid, Acidity Regulator (Cream of Tartar), Thickener (Carboxymethylcellulose), Flavourings, Artificial Sweetener (Sodium Saccharin), Colours (Annato, Betanin).
Custard Powder: Cornflour, Salt, Flavourings, Colour (Annatto).
Trifle Topping Mix: Hydrogenated Vegetable Oil, Sugar, Emulsifiers (Propylene Glycol Monostearate, Lecithin), Modified Starch, Whey Powder, Lactose, Caseinate, Thickener (Carboxymethylcellulose), Flavourings, Colour (Beta-Carotene).
Sponge Fingers Contain: Wheatflour, Eggs, Raising Agent (Ammonium Bicarbonate), Flavouring.
Decorations: with Colour (Cochineal).

145 g ℮

Examples of colourings used are:
E142 Green S (Acid Brilliant Green BS or Lissamine Green)
E150 caramel, the most used of the 52 permitted colours
E160a beta-carotene, a natural yellow colour often used in margarine
E174, the silver in edible cake decorations

Baby foods are only allowed to use the three colours which are also vitamin sources (e.g. beta carotene).

b *Flavour enhancers* (E600 numbers). For example, monosodium glutamate (E621) is used to bring out flavour in foods.

c *Sweeteners* do not have E numbers but there is a list of artificial sweeteners, including saccharin, acesulfame K, and aspartame, which are permitted in the UK.

Additives for miscellaneous purposes

These include anti-foaming agents (to prevent pineapple juice from frothing too much), flour improvers, acids, raising agents, and glazing agents (to give a shine to confectionery).

Composition of foods

Certain regulations lay down standards for the make-up of foods. Meat products regulations state, for example, that a pork sausage must contain 65% meat, but a beef sausage need contain only 50% meat. The bread and flour regulations require that all flours contain certain amounts of thiamin, niacin, iron, and calcium, so these are added to all flours except wholemeal to bring them up to the prescribed level. (Wholemeal flour already contains more than these levels.) The margarine regulations require that vitamins A and D are added to all margarine. You can send for a booklet about food additives (see p. 234).

QUESTIONS

1 How is the use of food additives controlled by law?
2 What are the four main types of additives used?
3 What would happen to a jar of salad cream without emulsifier?
4 What series of E numbers is given to colourants which are natural rather than artificial? Name three natural colourants.
5 Why do you think baby foods are only allowed very few additives?
6 What additives are added by law to flour and margarine? Why is this done?
7 Look in your cupboards and fridge at home. List 15 different food additives and which foods they are in.

Cold starters

Mackerel pâté *Serves 3–4*

1 tin mackerel or 150–200 g smoked mackerel fillets
25 g butter
1 lemon
1 tablespoon vinegar
Salt and pepper
Cress or parsley and lemon slice to garnish

Method

1 Open tin of mackerel, remove skin and bone, drain off the liquid.
2 Cut the lemon in half, cut off one or two neat slices for garnish. Squeeze the juice from the rest of the lemon.
3 Mix the mackerel, butter, lemon juice, vinegar, salt, and pepper in a basin. Beat very thoroughly with a fork and then with a wooden spoon until smooth, or use a food processor.
4 Turn into a small dish and smooth the top. Chill.
5 Garnish with a little cress or parsley and a twist of lemon.

Serve with fingers of toast or fresh bread buns, or in a baked potato.

Florida cocktail *Serves 3–4* (v)

2 oranges
1 grapefruit

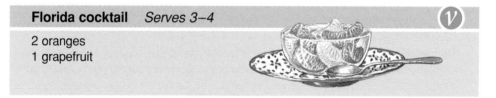

Method

1 Cut the top and bottom from the grapefruit, stand it flat on the board, and remove the skin with a sharp knife.

2 Carefully remove all the segments between the dividing skins. Hold over a bowl as you do this to collect any juice.
3 Prepare the oranges in the same way, mix with the grapefruit, and chill.
4 Serve in individual glass dishes, standing on a doily on a small plate, with a teaspoon. For a decorative effect you can dip the rim of the empty glass dish into egg white and then into caster sugar, to 'frost' the rim.

Ham and cheese roll-ups   *Serves 4*

4 slices cooked ham
1 small carton cottage or cream cheese
Lettuce leaves
1 tomato

Method

1   Spread the cheese over the slices of ham and roll them up.
2   Wash the lettuce leaves carefully under cold running water, then gently shake
    them dry. Arrange on a flat serving plate. Slice the tomato thinly.
3   Place the ham rolls neatly on the lettuce and place the tomato slices on top.

You would serve these with thinly cut brown bread and butter.

Ham and coleslaw roll-ups Use coleslaw (see p. 192 for the recipe) instead of
cottage cheese. Make and serve in the same way.

Stuffed eggs   *Serves 2*

2 eggs
25 g cheese
1 level tablespoon salad cream
Lettuce for serving

Method

1   Put the eggs in a small pan, cover with cold water. Bring to the boil and simmer
    gently for 10 minutes. Leave to cool.
2   Wash the lettuce leaves carefully under the cold tap. Gently shake them to
    remove the water. Grate the cheese very finely.
3   Shell the eggs, then cut them in half lengthwise.
4   Remove the yolk from the eggs. Mix it with the cheese and salad cream. Either
    spoon it or pipe it back into the whites. Arrange neatly on the lettuce.

Stuffed tomatoes   *Serves 4*

4 firm tomatoes
2 slices of bread
50 g cheese
Salt and pepper
Lettuce for serving

Method

1   Wash and dry the tomatoes. Slice the top off to make a lid (not the stalk end).
2   Use a grater or blender to make breadcrumbs. Grate the cheese.
3   Using a teaspoon, remove the inside of the tomatoes and mix this with the
    crumbs and cheese. Add a little salt and pepper.
4   Spoon this filling back into the tomatoes, put the lid on.
5   Wash the lettuce and gently shake it dry. Serve the tomatoes on the lettuce.

To serve hot Stand the filled tomatoes on a greased baking tray. Brush with oil or
melted butter and bake at Gas 4, 180°C, for about 20 minutes.

Melon *Serves 4–6*

One small melon, or about half a larger melon
Maraschino or glacé cherries
(if you like them)

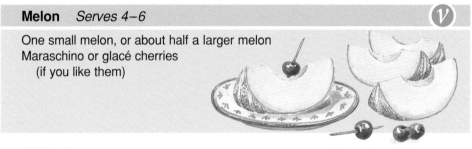

Method

1   Cut the melon into quarters, or cut it into six if it is large.
2   If you want to garnish it with a cherry, spear the cherry on to a cocktail stick and push into the centre of the melon slice.
3   Serve cool.

Avocado

One avocado serves 2 people

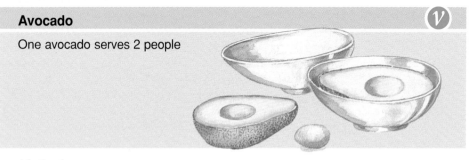

Method

Cut the avocado in two, remove the stone. Place on a small dish and serve (eat it with a teaspoon). It is important not to cut the avocado until just before you are going to serve it, because it starts to discolour straight away (like a cut apple).

Some people like to sprinkle a little French dressing (see p. 190) over the avocado, or to put a few prawns in the hollow where the stone was.

Prawn (or tuna) cocktail *Serves 4*

200 g can tuna or prawns, or frozen or fresh prawns
2 tablespoons natural yoghurt
1 tablespoon mayonnaise
1 teaspoon tomato ketchup
A few lettuce leaves

Method

1   Wash the lettuce and cut into shreds with a knife. Place in the bottom of 4 glass dishes.
2   If using tuna, drain any oil or water from it. Put the tuna into a dish and flake with a fork.
3   Mix the yoghurt, mayonnaise, and ketchup together, stir in the tuna or prawns. Divide between the 4 dishes and serve cool.

Lentil and hazelnut pâté   *Serves about 6*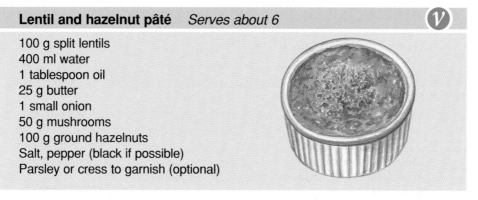

100 g split lentils
400 ml water
1 tablespoon oil
25 g butter
1 small onion
50 g mushrooms
100 g ground hazelnuts
Salt, pepper (black if possible)
Parsley or cress to garnish (optional)

Method

1   Put the lentils into a sieve and wash under the cold tap. Put into a pan with the water and boil rapidly for about 15 minutes until the lentils are soft and the water is absorbed. Check from time to time that the lentils do not stick to the pan.
2   Heat the butter and oil in a pan. Peel the onion, chop it finely, and fry gently until soft. Cut the mushrooms into fine slices and add to the onions.
3   When the lentils are cooked, beat them well until smooth. Add the onions and hazelnuts. Taste, add salt and pepper, and mix well. (If you wanted a smoother pâté you could now blend in a food processor, but it is not necessary if you have chopped the onions finely.)
4   Put into a serving dish, or 6 small ramekins and smooth the top. Leave to cool. Garnish with parsley or cress if you are using it.

Stuffed mushrooms   *Serves 4*

2 teaspoons oil
25 g butter
½ a small onion
50 g bread (crusts off)
1 tomato
Pinch of herbs
Salt, pepper (black if possible)
4 large flat mushrooms

Method

1   Light the oven, Gas 6, 200°C. Put the shelf near the top. Brush a baking tin with oil. Put a kettle of water on to boil.
2   Warm the oil and butter in a pan. Peel the onion and chop it finely. Fry gently.
3   Make the bread into crumbs with a grater, blender, or food processor. Add to the pan.
4   Put the tomato into a small jug or basin, cover with boiling water, and leave for about a minute. Remove it from the water with a spoon, then peel off the skin. Cut the tomato in half, then into very small dice. Add to the pan.
5   Turn off the heat and add the herbs. Taste, adding salt and pepper as needed.
6   Put the mushrooms into the baking tin, add a little salt, then put the stuffing onto the mushrooms. Brush the edges with a little oil, then bake in the oven for 20 minutes. Carefully lift out onto hot plates to serve.

If you were short of time you could make these with a packet of stuffing.

Soups

It is easy to make soup at home, and it always has a good flavour when made with fresh ingredients. With many soup recipes you can adapt the vegetables to make best use of those which are cheap and in season.

Always taste the soup before you serve it, to make sure it has enough salt and pepper. If it is too thick, it can be thinned with a little water or milk. If too thin, it can be thickened by blending a level tablespoon of cornflour or plain flour with about 3 tablespoons of cold milk or water in a small basin. Pour this into the soup, bring to the boil, and simmer for a few minutes to thicken.

Serve the soup in a soup tureen, garnished with chopped parsley or a few thinly-sliced vegetables. For a special occasion, a little single cream poured over the top of the soup looks attractive.

Tomato soup *Serves 3–4* Ⓥ

1 medium-sized can of tomatoes	1 potato, 1 onion, 1 carrot
500 ml water	Salt and pepper
1 stock cube	Chopped parsley

Method

1 Peel and chop the potato, onion, and carrot. Put them in a pan with the tomatoes, water, and stock cube, and stir to dissolve the stock cube.
2 Simmer gently with the lid on for about 20 minutes until soft.
3 Liquidize or sieve the soup. Check the flavour, adding salt and pepper if needed. Reheat if necessary.
4 Serve in a warm soup tureen, sprinkled with chopped parsley.

Golden vegetable soup *Serves 3–4* Ⓥ

1 potato	2 sticks celery or 1 leek (optional)
1 carrot	1 onion (2 if not using celery or leek)
1 tablespoon oil	1 stock cube
750 ml water	Salt and pepper
Chopped parsley	1 level tablespoon plain flour or cornflour

Method

1 Peel all the vegetables, grate the carrot and finely chop the other vegetables. Fry in the oil for 10 minutes.
2 Add the water and stock cube, bring to the boil, and simmer for about 25 minutes until all the vegetables are soft.
3 Blend the flour with 4 tablespoons water until smooth. Pour into the soup and simmer for 5 minutes. Check the flavour, adding salt and pepper if needed.
4 Blend in a liquidizer until smooth.
5 Serve in a warm soup tureen, sprinkled with parsley.

Onion soup   *Serves 3–4*   ⓥ

500 g onions	1 stock cube
1 tablespoon oil	Salt and pepper
1 medium-sized potato	Chopped parsley
750 ml water	

Method

1 Peel and roughly chop the onions and potato.
2 Heat the oil in a fairly large pan and gently fry the vegetables for 10 minutes.
3 Add the water and stock cube, and bring to the boil. Simmer with the lid on for about 30 minutes until cooked.
4 Put into a blender and run for a few seconds until smooth (or sieve). Check the seasoning, adding salt and pepper if necessary. Reheat if necessary.
5 Serve in a warm soup tureen, garnished with chopped parsley.

Mushroom soup   *Serves 3*   ⓥ

100 g mushrooms	1 stock cube
15 g butter	Salt and pepper
½ a small onion	1 level tablespoon plain flour or cornflour
500 ml water	125 ml milk

Method

1 Carefully wash the mushrooms in cold water. Slice one of them very thinly to use as a garnish, and roughly chop the rest. Peel and chop the onion.
2 Melt the butter in a pan and gently fry the vegetables for 5 minutes. Add the water and stock cube.
3 Bring to the boil and simmer with the lid on for 25 minutes.
4 Mix the flour with the milk until smooth. Check the seasoning, pour into the pan, and boil for a few minutes. Blend for a few seconds until smooth.
5 Serve in a warm soup tureen, garnished with mushroom slices.

Lentil soup   *Serves 3–4*   ⓥ

75 g lentils	1 tablespoon oil
1 large carrot	750 ml water
1 onion	1 stock cube
1 medium potato	Salt and pepper
½ a small turnip or swede	Chopped parsley
1 celery stalk (optional)	

Method

1 Wash the lentils in a sieve and drain.
2 Thinly slice the carrot, onion, celery. Cut the potatoes and turnip into small dice.
3 Heat the oil in a large pan and fry the vegetables for about 5 minutes. Add the lentils, water, and stock cube. Bring to the boil, stirring, lower the heat and cover.
4 Simmer very gently for 45 minutes (or pressure cook at H pressure for 30 minutes, then reduce the pressure at room temperature).
5 Liquidize or sieve. Check the flavour, adding salt and pepper if necessary.
6 Serve hot, sprinkled with chopped parsley.

Leek and potato soup   *Serves 4*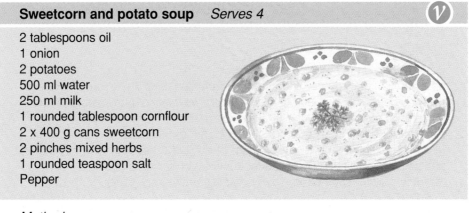

2 tablespoons oil	1 stock cube
1 onion	1 rounded teaspoon salt
3 potatoes	Pepper
2 leeks	125 ml milk
700 ml water	1 rounded tablespoon cornflour

Method

1 Warm the oil in a large pan, peel and chop the onion, and fry without browning.
2 Peel the potatoes and cut them into slices no more than 1cm thick. Add to the pan.
3 Trim the ends off the leeks and slice them. Put into a colander one at a time and wash carefully under cold running water. Add to the pan.
4 Add the water and stock cube to the pan.
5 Simmer with the lid on for 20–30 minutes until the vegetables are cooked.
6 Mix the milk and cornflour until smooth. Pour into the soup, stirring, until it thickens.
7 Check the flavour, adding salt and pepper if needed.

Sweetcorn and potato soup   *Serves 4*

2 tablespoons oil
1 onion
2 potatoes
500 ml water
250 ml milk
1 rounded tablespoon cornflour
2 x 400 g cans sweetcorn
2 pinches mixed herbs
1 rounded teaspoon salt
Pepper

Method

1 Warm the oil, peel and chop the onion. Fry gently without letting it brown.
2 Peel the potatoes and cut to 1cm dice. Add to the pan, add the water and bring to the boil, then simmer for about 10 minutes until the potatoes are cooked.
3 Mix the milk and cornflour until smooth. Pour into the pan and bring to the boil, stirring all the time to thicken. Add the sweetcorn, herbs, salt, and pepper, checking the taste. Simmer for a further five minutes.

Fish

A wide variety of fish is available in Britain. If you don't have a fishmonger near you, you can buy frozen fish from a supermarket or freezer centre. Frozen fish is a good substitute for fresh, though there may be less variety to choose from. The fish is usually frozen quite soon after being caught, so not much flavour is lost. There are three main types of fish: white fish, oily fish, and shellfish.

White fish

These are fish which have white flesh, and include cod, haddock, whiting, plaice, sole, and coley or saithe. Coley is becoming more popular, as cod and haddock become more expensive. Its flesh is less white before cooking, but when cooked it has a good flavour and colour and can be used in any recipe which normally uses the more expensive fish.

Food value
White fish is a good source of protein, phosphorus, and iodine. As there is little fat or oil in the flesh of white fish it is easily digested. This makes it a suitable food for invalids and elderly people. The liver of the cod is used to make cod-liver oil, which is a very good source of vitamins A and D.

Oily fish

This group includes herring, mackerel, sardines, pilchards, salmon, trout, and tuna. These fish are called oily as they have oil dispersed through the flesh. They are usually darker in colour than white fish. Oily fish are a rich source of essential fatty acids (see p. 16) so we are advised to eat them a couple of times a week as part of a healthy diet. This can easily be done by having, for example, sardines on toast, tuna sandwiches, mackerel pâté, or a cooked fish dish.

Other nutrients
They are a good source of protein, phosphorus, iodine, polyunsaturated fats (in the form of oil), and vitamins A and D. They are particularly useful as a source of vitamin D as this is not found in many other foods. Canned fish, where the bones have been softened and may be eaten, are also a good source of calcium.

Shellfish

Shellfish are protected by a hard external shell. Lobster, crabs, prawns, shrimps, cockles, mussels, and oysters are all shellfish. They are a good source of protein but not of vitamins and minerals, and they are fairly hard to digest. They must be eaten very fresh, or they may cause food poisoning. Most of them are sold cooked, except for oysters, mussels, and scallops.

Smoked fish
Some fish may be smoked. This adds flavour and it helps the fish to stay fresh for longer. Examples are smoked haddock, kippers (which are smoked herrings), smoked mackerel, smoked salmon, and smoked trout.

Choosing fish

It is important that the fish you buy is really fresh, as it does not keep well. Look for these signs:

1 The flesh should be firm and moist.
2 Whole fish should have bright red gills and sparkling scales, and the eyes should be prominent, not sunken.
3 The fish should have a fresh smell.
4 When choosing smoked fish, look for firm flesh, a glossy skin, and a wholesome smoky smell.

Storing fish

As fresh fish does not keep well, it should be eaten the day it is bought, or the following day at the latest if kept in a refrigerator. A supply of canned fish such as sardines, mackerel, or salmon is useful in the store cupboard. Frozen fish may be stored in the freezer if you have one. Several kinds are available, and it is quite cheap if bought in bulk from a freezer centre.

Serving

White fish can sometimes lack flavour and colour. This can be overcome by:

1 using a method of cooking which adds flavour, such as frying in breadcrumbs or butter;
2 serving with a well-flavoured sauce, such as cheese or tomato sauce;
3 serving with plenty of colourful garnish, such as parsley, cress, lemon slices or wedges, or tomatoes.

Recipes using fish

As well as the recipes below, fish is also included in: mackerel pâté (p. 128), pizza (p. 228), quick cheese pizza (p. 174), tuna fish salad (p. 193), sardine and tomato sandwiches (p. 211), sardine and tomato salad (p. 193).

QUESTIONS

1 Give some examples of white fish and list the nutrients they contain.
2 Make a list of the types of oily fish you have eaten or seen on sale. List the nutrients they contain.
3 Name as many recipes as you can in which you would use (a) white fish, (b) oily fish.
4 Why are fish sometimes smoked? Give some examples.
5 What signs would you look for when choosing fresh fish?
6 What foods can be served with fish to add colour and flavour?

Recipes

Fried fillets of fish   *Serves 3*

3 fillets of any white fish, about 100 g each
1 egg   Oil for frying
50 g fresh white bread   1 lemon
Flour for coating   Parsley or cress

Method
1   Wash and dry the fish. Make the bread into crumbs. Beat the egg and put into a shallow dish. Put the flour on to a plate.
2   Dip the fish into the flour, then brush with the beaten egg. Coat with the crumbs, pressing them on to the fish. Shake off any loose crumbs.

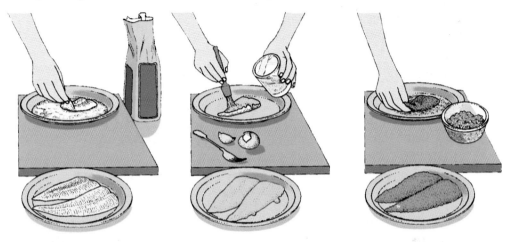

3   Heat the oil in a frying pan. There should be enough to cover the bottom of the pan to about 0.5 cm depth.
4   Carefully lower the fish into the hot oil, placing the skin side of the fish upwards. Cook gently for about 7 minutes, then turn over and cook the other side. When cooked the fish should be white and no longer transparent.
5   While the fish is cooking, cut the lemon into wedges or slices, and wash the parsley.
6   Drain the fish fillets on kitchen paper to remove any excess oil. Place them on paper on a warm, flat serving dish, and garnish with the lemon and parsley.

To cut the lemon wedges or twists for garnishing fish dishes:

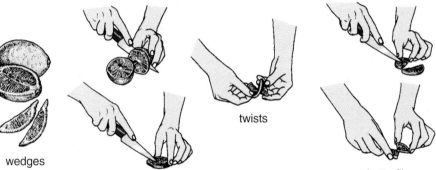

twists

wedges

butterflies

Fish and cheese sauce   *Serves 2–3*

250 g white fish
Small packet instant potato (optional)
Parsley to garnish

Sauce
250 ml milk
25 g plain flour
25 g margarine
Salt, pepper, pinch of mustard
100 g cheese

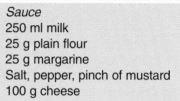

Method

1   Wash the fish, place it between two plates, and steam it over a pan of simmering water until cooked (about 15 minutes).
2   Grate the cheese. Make up the instant potato if you are using it.
3   Put the sauce ingredients into a pan. Bring to the boil, whisking all the time. Simmer for 2–3 minutes until thick. Stir in half the cheese.
4   When the fish is cooked, place it in a shallow ovenproof dish. Pour the sauce over, sprinkle the rest of the cheese on top. Pipe the potatoes around the edge.
5   Either grill under a medium heat, or place near the top of a hot oven until golden brown. Garnish with a sprig of parsley.

Fish cakes   *Makes 6*

100 g white fish (or a can of mackerel, tuna, or salmon)
250 g potatoes (or small packet instant potato)
15 g margarine
Salt and pepper
1 level tablespoon parsley (optional)
1 sprig of parsley for garnishing

For coating
Flour, 1 beaten egg, breadcrumbs
Oil for frying

Method

1   Wash and peel the potatoes. Cut them into even-sized pieces, put in a pan, and cover with cold water, adding a little salt. Simmer for about 20 minutes until cooked.
2   Wash the fish and place between two plates over the potatoes. Steam for about 15 minutes until cooked.
3   Wash and chop the parsley. Keep a sprig for garnishing.
4   Mash the cooked potatoes, flake the fish and add to the potatoes with the margarine, salt, pepper, and parsley.
5   Divide the mixture into 6 pieces, and shape into fish cakes. Coat each with flour, beaten egg, and crumbs (see p. 137).
6   Heat the oil in a frying pan. Fry the fish cakes carefully, turning over once. Drain well on kitchen paper.
7   Serve on a shallow dish, garnished with the sprig of parsley.

If you are using a can of fish, just open the can, drain the liquid, remove any skin and bone, and mix with the cooked, mashed potato.

Fish and tomato casserole   *Serves 3–4*

About 500 g white fish fillet (e.g. cod, coley, haddock)
Salt and pepper
1 onion
1 medium-sized tin of tomatoes
25 g butter
1 rounded tablespoonful chopped parsley
25 g fresh white or brown breadcrumbs
50 g cheese

Method
1 Wash the fish, place in an ovenproof dish, sprinkle with salt and pepper.
2 Peel and slice the onion, wash and chop the parsley. Drain most of the juice off the tomatoes. Put the tomatoes, onion, parsley, and butter into a small pan, and simmer gently for 10 minutes.
3 Grate the cheese. Grate the bread to make breadcrumbs.
4 Pour the tomatoes over the fish. Mix the cheese and crumbs, and spread them over the tomato mixture.
5 Bake in the centre of the oven, Gas 4, 180°C for 30 minutes.

Serve with mashed potatoes and fresh vegetables.

Crispy fish bake   *Serves 2–3*

1 tin mackerel or tuna fish
1 tin condensed mushroom or chicken soup
50 g bread
50 g cheese
1 packet of plain crisps
Lemon and parsley to garnish

Method
1 Light the oven, Gas 5, 190°C. Place the shelf in the centre of the oven.
2 Remove any skin or bone from the fish. Place the fish in a greased 500 ml ovenproof dish.
3 Pour the soup over the fish.
4 Make the bread into crumbs (using blender or grater). Grate the cheese. Crush the crisps in the packet.
5 Mix the bread, cheese, and crisps together, and place over the soup.
6 Bake in the oven for about 30 minutes until hot and lightly browned.
7 Garnish with parsley and lemon twists (see p. 137). Serve with freshly cooked vegetables.

Meat

The meat we eat in Britain today comes mainly from the cow (beef), the calf (veal), the sheep (mutton and lamb), and the pig (pork and bacon).

The food value of meat

Meat is a valuable food as it supplies many nutrients. It is a good source of:

- *protein,* in the lean part of all meats;
- *fat,* both in the fat you can see on the meat and in the fat spread through the meat;
- *iron,* particularly in liver and kidney, corned beef, black pudding, and red meat;
- *B vitamins,* in most meats.

Storing meat

1 Meat must be kept in a cold place, preferably in a fridge.
2 Cover meat loosely with foil before placing in the fridge, so that it does not dry out.
3 Uncooked beef, pork, and lamb will keep for 2–3 days in a refrigerator.
   Mince and liver can only be kept for one day uncooked.
   Sausages should only be kept for up to three days.
   Cooked meats should only be kept for 2–3 days.
4 Frozen meat keeps for varying lengths of time, depending on what kind it is.

Cuts of meat

Meat is cut into different joints or cuts. The more expensive cuts are leaner and more tender. They can be cooked by quicker, dry methods such as roasting, frying, or grilling. Cheaper cuts usually cost less because they are tougher or have more fat. They need to be cooked more slowly, by a moist cooking method such as stewing, boiling, or in a casserole. They have a good flavour and are just as nutritious as expensive cuts.

Beef

Beef should be a bright red colour when freshly cut. It darkens a little when it is exposed to the air but this does no harm. The fat may be creamy coloured or white. There should not be too much gristle in the meat.

Methods of cooking beef
Roasting: sirloin, rib, silverside.
Grilling or frying: sirloin, rump, or fillet steak.
Stewing or in a casserole: blade, buttock, or chuck steak (these may be labelled 'braising steak'); shin (often just labelled 'stewing steak').

Mince is made from flank or other cheaper cuts. If it is very fatty it is not very good value for money. You can buy lean stewing steak instead and ask the butcher to mince it for you, so that you can see what you are buying.

Foods served with beef

With roast beef it is traditional to serve Yorkshire pudding and sometimes horseradish sauce. With boiled silverside it is traditional to eat dumplings.

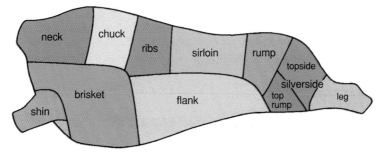

Veal

Veal is meat from the young calf. It is a pale pink colour with a small amount of white fat. The calf is specially fed to produce the delicate flavour and colour. Veal is very lean and tender. It is very expensive and is not eaten much in the UK.

Lamb and mutton

Most lamb is from young sheep up to about 6 months old. Mutton is from sheep about 18 months old. The meat of lamb should be pink. In an older animal it is darker. The fat should be a creamy white colour.

Methods of cooking lamb

As lamb is young, most cuts are tender enough to be fried, grilled, or roasted. The only exceptions are the middle or scrag end of neck, sometimes sold as 'stewing chops'.
Roasting: leg, shoulder, breast, loin, best end of neck.
Grilling or frying: loin chops, chump chops, cutlets.
Stewing or in a casserole: middle neck, scrag end of neck.

The traditional sauce to serve with roast lamb is mint.

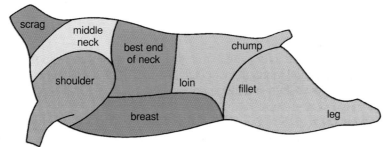

Pork

Pork is meat from the pig. It should have firm, pink meat and white fat. The skin should be smooth and free from hairs. Pork is a rich meat, containing a lot of fat dispersed through the flesh as well as the fat you can see around the meat. Apple sauce is the traditional sauce served with roast pork. Its sharp, tangy flavour balances the richness of the meat. Sage and onion stuffing, too, is usually served with roast pork. Pork must always be thoroughly cooked.

Methods of cooking pork
Roasting: leg, fillet, loin, spare rib, hand or shoulder, belly (this is a cheaper cut as it is more fatty).
Grilling or frying: loin chops, chump chops, spare rib chops.
In a casserole: belly pork, spare rib.
  Sausages may be made from pork or beef. The meat is mixed with a cereal such as breadcrumbs and seasoning.

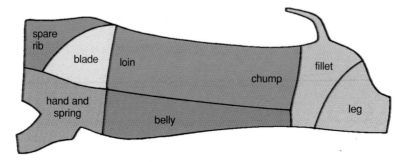

Bacon and ham

Bacon is pork which has been 'cured' so that it stays fresh for a longer time. The pork is cut into two sides and cured in brine (a solution of salt and water) for about two weeks. It is either sold as 'green' bacon after curing, or it is further treated by smoking, and sold as 'smoked' bacon. Smoked bacon has a stronger flavour than green bacon.
Gammon is the leg from the side of bacon.
Ham is also the leg of the pig. It is removed from the side of the pig before the pig is cured for bacon, and is then cured separately. The way it is cured decides the type of ham it will be. York ham, for instance, has a mild flavour. You can also buy 'honey cured' ham or Virginia ham.

Choosing bacon
Look for a deep pink colour and firm white fat. Avoid any which has brownish meat or which has salt crystals on it.

To store bacon
It must be well covered to prevent it from drying out. It may be wrapped in greaseproof paper and then put in a polythene bag or box, or it may be wrapped in suitable cling film. Store in a fridge or cool larder.

Cooking bacon
Most bacon is sold in rashers or thin slices. Cuts include back bacon, middle cut, streaky, or collar (shoulder) bacon. Bacon chops may be cut from the back. Rashers or bacon chops are best cooked by grilling to allow any excess fat to drain away. If fried, it should be slowly 'dry' fried without any extra fat added.
  Joints of bacon, for example, collar, back, or gammon, should first be soaked in cold water to remove any excess salt.

The food value of bacon
It is a good source of protein, fat, and B vitamins.

Offal

Offal is the term for the internal organs of the animal. It includes liver, kidney, tongue, heart, brains, sweetbreads, and tripe.

Other meat products include pigs' trotters, brawn, oxtail, sausages, and black pudding.

The food value of offal

All offal is very nutritious, and it is good value for money. It is a good source of protein, iron, B vitamins, and vitamins A and C in liver and kidney.

Poultry

Poultry includes chicken, turkey, duck, and goose. Chicken is widely available, both fresh and frozen, and is usually good value for money. It provides a good supply of protein but is fairly low in fat content, so it is a useful food to include often in meals if you are trying to cut down the amount of fat you eat. Chicken is available in joints (for baking, frying, casseroles, or grilling) and as whole birds (for roasting). Roast chicken is usually served with stuffing. Bread sauce, bacon rolls, and chipolata sausages are other traditional accompaniments.

A frozen chicken must be completely thawed before cooking, otherwise the centre may not reach a high enough temperature to kill any bacteria. This could cause food poisoning. Once the chicken is thawed, remove the giblets and wash the chicken inside and out in cold running water. Dry with kitchen paper.

QUESTIONS

1 What nutrients does meat contain?
2 Describe how you would wrap each of the following before placing them in the refrigerator. Say how long you would expect each one to keep fresh:
a) lamb's liver
b) a large joint of beef
c) 500 g mince
d) a packet of pork sausages
3 Name a cheap cut of (a) beef, (b) pork, (c) lamb which would be suitable for cooking in a casserole or stewing.
4 Name a roasting joint of (a) beef, (b) pork, (c) lamb.
5 Suggest meat dishes for the seven main meals in a week. Include a variety of meats from different animals, cooked by different methods. Include some inexpensive meat dishes.
6 What are the traditional foods or sauces served with (a) roast beef, (b) roast lamb, (c) roast pork, and (d) roast chicken?
7 What is offal? Give four examples. Name the nutrients which are found in one of these examples.
8 Why are some cuts of meat less expensive than others? Give three possible reasons.
9 What is the difference between
a) gammon, ham, and a leg of pork?
b) green bacon and smoked bacon?
10 Name five meats or meat products which are good sources of iron.

Recipes

As well as the meat recipes here, there are many others in the Rice, Pasta, and Pulses sections.

Sausage goulash   *Serves 3–4*

250–500 g sausages
1–2 tablespoons oil
2 onions
1 pepper
100 g mushrooms
1 rounded teaspoon paprika
1 level tablespoon plain flour
400 g can tomatoes
Bay leaf (if you have one)
1 level teaspoon sugar
125 ml water
1 small carton plain yoghurt
Salt and pepper

Method

1   Put the sausages to grill under a medium heat, or fry using a very little oil.
2   Put 1 tablespoon oil in a pan to warm. Peel and chop the onions and fry in the oil.
3   Cut the pepper in half, scoop out seeds, and remove stalk. Chop and add to the onions. Chop the mushrooms and add them to the onions.
4   Stir in the paprika, then stir in the flour. Pour in the tomatoes. Add the bay leaf (if you are using it), the sugar, and the water.
5   Cover the pan and simmer gently for about 20 minutes.
6   When the sausages are brown, cut into chunks and add to the pan.
7   When cooked, taste, and add salt and pepper if you wish. Stir in the yoghurt at the end of cooking but be very careful not to let it boil or it will separate.

This can be a meat or vegetarian dish, depending on the sausage you use. You could also use salami-style ready-cooked sausage. Serve with boiled rice or mashed potatoes.

Burgers   *Makes 4*

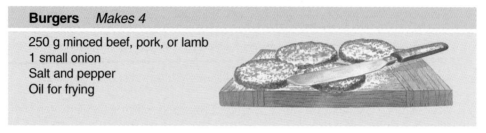

250 g minced beef, pork, or lamb
1 small onion
Salt and pepper
Oil for frying

Method

1   Peel and grate the onion. Mix with the meat, add salt and pepper.
2   Divide into 4 and shape each into round cakes about 2 cm thick, on a floured board.
3   Either grill for about 10 minutes, turning once, or fry for 5 minutes each side.

Serve with barbecue sauce or tomato sauce.

Burgers with barbecue sauce   *Makes 4*

4 burgers as above
1 small onion
15 g margarine
2 tablespoons tomato ketchup
1 tablespoon vinegar

1 teaspoon Worcester sauce
Salt and pepper
4 tablespoons water
Tomato and parsley or cress to garnish

Method

1. Grate the onion. Put in a small pan with the other ingredients. Simmer very gently for 10 minutes, stirring occasionally.
2. Make the burgers as above. Put them in a grill pan without the grid. Spoon the sauce over and grill gently for about 10 minutes each side, basting occasionally with the sauce.
3. Serve in bread buns or in a warm, shallow serving dish, garnished with slices of tomato and parsley.

Tomato sauce   Ⓥ

1 medium can tomatoes
1 onion
1 rasher of bacon (optional)

15 g margarine
1 level tablespoon cornflour or plain flour
Salt, pepper, level teaspoon of sugar

Method

1. Peel and chop the onion. Chop the bacon.
2. Melt the margarine in a small pan, fry the onion and bacon (if using) gently until softened (about 5–10 minutes).
3. Add the can of tomatoes, bring to the boil and simmer gently for about 20 minutes until cooked.
4. Blend the flour to a smooth paste with 3 tablespoons cold water. Pour into the pan, reboil, and simmer for 5 minutes until thickened.
5. Blend in a liquidizer until smooth, or sieve. Check the flavour, and add the salt, pepper, and sugar as required.

Grilled kebabs   *Serves 2*   Ⓥ

4 sausages or burgers or 100–200 g chicken, pork, or lamb
2 small onions
1 pepper
100 g mushrooms

4 small tomatoes
Oil, salt, and pepper

Method

1. Peel the onions, and cut into quarters, leaving the root on to hold them together.
2. Remove stalk and seeds from the pepper. Cut it into pieces about 2.5 cm square.
3. Cut the burgers into quarters, or the sausages or meat into chunks about 2.5 cm long.
4. Put all ingredients onto skewers, brush with plenty of oil, and season.
5. Pre-heat the grill (or barbecue) and grill for 10–20 minutes until cooked.
   Watch the kebabs carefully, turning from time to time and brushing with oil as necessary.

These can be made with or without meat. Serve on a bed of cooked rice or with baked potatoes.

Corned beef and potato pie   *Serves 4*

1 kg potatoes
1 small can corned beef
4 tomatoes
1 small onion (optional)
25 g butter
25 g cheese

Method

1   Peel the potatoes and cut into slices about 1cm thick. Put in a pan, just cover with cold water, and simmer for about 10–15 minutes, until soft.
2   Cut the corned beef into 2 cm cubes and put into a shallow oven proof dish. Slice the tomatoes and put over the corned beef.
3   Grate the onion, or chop it very finely. Grate the cheese.
4   When the potatoes are cooked, drain them and mash with the butter. Stir in the onion. Spread them over the tomatoes and sprinkle with the cheese.
5   Either grill until golden brown, or bake in a hot oven, Gas 6, 200°C for 15–20 minutes until golden brown.

Minced beef and dumplings   *Serves about 3*

250 g minced beef or vegetarian mince
1 large onion
15 g margarine
1 level tablespoon plain flour
250 ml water
Salt, pepper, stock cube

Dumplings
100 g self-raising flour
50 g suet
Pinch of salt

Method

1   Peel and chop the onion. Fry in the margarine in a saucepan for 5 minutes.
2   Put the mince into the saucepan and stir gently over a low heat until it is brown. Stir in the flour.
3   Add the water, stock cube, salt, and pepper. Bring to the boil, stirring. Simmer gently with the lid on for 10 minutes, stirring occasionally. Light the oven, Gas 6, 200°C.
4   Make the dumplings: mix the flour, suet, and salt, and add enough water to make a firm dough. Divide into about 6 dumplings.
5   Pour the meat into an ovenproof dish or tin, adding a little gravy browning if necessary. Place the dumplings on top of the mince and bake near the top of the oven for about 20 minutes until the dumplings are golden brown and crisp.

For soft dumplings, leave the mince in the pan, place the dumplings on top, and cook with the lid on for 15–20 minutes.

You would serve this with freshly cooked vegetables.

Toad in the hole   *Serves about 3*

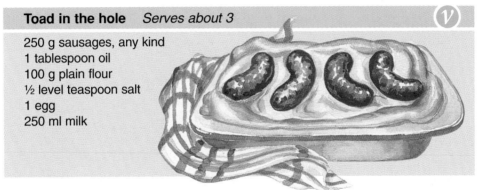

250 g sausages, any kind
1 tablespoon oil
100 g plain flour
½ level teaspoon salt
1 egg
250 ml milk

Method

1 Light the oven, Gas 7, 220°C. Put the shelf near the top of the oven.
2 Put the sausages into a large shallow tin or dish. Add the oil and place in the oven.
3 Sieve the flour and salt into a bowl. Drop the egg into the centre of the flour. Add a little milk, and beat well until smooth.
4 Add the rest of the milk a little at a time and beat well.
5 When the oil in the tin is really hot and has a faint haze over it, pour the batter into the tin.
6 Bake for about 40 minutes until well risen and golden brown.

Serve with freshly cooked vegetables.

Yorkshire puddings

(To make enough for a 4-hole Yorkshire pudding tin)

50 g plain flour, preferably strong flour
Pinch of salt
1 egg
100 ml milk
Oil

Method

1 Light the oven, Gas 8, 240°C. Place the shelf at the top of the oven.
2 Put a teaspoon of oil into each part of the tin and heat in the oven until a haze appears.
3 Sieve the flour and salt into a basin and beat in the egg. Add the milk a little at a time, beating well until smooth.
4 When the oil is hot enough, pour the mixture into the tin and put back into the oven.
5 Bake for about 20 minutes until well risen, firm, and golden brown, and serve with roast beef, or as a starter with gravy.

Yorkshire pudding (to make one large pudding)
Make in exactly the same way but use 100 g flour, 1 egg, 250 ml milk. Bake in the same way but cook for 40 minutes.

Sausage and onion casserole   *Serves 3–4*

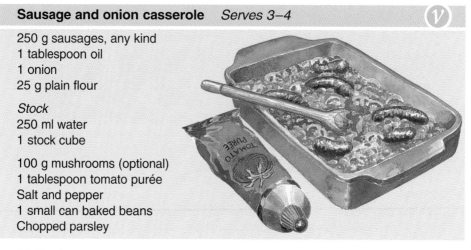

250 g sausages, any kind
1 tablespoon oil
1 onion
25 g plain flour

Stock
250 ml water
1 stock cube

100 g mushrooms (optional)
1 tablespoon tomato purée
Salt and pepper
1 small can baked beans
Chopped parsley

Method
1   Fry the sausages gently in the oil for 10 minutes until browned.
2   Peel and chop the onion, wash and slice the mushrooms, chop the parsley.
3   Put the sausages on to a plate and keep them warm. Add the onion to the pan and fry till lightly browned.
4   Stir in the flour, add the stock, tomato purée, and mushrooms, and stir well.
5   Add the sausages and beans. Cover and simmer very gently for 10 minutes. Taste and season, if necessary.
6   Pour into a serving dish, sprinkle with chopped parsley, and serve with mashed potatoes and vegetables.

Baked chicken joints

1 chicken joint per person
Flour, seasoned with salt and pepper
1 egg
25 g breadcrumbs for each joint
2 tablespoons oil
To garnish: 1 tomato per person, cress

Method
1   Light the oven, Gas 5, 190°C. Place the shelf above the centre. Put the oil into a small roasting tin and place it in the oven.
2   Make the breadcrumbs. Beat the egg and put it in a shallow dish. Wash and dry the chicken joints.
3   Coat each chicken joint in flour, then in egg, then in breadcrumbs.
4   When the oil is hot add the chicken joints, basting them with hot oil.
5   Bake for 35–45 minutes until tender. Baste during cooking.
6   Cut the tomatoes in half and warm in the oven for the last 10 minutes of cooking time.
7   Place the cooked chicken on kitchen paper to remove any excess oil, then place on a shallow serving dish.
8   Garnish with the tomatoes and plenty of cress.

Creamy chicken and mushroom   *Serves about 3*

2 tablespoons oil
1 onion
250 g chicken or turkey breast
100 g mushrooms
250 ml milk
½ chicken stock cube
Salt and pepper
2–3 tablespoons cream (any kind)

Method

1   Heat the oil in a large pan. Peel and chop the onion, and fry gently without letting it brown.
2   Cut the chicken into small pieces and add to the pan. Fry for five minutes until the colour changes.
3   Cut the mushrooms into quarters, add to the pan, and fry for a couple of minutes.
4   Take the pan off the heat and slowly add the milk a little at a time, stirring all the time. Stir in the stock cube.
5   Return to the heat and simmer *gently*, stirring occasionally, for 10 minutes.
6   Taste, adding salt and pepper if needed, and stir in the cream.

Serve on a bed of rice or pasta, cooking 75 g per person.

For a lower calorie version, leave out the cream or replace it with plain yoghurt, added at the end of cooking.

Chicken tikka masala   *Serves about 3*

2 tablespoons oil
1 onion
250 g chicken or turkey breast
2 teaspoons tikka paste
1 teaspoon tandoori paste (optional)
150 ml water
Small carton single cream or yoghurt

Method

1   Heat the oil in a large pan. Peel, chop, and fry the onion.
2   Cut the chicken into small cubes or strips and fry for five minutes, stirring, until it is all white in colour.
3   Stir in the pastes and fry for 2 minutes. Add the water, bring to the boil, and simmer with the lid on for 10–15 minutes. Turn off the heat and stir in the cream.
4   Serve on a bed of rice. Sprinkle with fresh coriander if you have some.

Cream is traditionally added but you can make a much lower fat version by using water, then stirring in a carton of yoghurt or fromage frais at the end of cooking.

Lamb do-piaza   *Serves 2*

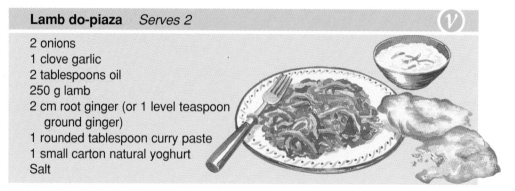

2 onions
1 clove garlic
2 tablespoons oil
250 g lamb
2 cm root ginger (or 1 level teaspoon
   ground ginger)
1 rounded tablespoon curry paste
1 small carton natural yoghurt
Salt

Method

1   Peel and chop the onions and garlic. Fry in fairly hot oil until brown.
2   Cut the lamb into thin strips. Peel and grate the ginger.
3   When the onions are brown, add the lamb and ginger, stirring over a high heat until brown.
4   Lower the heat, and stir in the curry paste and yoghurt. Simmer gently with the lid on for 10 minutes. You may need to add up to 3 tablespoons of water.
5   Taste, adding salt if necessary.

Serve with rice or chapattis, and mint or cucumber raita if you wish.

Instead of lamb you could use chicken, pork, beef, Quorn pieces, or tofu. The meat must be of frying or grilling quality to cook in this time.

Spiced lamb with lime and coconut   *Serves 2*

250 g lamb steaks
1 clove garlic
2 cm root ginger (or 1 level teaspoon
   ground ginger)
1 lime
25 g creamed coconut
150 ml water
1 teaspoon oil
1 rounded tablespoon curry paste
1 tablespoon fresh coriander (optional)
Salt

Method

1   Half fill the kettle and put on to boil.
2   Cut the lamb into very thin strips. Peel the garlic and chop it finely. Peel and grate the root ginger. Grate the zest off the lime, then cut it in two and squeeze out the juice. Dissolve the coconut in hot water.
3   Heat the oil in a large frying pan (or wok) until very hot. Add the lamb, garlic, and ginger and stir-fry for 3 minutes.
4   Stir in the curry paste, lime zest and juice, and coconut. Bring to the boil, and simmer gently for 5 minutes.
5   Chop the coriander if you are using it, and stir it in. Taste and add salt if you need it.

Serve with rice, chapattis, or naan bread, and raita if you wish.

Use frying or grilling lamb, pork, or beef. Vegetarians could use Quorn or tofu pieces.

Liver casserole   *Serves 3–4*

250 g liver	*Stuffing*
2 rashers bacon	25 g fresh breadcrumbs
250 ml water	1 dessertspoon chopped parsley
1 stock cube	1 small onion
1 teaspoon Worcester sauce	About 3 tablespoons milk or beaten egg
1 level tablespoon plain flour	
Parsley	

Method

1 Light the oven, Gas 5, 190°C. Place the shelf just above the centre of the oven.
2 Wash and dry the liver, cut off any skin. Cut into 3 or 4 portions and lay it in a greased dish or baking tin.
3 Make the breadcrumbs, chop the parsley, finely chop the onion. Mix these ingredients and add enough egg or milk to bind them together.
4 Place some stuffing on each piece of liver and cover it with a piece of bacon.
5 Pour the stock around the liver, cover with a lid or foil, and bake for about 30 minutes until the liver is tender. Remove the lid for the last 10 minutes to allow the bacon to brown slightly.
6 Place the meat carefully on a hot serving dish and keep it warm. Add the Worcester sauce to the stock in the tin. Blend the flour with a little cold water and add it to the gravy. Bring to the boil, stirring all the time, and pour round the liver. Garnish with parsley.

Serve hot, with potatoes and vegetables.

Pork with noodles   *Serves 2–3*

1 tablespoon soy sauce	100 g noodles
2 cloves garlic	1 tablespoon soy sauce
250 g pork steak	1 teaspoon sugar
1 carrot	1 teaspoon sesame oil (optional)
1 bunch spring onions	
Small can waterchestnuts and/or 50 g beansprouts	
50 g frozen peas or mangetout	
2 teaspoons oil	

Method

1 Peel and finely chop the garlic. Put it in a bowl with 1 tablespoon of soy sauce. Cut the pork into thin strips and put in the bowl.
2 Peel the carrot, and cut into very thin strips or slices. Trim and slice the spring onions. Cut the water chestnuts into two. Trim the mangetout (if using), or allow the peas to thaw.
3 Put the water on to boil for the noodles and cook as on the directions on the packet, then drain them.
4 Heat the oil in a large frying pan or wok until hot. Add the pork and stir-fry for 3–4 minutes over high heat until brown. Add the vegetables and stir-fry for 3 more minutes.
5 Stir in the cooked noodles, soy sauce, sugar, and sesame oil, and heat the noodles through. Serve straight away onto hot plates.

Rice

Rice is the staple food in the diet of many millions of people in the East. It is becoming more popular in this country, as it is economical, easy to prepare and cook, and keeps well.

For cooking, there are three main kinds of rice: long, medium, and short grain. Long grain rice such as Patna and Basmati stays fluffy and separate when cooked, so it is best for savoury dishes. Medium and short grain rice (e.g. Carolina rice) become softer and stickier when cooked, so are best for rice puddings.

Brown rice is the whole grain of rice, with only the husk removed. White rice has had the bran and germ removed during milling and polishing. Because of this it is less nutritious than brown rice, having fewer B vitamins, minerals, and proteins, and less NSP. Brown rice takes longer to cook than white rice, about 40 minutes instead of 11. It has a nutty flavour and a more chewy texture.

To cook rice

Allow about 75 g for each person. Wash the rice in a sieve under cold running water. Put it into plenty of boiling, salted water, bring back to the boil, then cook for 11 minutes. Drain in the sieve, then serve.

Brown rice is cooked in the same way, but takes 40−45 minutes to cook.

Recipes

As well as the recipes below, see rice pudding (p. 221), rice salad (p. 192), stuffed peppers (p. 168), chilli con carne (p. 159), creamy chicken and mushroom (p. 149), chicken tikka masala (p. 149), kebabs (p. 145).

Vegetable curry *Serves about 3*	Ⓥ
2 tablespoons oil	2 cm root ginger or 1 level teaspoon ground ginger
2 onions	1 rounded tablespoon curry paste
1 clove garlic	250 ml water
2 potatoes	50 g creamed coconut
2 carrots	Salt
¼ to ½ cauliflower	2 tablespoons fresh coriander (optional)

Method

1 Put the kettle on to boil.
2 Warm the oil in a fairly large pan. Peel and chop the onion, and fry until brown. Peel and chop the garlic, and add to the pan.
3 Peel the potatoes and cut to dice about 1cm. Add to the pan. Peel the carrots, cut to thin slices, and add. Cut the cauliflower to florets and add. Peel and grate the ginger, and add. Stir in the curry paste.
4 Dissolve the creamed coconut in the hot water, add to the pan, bring to the boil, then simmer gently with the lid on for about 20 minutes. You may need to add more water.
5 If you are using coriander, chop it and add to the finished dish.
6 Taste, and add salt if required. Serve with rice or chapattis.

You can make this with different vegetables if you like. Try using okra, aubergine, peas, beans of any kind, or broccoli, for a change.

Chicken curry Add 100–200 g chicken (cut into thin strips or small pieces) with the onions, and fry over fairly high heat until coloured. Alternatively, use left over cooked chicken.

Mushroom risotto   *Serves 3–4*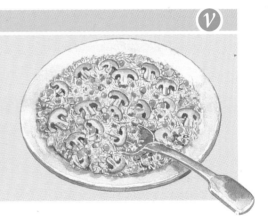

4 tablespoons oil
250 g mushrooms
2 cloves garlic (optional)
1 onion
175 g risotto (or other) rice
1 litre hot water
1 vegetable stock cube
50 g cheese
Salt and pepper
1 rounded teaspoon mace (optional)

Method

1 Put the oil into a fairly large pan and heat gently. Roughly chop the mushrooms and fry for 4 minutes, then spoon them onto a plate.
2 Put the rice in a sieve and wash it under the cold tap. Fill the kettle and when it boils, measure 1 litre water into a jug, and stir in the stock cube.
3 Peel and chop the onion and garlic (if you use it). Add to the pan and fry gently for 6 minutes, then add the rice and stir well.
4 Add the liquid to the rice and simmer very gently until the rice is cooked. White rice will take 15–20 minutes, brown rice about 40 minutes. Stir occasionally. You may need to add up to a further 125 ml hot water.
5 Grate the cheese.
6 When the rice is cooked stir in the mushrooms, cheese, and mace. Taste, add salt and pepper as needed, and serve on hot plates.

For a change you could add a chopped pepper to the mushrooms, or add some broccoli for the last ten minutes while the rice is cooking.

Chicken risotto Make in the same way, but add about 200 g cooked chicken with the cooked mushrooms, or add 200 g uncooked finely sliced chicken with the onions when you fry them.

Sweet and sour chicken *Serves about 3*

2 tablespoons oil
2 onions
250 g chicken breast (or turkey)
1 can pineapple pieces
2 level tablespoons sugar
2 tablespoons vinegar
1 tablespoon soy sauce
1 level tablespoon tomato purée or ketchup
1 level tablespoon cornflour
Salt and pepper

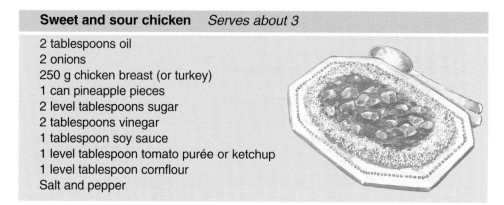

Method

1   Heat the oil in a large pan or wok. Peel, chop, and fry the onions.
2   Cut the chicken into small pieces, add to the pan, and fry over fairly high heat for
    five minutes, stirring occasionally.
3   Drain the juice from the pineapple into a measuring jug, add enough water to
    make it 250 ml. Add the pineapple to the chicken.
4   Add all the other ingredients to the jug and mix until smooth. Pour into the pan
    and bring to the boil, stirring, until the sauce thickens.
5   Simmer for ten minutes with the lid on, stirring occasionally.

Serve on a bed of rice (cook 75 g per person).

Pork and apricots *Serves about 3*

250 g pork fillet
1 rounded tablespoon plain flour
1 tablespoon oil
Salt and pepper
2 teaspoons Worcester sauce
1 can apricots
150 g long grain rice

Method

1   Cut the meat into small cubes or thin strips, removing any skin and bone. Coat in
    the seasoned flour.
2   Heat the oil in a frying pan and fry the meat for about 10 minutes until golden
    brown and cooked.
3   Open the tin of apricots and pour the syrup into a measuring jug. Add enough
    water to make 250 ml liquid. Save four apricot halves for garnishing and chop the
    others into small pieces.
4   Put the meat on to a plate. Add the rest of the flour to the pan and stir until
    smooth. Add the liquid a little at a time, stirring, and boil. Add the Worcester
    sauce, meat, and apricots to the pan and simmer very gently for about 5 minutes.
5   Cook the rice in boiling water (see p. 152), then drain. Place on a hot serving
    dish. Pour the meat over the rice and garnish with the apricot halves.

You could serve this with a salad.

Pasta

Pasta can be bought in many different shapes and sizes. Some of the best known kinds of pasta are macaroni, spaghetti, noodles, lasagne, ravioli, cannelloni, and vermicelli.

They are made from a dough of wheat flour and water, sometimes with egg added. The dough is made into different shapes, then dried.

You can buy traditional white pasta made from white flour, or brown pasta made with wholemeal flour. Like brown flour or brown bread, brown pasta contains more NSP than white pasta. Green pasta, for example, 'lasagne verdi', is made by adding cooked spinach to the basic dough.

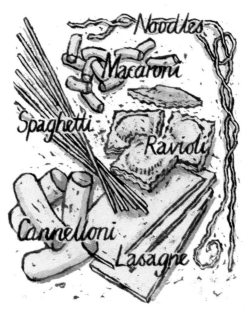

To cook pasta

Allow about 50–75 g for each person. Drop the pasta into plenty of boiling water and cook for the time directed on the packet, with the lid off the pan. The water should be kept boiling quite vigorously to prevent the pasta sticking. A dessertspoon of oil added to the water will help keep the pieces separate.

Recipes

As well as the recipes below, see vegetarian lasagne (p. 163), ratatouille pasta (p. 167), and pork with noodles (p. 151).

Macaroni cheese	Serves about 2	
100 g macaroni	25 g margarine	
100 g cheese	Salt, pepper, pinch of mustard	
375 ml milk	Parsley	
25 g plain flour		

Method
1   Cook the macaroni in a large pan of boiling water for about 12 minutes until tender.
2   Grate the cheese.
3   Make the cheese sauce: put the milk, flour, margarine, salt, pepper, and mustard into a pan. Bring to the boil, whisking all the time. Stir in most of the grated cheese, saving a little for the top.
4   Drain the macaroni, then put into an ovenproof dish with the cheese sauce.
5   Put the remaining cheese on top and grill until golden brown. Garnish with a sprig of parsley.

Quick spaghetti snack   *Serves 2*

175 g spaghetti
Salt
3 tablespoons olive oil
50–100 g cheese
Freshly ground black pepper

Method

1   Put a large pan of water on to boil.
2   Add the spaghetti and cook for 9 minutes until cooked (see instructions on packet).
3   Grate the cheese.
4   When the spaghetti is cooked, drain it in a sieve and put back in the pan on a very low heat. Add the oil and cheese and gently warm through.
5   Add lots of black pepper and serve straight away onto hot plates.

Serve with tomato or lettuce salad, and some crisp, fresh bread.

You could add a tablespoon of freshly chopped herbs such as parsley or basil, or two crushed cloves of garlic, or some chopped sun dried tomatoes, or a spoonful of pesto.

Vegetable and pasta bake   *Serves 2–3*

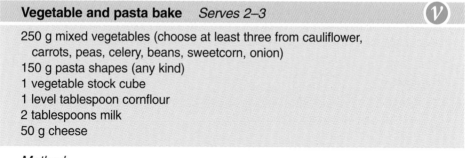

250 g mixed vegetables (choose at least three from cauliflower, carrots, peas, celery, beans, sweetcorn, onion)
150 g pasta shapes (any kind)
1 vegetable stock cube
1 level tablespoon cornflour
2 tablespoons milk
50 g cheese

Method

1   Prepare the vegetables and cut into bite sized pieces. Cook in boiling water until tender, then drain the water into a measuring jug.
2   Cook the pasta in boiling water until cooked (read packet instructions) then drain.
3   Grate the cheese.
4   Mix the cooked vegetables and pasta in one pan.
5   Dissolve the stock cube in the measuring jug, add enough water to make 250 ml, and pour into the empty pan.
6   Mix the cornflour and milk until smooth, add to the stock in the pan, and bring to the boil, stirring all the time. Add half the cheese, then stir in the pasta and vegetables.
7   Put into an ovenproof dish, and sprinkle the rest of the cheese on top.
8   Either grill until golden brown, or bake in a hot oven, Gas 6, 200°C for about 20 minutes.

For a change, you could stir in a drained can of tuna or salmon.

Spaghetti bolognese   *Serves about 3*   (V)

200 g spaghetti
250 g minced beef or vegetarian mince
1 onion
100 g mushrooms
1 green pepper (optional)
2 tablespoons oil
1 rounded tablespoon flour
1 large can tomatoes
100 ml water
1 stock cube
Salt, pepper

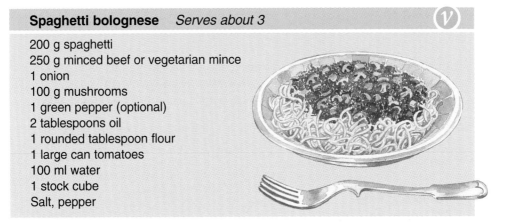

Method

1   Peel and chop the onion and pepper. Wash and slice the mushrooms.
2   Heat the oil in a large pan. Fry the onions, pepper, and mushrooms for 5 minutes.
3   Add the mince and fry, stirring gently, until it is brown.
4   Stir in the flour, tomatoes, and stock cube. Add the water if it seems necessary, then add salt and pepper.
5   Bring to the boil, then simmer very gently with the lid on, stirring occasionally, for 30 minutes.
6   Cook the spaghetti: put a large pan of water on to boil. Add the spaghetti and when the water comes back to the boil, cook for 10 minutes. Drain in a colander and put on a hot dish.
7   Pour the sauce on top of the spaghetti and serve.

Lasagne   *Serves 4*   (For vegetarian lasagne see p. 163)

175 g lasagne (ready to use)

Cheese sauce
375 ml milk
25 g margarine
25 g plain flour
½ level teaspoon mustard
100 g cheese

Meat sauce
250 g mince, any kind
1 tablespoon oil
1 level tablespoon flour
1 can tomatoes
1 heaped teaspoon tomato
  purée or ketchup
1 heaped teaspoon sugar
Pinch of mixed herbs

Method

1   Make the meat sauce. Brown the mince in the oil, then stir in the flour. Stir in the other ingredients and simmer gently for 15 minutes.
2   Make the cheese sauce by the all-in-one method: put the milk, flour, margarine, and mustard into a saucepan. Bring to the boil, whisking all the time, until thickened. Add most of the cheese, saving a little for the top. Check the seasoning.
3   Put layers of cheese sauce, lasagne, and meat into a shallow ovenproof dish, finishing with a layer of cheese sauce. Sprinkle with the remaining cheese.
4   Bake in the oven Gas 4, 180°C, for about 30 minutes until golden brown.

Serve with a salad.

Pulses

Dried beans, peas, and lentils of many kinds are widely available and are becoming more popular. They are inexpensive, easy to store and cook, and high in food value. They are a good source of protein, carbohydrate, iron, and B vitamins. They are also low in fat and high in NSP.

Pulses include orange and green lentils, green and yellow split peas, chick peas, haricot beans, cannellini beans, butter beans, red kidney beans, and soya beans.

To cook pulses

As they are usually dried, all pulses except lentils must be soaked before cooking. Soak them either overnight in cold water, or for 2–3 hours in boiling water. Drain, then simmer gently in fresh water until soft.

This may take, for example:

Red kidney beans	1 hour
Split peas and lentils	30–45 minutes
Butter beans	1 hour
Soya beans	2–3 hours

A pressure cooker will save you a lot of time if you are cooking pulses. The cheapest way to prepare beans is to cook a large batch at once, then divide it into useful quantities such as 100 g or 200 g, put into bags, and freeze.

Red kidney beans *must* be boiled for at least 15 minutes, otherwise they can be dangerous. So never cook them in a slow cooker without boiling them first.

You can buy canned beans of all kinds now, as well as the popular baked beans in tomato sauce. They save a lot of time as they are already cooked, but they are rather more expensive. If you are using tinned beans in a casserole, add them about 20 minutes before the end of the cooking time to allow them to heat through.

Soya protein

As soya beans are particularly high in protein and low in fat, they are often used to make soya mince as a meat substitute. This can be used by vegetarians as a meat alternative or by anyone wanting to reduce their fat intake. It is also used by manufacturers of foods such as chicken or beef curry, or meat pies, as it is cheaper to produce than meat. You may see it on the ingredients list on meat products.

Soya proteins may have iron and B vitamins, especially B_{12}, added to make their nutritional value more like that of meat. In many recipes you can make a vegetarian alternative by using soya mince or pieces instead of meat, or simply by adding a can of beans or chick peas to a dish.

Recipes using pulses include those below, and also sausage and onion casserole, p. 148; kidney bean salad, p. 192; lentil soup, p. 133; chilli bean casserole, p. 166; spicy chick peas, p. 164; and cheese and lentil bake, p. 163.

Chilli con carne   *Serves about 3*

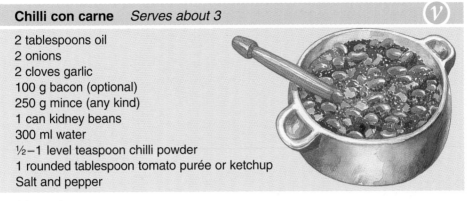

2 tablespoons oil
2 onions
2 cloves garlic
100 g bacon (optional)
250 g mince (any kind)
1 can kidney beans
300 ml water
½–1 level teaspoon chilli powder
1 rounded tablespoon tomato purée or ketchup
Salt and pepper

Method

1   Peel and chop the onions, and fry in the hot oil until brown. Peel and chop the garlic, and add to the onions. Chop the bacon and add. Add the mince and fry until brown.
2   Add the water, tomato purée, and chilli powder. Drain the beans and add to the pan. Bring to the boil then simmer gently for 15–20 minutes.
3   Check the flavour, adding salt and pepper to taste.

Serve with rice, or baked or boiled potatoes.

Cassoulet   *Serves 4*

1 tablespoon oil
200 g pork sausages (or cooked smoked sausages)
100 g bacon
2 onions
2 cloves garlic
1 can cannellini or butter beans
1 level tablespoon cornflour
1 rounded tablespoon tomato purée
   or ketchup
2 pinches dried thyme or mixed herbs
75 g bread
25 g butter

Method

1   Fry the sausages in the oil in a large frying pan. Chop the bacon and add to the pan.
2   Peel and chop the onions and garlic and add to the pan. Fry until the sausages and onion are brown and cooked, 10–15 minutes.
3   Drain the liquid from the beans into a jug, and add enough water to make 300 ml. Add the cornflour to the liquid and stir until smooth. Stir in the tomato purée, and pour the liquid into the pan. Stir in the herbs and beans.
4   Bring to the boil and simmer for 5 minutes, stirring occasionally. Meanwhile, make the bread into crumbs.
5   Pour the meat into a heatproof dish, put the crumbs on top and dot with the butter.
6   Either grill until golden brown, or brown in a hot oven, Gas 6, 200°C, for about 20 minutes.

Serve with green vegetables.

Potato, chick pea, and chorizo stew   *Serves 4*

170 g chorizo sausage (or other spicy, cooked sausage)
2 tablespoons oil
1 large onion
2 cloves garlic (optional)
3 large potatoes
1 rounded teaspoon paprika
1 tablespoon vinegar
400 g tin tomatoes
400 g tin chick peas
Salt and pepper

Method

1   Warm the oil in a fairly large pan. Peel and roughly chop the onion (and garlic if you use it). Fry for about 5 minutes.
2   Cut the sausage into small chunks or slices, add to the pan and warm for about 3 minutes.
3   Peel the potatoes and cut to roughly 1cm dice. Add to the pan.
4   Stir in the paprika, vinegar, and tomatoes.
5   Drain the liquid from the chick peas, then add them to the pan. Add the lid and simmer for about 20 minutes, stirring occasionally, until the potatoes are cooked.
6   Check the taste, adding salt and pepper if you need to. Serve onto hot plates.

Three bean bake   *Serves 3–4*

500 g potatoes
Salt
1 tablespoon oil
1 onion
1 can tomatoes
2 cans mixed beans (e.g. flageolets, aduki, chick peas)
1 rounded tablespoon fenugreek (optional but adds interesting flavour)
Pepper, black if possible
25 g butter

Method

1   Peel the potatoes, and cut to slices about 1cm thick. Cover with water and simmer for about 10–15 minutes, until soft.
2   Heat the oil, peel and chop the onion, and fry for a few minutes until soft. Then add the tomatoes, beans, and fenugreek and simmer very gently while you wait for the potatoes to cook.
3   Put the beans into an ovenproof dish. Drain the potatoes and put the slices on top of the beans. Dot with the butter and either grill gently to brown the potatoes or brown in a hot oven, Gas 6, 200°C for about 20 minutes.

If you can't get fenugreek, add 2 pinches of dried mixed herbs. Meat eaters could add about 100 g spicy cooked sausage such as salami, Bratwurst, or chorizo to the beans.

Hummus

This is a thick, creamy paste made from chick peas and flavoured with tahini (made from sesame seeds). It is popular in the Middle East where it is often served as a dip, eaten with pitta bread. As chick peas have to be soaked overnight and then boiled for one or two hours, you may prefer to use a can of chick peas.

200 g chick peas or 1 can (about 400 g size)
1 clove of garlic
1 rounded tablespoon of tahini
1 lemon
Salt
Paprika pepper

Method
1 If using dried chick peas, soak overnight then boil for 1 or 2 hours until soft. (A pressure cooker may be used.)
2 If using a can of chick peas, open and drain off the liquid.
3 Peel and crush the garlic, squeeze the juice from the lemon.
4 Keep a few peas back to decorate the finished dish and use a blender or processor to make a purée with the rest.
5 Beat in the garlic, tahini, lemon juice, and salt and turn into a serving dish. Decorate with the chick peas and a little paprika sprinkled on top.

Dal *Serves 2–3*

200 g lentils	1 green pepper
700 ml water	25 g butter
1 rounded teaspoon each of ground ginger, ground cumin, and turmeric	1 level teaspoon curry powder or paste
4 tomatoes (optional)	1 clove garlic
2 potatoes	1 extra teaspoon ground ginger
1 large onion	Salt

Method
1 Put the water into a pan and add the ginger, cumin, and turmeric. Bring to the boil.
2 Wash the lentils in a sieve under running water and add to the pan. Bring back to the boil and simmer for 5 minutes.
3 Meanwhile, peel the potatoes and cut into 1cm dice. Add them to the pan and leave to simmer, stirring occasionally to prevent sticking.
4 Peel and chop the onion, garlic, and pepper. Melt the butter in another pan and fry them over a fairly high heat until brown.
5 Cut the tomatoes into quarters and add them, with the curry powder and the extra ground ginger, to the onions. Cook for a minute then add to the lentil mixture.
6 Taste and add a little salt. Cook gently for another 5–10 minutes, stirring occasionally.
7 Serve with rice (see p. 152) and/or chapatis and natural yoghurt if you wish.

Chilladas   *Serves 3*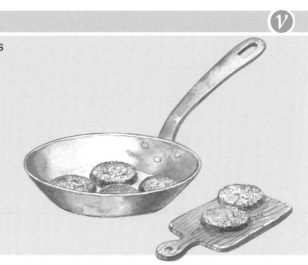

100 g red or orange lentils
250 ml water
25 g butter
1 small onion
½ pepper
1 small carrot
Pinch of mixed herbs
Pinch of cayenne pepper
1 teaspoon tomato purée
Salt and pepper

To fry
Breadcrumbs, 1 egg
Oil

Method

1   Wash the lentils in a sieve, put in a pan with the water. Bring to the boil and simmer gently for about 15 minutes until mushy and the water is all absorbed.
2   Peel the carrot and onion and chop finely. Fry in a little oil until soft.
3   Remove seeds from the pepper and chop it finely. Add to the onion and fry for 5 minutes more.
4   When the lentils are cooked, beat to a pulp then stir in the vegetables, herbs, and purée. Add a little salt and pepper to taste.
5   If you have time, leave the mixture in a cool place as this makes it easier to handle. Then divide into 6 and shape into rounds.
6   Brush with beaten egg, then coat with crumbs (see p. 137).
7   Shallow fry in hot oil until golden brown on each side.

Serve with tomato sauce (see p. 145) and a salad.

Rice and peas   *Serves 4*

This is a popular dish from Jamaica. The 'peas' are actually kidney beans. You can use a fresh coconut instead of desiccated; crack it open and grate the flesh. Use the coconut milk to replace some of the water.

1 coconut or 100 g desiccated coconut
300 g long grain rice
1 medium can of kidney beans (about 400 g)
1 chopped onion
Sprig of thyme or pinch of dried thyme
½ level teaspoon salt
600 ml hot water
    (including coconut milk if used)

Method

Drain the liquid from the beans, put them into a pan with all the other ingredients. Cover and cook over a low heat until all the water is absorbed. Serve hot.

Courgette and tomato bake   *Serves about 3*

450 g courgettes
75 g butter
250 g tomatoes
1 tablespoon chopped parsley
Salt and pepper
Pinch of sugar
50 g cheese
75 g breadcrumbs

Method

1   Wash and dry the courgettes, and cut into 0.5 cm slices. Melt 50 g of the butter and gently fry the courgettes until soft, about 10–15 minutes.
2   Chop the parsley and grate the cheese. Cut the tomatoes into quarters.
3   Melt the rest of the butter, add the tomatoes, parsley, and sugar, and cook until soft. Taste, and add salt and pepper if necessary.
4   Put the courgettes into an ovenproof dish and pour the tomato mixture over. Sprinkle with the cheese and crumbs and grill until golden brown.

Ratatouille   *Serves about 3*

1 large onion
1 clove of garlic (optional)
2 tablespoons vegetable oil
1 aubergine
1 green pepper
3 courgettes
1 medium can tomatoes
    or 250 g fresh tomatoes
1 level tablespoon tomato purée
Salt and black pepper

Method

1   Peel and chop the onion. Peel the garlic and chop very finely. Fry both in the oil in a large pan for 5–10 minutes until soft.
2   Wash and dry the other vegetables. Cut the aubergine into chunks and add to the pan. Fry for 5 minutes.
3   Remove the top and seeds from the pepper, then chop it. Slice the courgettes 0.5 cm thick. Quarter the fresh tomatoes if you are using them or discard the juice from the canned tomatoes. Add all the vegetables to the pan, then add the tomato purée.
4   Simmer very gently with the lid on for 30 minutes until the vegetables are soft but not mushy. Check the taste, adding salt and pepper as required.

You can serve this either hot or cold, on its own with fresh bread rolls, or as a vegetable dish, for example with cheese and lentil bake.

Ratatouille pasta Make the ratatouille as above. Cook 100 g of any pasta, drain, and put into a warm serving dish. Pour the ratatouille over, sprinkle with 75 g grated cheese, and grill until golden brown.

Stuffed peppers   *Serves 4*

4 peppers, red or green. When you buy them, choose
  ones which will stand up in the dish.
100 g rice, brown or white
1 tablespoon oil
1 large onion
100 g mushrooms
A pinch of dried thyme
Salt and pepper

Method

1 Cook the rice: put a pan of water on to boil and wash the rice in a sieve under the
   cold tap. Tip in to the boiling water, bring back to the boil, and simmer, 11 minutes
   for white rice, 35 minutes for brown rice. Drain in the sieve when cooked.
2 Wash and dry the peppers. Cut a 'lid' off the stalk end. Remove the seeds from
   inside the peppers.
3 Light the oven, Gas 4, 180°C. Lightly oil or grease a deep ovenproof dish.
4 Make the stuffing: peel and chop the onion, fry in the oil in a pan for 5–10
   minutes until brown. Wipe and slice the mushrooms and add them to the onions,
   frying for a further 5 minutes. Add the thyme and a little salt and pepper. Add this
   mixture to the cooked rice.
5 Fill the peppers with the stuffing mixture. Place them in the dish and brush with a
   little oil or a knob of butter to prevent the skin from shrinking. Cover with a lid or
   foil and bake for 30 minutes.

If you wish, you could make some tomato sauce (see p. 145) and pour it around
the peppers while they are baking in the oven. This would then make a complete
main course dish, perhaps served with baked potatoes.

Stir fried vegetables and noodles   *Serves about 3*

250 g noodles   50 g bamboo shoots (if you wish)
50 g Chinese leaves   4 spring onions
1 carrot   2 tablespoons oil
100 g mushrooms   2 tablespoons soy sauce
50 g bean sprouts

Method

1 Put a large pan of water on to boil, ready for the noodles.
2 Wash the Chinese leaves and shake dry. Peel the carrot, wipe the mushrooms,
   wash the bean sprouts and spring onions, trim the ends of the onions.
3 Drop the noodles into the boiling water, bring back to the boil, and simmer for
   about 7 minutes or as directed on the packet. Drain when cooked.
4 Cut all the vegetables (except the bean sprouts) into fine slivers, about the size of
   matchsticks.
5 Heat the oil in a wok if you have one, or in a large frying pan. The oil should be
   really hot. Add all the vegetables except the bean sprouts and spring onions and
   stir fry over a high heat for 2 minutes. Add the bean sprouts and spring onions
   and cook for a further minute.
6 Add the soy sauce and the noodles, gently warm through to heat the noodles.
   Turn on to a hot dish and serve straight away.

Vegetable samosas   *Makes 6*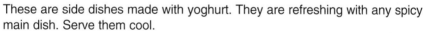

Chapatis as in the recipe below

1 level teaspoon plain flour mixed
   to a paste with a little water
Oil for shallow frying

Filling
500 g potatoes
100 g frozen peas
50 g butter
2 level teaspoons curry powder
½ level teaspoon salt
1 tablespoon fresh chopped
   coriander (optional)

Method
1. Make the chapatis according to the recipe below. While the dough is resting, make the filling.
2. Peel the potatoes and cut into dice about 1cm square. Simmer gently in boiling water for 5 minutes, then add the peas to the pan and simmer for a further 3 minutes until the potato is cooked. Drain.
3. Melt the butter in a frying pan and fry the potato cubes, peas, curry powder, coriander, and salt gently for 10 minutes.
4. Roll out the chapatis to circles about 15 cm across and cut each in half. To shape the samosas, fold over one third, fold the next third on top, and seal with the flour paste. Add some filling to the cone and seal the top flap.
5. Repeat until all the samosas are filled. Pour about 1cm oil into the cleaned frying pan and heat. Fry the samosas in hot oil, turning over once, until golden brown.

Raita

These are side dishes made with yoghurt. They are refreshing with any spicy main dish. Serve them cool.

Mint raita
Mix 1 tablespoon of chopped fresh mint (plus 1 tablespoon of chopped fresh coriander if you wish) with a small carton of plain yoghurt.

Cucumber raita
Slice, grate, or cut to small dice half a cucumber. Mix with a small carton of plain yoghurt.

Banana raita
Slice a banana thinly and mix with plain yoghurt.

Chapatis   *Makes 6*

100 g wholemeal flour
Pinch of salt

100 ml water
Oil for cooking

Method
1. Mix the flour and salt in a bowl.
2. Stir in the water and mix to a stiff dough adding more flour or water if needed.
3. Knead until smooth, cover, and leave to rest for 30 minutes if possible.
4. Divide into 6 balls. Roll each ball out to a circle about 15 cm in diameter.
5. Heat a little oil in a frying pan until very hot and fry each chapati for 1 or 2 minutes on each side, until small bubbles appear on top.
6. Serve as soon as possible, keeping them warm in a tea towel.

Microwave recipes

Page 219 tells you how to cook steamed puddings very quickly in the microwave.

Baked potato ⓥ

1 medium potato	Salt and pepper
A little butter	Parsley to garnish

Method
1. Scrub the potato, and make a large cross on the top with a knife.
2. Place on kitchen paper and cook for 6 minutes on full power until soft.
3. Open the top and add seasoning, butter, and parsley.

Depending on their size, four potatoes might take about 20 minutes.

Chicken in tomato sauce *Serves 2*

2 chicken breasts	50 g mushrooms
Salt and pepper	Pinch of mixed herbs
Can of tomatoes (400 g)	Parsley
1 small onion	

Method
1. Drain the juice off the tomatoes. Peel and finely chop the onion. Wipe and slice the mushrooms.
2. Place the chicken in a dish, add salt and pepper. Add the tomatoes (not the juice), onion, mushrooms, and herbs.
3. Cover with a lid or cling film (pierce the cling film) and cook for 12–14 minutes. Allow to stand for 5 minutes, then sprinkle with chopped parsley and serve. Potatoes and a green vegetable go well with this.

Cheese sauce ⓥ

It is easy and quick to make any white sauce in the microwave and washing up the jug afterwards is much easier than washing up a saucepan. To make sure the sauce is smooth, it is important to stop cooking every minute to stir the sauce well.

250 ml milk	Salt, pepper
25 g cornflour or plain flour	Pinch of mustard
25 g butter	50 g cheese

Method
1. Put the butter into a 500 ml jug. Cook for about ½ minute to melt.
2. Stir in the flour and mix well until smooth.
3. Mix in the milk, a little at a time. Cook for 1 minute on full power, then stir well. Cook for another 2 minutes. The sauce should boil and thicken. If necessary, cook for another minute.
4. While the sauce is cooking, grate the cheese. When the sauce is cooked, add the seasonings and the cheese. Cook for 1 minute to melt the cheese, stir well and serve.

Custard

250 ml milk
1 level tablespoon custard powder
1 level tablespoon sugar

Method
1 Put the milk into a 500 ml jug. Stir in the custard and sugar, and mix until smooth.
2 Cook on full power for 1 minute, stir. Cook for 2 minutes and stir. If necessary cook for a further minute until thick and smooth. Serve.

Chocolate cake

100 g self-raising flour
100 g sugar
100 g soft margarine
2 eggs plus 3 tablespoons milk
25 g cocoa
Pinch of salt
½ teaspoon vanilla essence

Method
1 Line the base of an 18 cm microwave dish, or a ring mould.
2 Sieve the flour, cocoa, and salt together. Add all the other ingredients and beat well until smooth and light. Spoon into the container and level the top. Stand on an upturned plate to help the middle of the cake cook, unless you are using a ring mould.
3 Cook on full power for 6 minutes. Leave to stand for 5 minutes in the container before turning on to a wire tray to cool.

Chocolate fudge frosting

50 g sugar
2 tablespoons water
40 g butter
75 g icing sugar
25 g cocoa

Method
1 Heat sugar, water, and butter for 1 minute on full power. Stir, then cook for a further ½ minute.
2 Sieve the icing sugar and cocoa together. Stir into the water and butter, and beat well. Allow the mixture to cool until it will coat the back of a wooden spoon, then use a little of it to spread in the centre of the cake and spread the rest on top.

Cheese

Cheese can be made from the milk of cows, goats, sheep, or other animals. Most cheese in the UK is made from cow's milk. It takes about ten litres of milk to produce one kilogram of cheese.

How cheese is made

A 'starter' is added to pasteurized milk to ripen it. Rennet is added and this separates the milk, as it ripens, into curds and whey. The curds are the solid part of the milk which eventually become the cheese. The liquid whey may be used for animal feeding. The curds are drained, and salt is added. The cheese is then pressed. If it is lightly pressed, a soft, crumbly cheese is produced. If the cheese is more firmly pressed, a harder cheese is produced. Then the cheeses are left to mature, to develop a good flavour and texture.

Types of cheese

Hard British cheeses include Cheddar, Cheshire, Double Gloucester, Leicester, and Derby. Softer British cheeses include Wensleydale, Lancashire, and Caerphilly. We import many foreign cheeses into the UK. Some of the best known are Edam, Camembert, Brie, Roquefort, Danish blue, Gorgonzola, Parmesan, and Gruyère.

Blue-veined cheeses like Danish blue, Stilton, and Roquefort have harmless moulds inserted in them, which spread through the cheese. Originally this kind of cheese was left to ripen in damp caves and the mould grew naturally.

The variations in the different types of cheese are due to the different milks used to make them and to differences in the traditional ways of making the cheeses in the areas from which they come.

Cottage cheese is made from pasteurized skimmed milk. It has a 'starter' added to separate it and to add flavour and texture. As it is made from skimmed milk (with the fat or creamy part removed), it is easy to digest. It is also low in calories and high in protein, so it is useful for a slimming diet.

The food value of cheese

Cheese is really a concentrated form of milk. It contains roughly $\frac{1}{3}$ protein, $\frac{1}{3}$ fat, and $\frac{1}{3}$ water. It is a good source of retinol (vitamin A) and the minerals calcium and phosphorus.

Storing cheese to keep it fresh

1   Wrap the cheese in cling film (be careful to use a suitable kind) or foil. Keep it in a cool place.
2   A cheese dish with a lid is also ideal for storing cheese, if it is kept in a cool place.
3   If you keep the cheese in a fridge or cold larder, leave it at room temperature for about half an hour before you eat it. This will bring out the full flavour.
4   Buy cheese in fairly small amounts, just enough to last for about a week.
5   Cheese can be frozen, but hard cheese may become crumbly when it thaws.

The usefulness of cheese as a food

1 It has high food value, containing many nutrients in good amounts.
2 It can be eaten raw, so is very useful for sandwiches and quick meals.
3 There is no waste.
4 It is relatively inexpensive compared with meat.
5 It has a very good flavour, and there are many kinds to choose from.
6 It can be used in cooking, for example in sauces, scones, cheese pastry, pies, flans, and cheesecake.

Digesting cheese

Some people feel that cheese is hard to digest as it contains a lot of fat (about ⅓). It can be made more easy to digest if:

1 it is grated before being eaten raw;
2 it is cooked lightly, but not for long;
3 it is eaten with a starchy food like bread, potatoes, or macaroni;
4 it is served or cooked with a highly flavoured seasoning, for example with mustard in cheese scones or sauce, or with pickle or chutney for a 'ploughman's lunch'.

QUESTIONS

1 Describe briefly how cheese is made.
2 List all the (a) British cheeses and (b) foreign cheeses you have tasted or seen for sale.
3 Although all cheeses are made from milk, they have different flavours and textures. Give 3 reasons for this.
4 Name (a) a French blue-veined cheese; (b) a cheese suitable for someone on a slimming diet; (c) the most popular hard British cheese; and (d) a crumbly Welsh cheese.
5 List the nutrients found in cheese.
6 How would you store cheese to make sure it did not become dry or mouldy?
7 Write out two menus for a family evening meal, both of which contain a hot or cold cheese dish.
8 Suggest two cheese dishes suitable for someone trying to lose weight.
9 Suggest three cheese dishes suitable for a party.
10 Describe fully why cheese is such a useful food.

Recipes

As well as the recipes below, cheese is used in: fish and cheese sauce (p. 138), fish and tomato casserole (p. 139), crispy fish bake (p. 139), ham and cheese roll-ups (p. 129), cottage cheese and pineapple salad (p. 193), cheese scones (p. 215), cheese and onion flan (p. 198), lasagne (p. 157), lemon cheesecake (p. 223), macaroni cheese (p. 155), pizza (p. 228), quiche Lorraine (p. 197), stuffed eggs (p. 129), sandwich fillings (p. 211), stuffed tomatoes (p. 129), and cheese and lentil bake (p. 163).

Quick cheese pizza *Serves about 3*

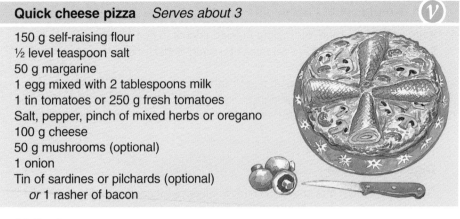

150 g self-raising flour
½ level teaspoon salt
50 g margarine
1 egg mixed with 2 tablespoons milk
1 tin tomatoes or 250 g fresh tomatoes
Salt, pepper, pinch of mixed herbs or oregano
100 g cheese
50 g mushrooms (optional)
1 onion
Tin of sardines or pilchards (optional)
    or 1 rasher of bacon

Method

1   Light the oven, Gas 5, 200°C. Place the shelf near the top of the oven. Grease a baking sheet.
2   Put the flour and salt in a bowl, rub in *half* of the margarine, add the egg and milk, and mix to a soft dough. Roll out to a large circle, about 22 cm in diameter, or make two smaller circles.
3   Drain the tomatoes (or slice if fresh). Grate the cheese. Peel and slice the onion and mushrooms and chop the bacon (if used). Fry in the other half of the margarine until soft.
4   Spread the tomatoes, cheese, salt, pepper, herbs, onions, mushrooms, and bacon over the base. Arrange the fish on top (if used).
5   Bake for about 20–25 minutes until the base is cooked. Cool on a wire tray. Serve warm or cold with a salad.

You can change the topping on a pizza as you like, using for example chopped cooked meat or chicken, olives, or peppers.

Cheese loaf

200 g self-raising flour
Pinch of salt
Pinch of mustard
50 g margarine
75 g cheese
1 egg
6 tablespoons of milk

Method

1   Light the oven, Gas 6, 200°C. Place the shelf above the centre. Grease a small loaf tin, and line the bottom with greaseproof paper.
2   Sieve the flour, salt, and mustard together. Rub in the margarine.
3   Grate the cheese and add it to the flour.
4   Beat the egg and milk and save a little to brush the top. Pour the rest into the flour and mix to a fairly soft dough. Shape to a loaf and put into the tin.
5   Bake for about 35 minutes until well risen and golden brown. Cool on a wire tray.

Serve sliced and buttered, the same day it is made. If kept to the next day, serve toasted and buttered.

Cheese and vegetable flan   *Serves about 3*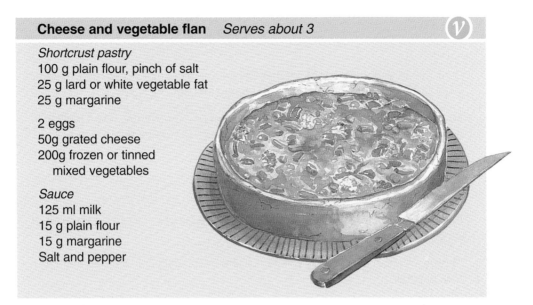

Shortcrust pastry
100 g plain flour, pinch of salt
25 g lard or white vegetable fat
25 g margarine

2 eggs
50g grated cheese
200g frozen or tinned
    mixed vegetables

Sauce
125 ml milk
15 g plain flour
15 g margarine
Salt and pepper

Method

1 Light the oven, Gas 6, 200°C. Position the shelf just above the centre. Grease an 18 cm flan ring and baking sheet (or use a sandwich cake tin).
2 Make the pastry and line the flan ring. Bake it blind (see p. 196).
3 Cook the vegetables as directed on the packet or tin. Grate the cheese. Beat the eggs.
4 Make the sauce: put the milk, flour, and margarine into a pan and bring to the boil, stirring all the time. Add the salt, pepper, and grated cheese. Remove from the heat.
5 Add the eggs and vegetables and mix carefully.
6 Pour into flan case. Turn the oven down to Gas 4, 180°C, and bake for about 30 minutes until the filling is firm and golden brown.

Cheese and potato bake   *Serves 3–4*

750 g potatoes	2 onions
50 g butter or margarine	Salt and pepper
2 tablespoons milk	2 tomatoes
150 g cheese (grated)	100 g bacon (optional)
1 egg	

Method

1 Peel the potatoes, cut to even-sized pieces. Put into a pan, cover with cold water, bring to the boil, and simmer for about 20 minutes until cooked. Drain and mash with the milk, butter, about half of the cheese, and the beaten egg.
2 Peel the onion and chop it finely. Add to the mashed potato. Add a little salt and pepper.
3 Put the potato into a shallow heatproof dish. Place the sliced tomato on top, then the chopped bacon (if used). Sprinkle the rest of the cheese on top.
4 Bake near the top of the oven, Gas 6, 200°C, for about 20–30 minutes until the top is golden brown. For a vegetarian dish, leave out the bacon.

Serve warm.

Eggs

Eggs are an extremely useful food as they are used in making so many different kinds of dishes. They can be used for many purposes, including:

Whisking They will hold a lot of air when whisked, for example when making a Swiss roll, a whisked sponge cake, or meringues. All the air held in the mixture by the eggs makes the cake light and well risen.

Eating on their own Eggs can be eaten boiled, fried, poached, or scrambled, to make a quick nutritious meal.

Setting Eggs enable a liquid mixture to set, for example in a quiche Lorraine or lemon curd.

Binding You can add an egg yolk to burgers or fish cakes. It will help them to stick together.

Coating Beaten egg can be used to coat fish or chicken portions before they are dipped into breadcrumbs and fried. This gives a crisp and attractive finish.

Emulsion When you add an egg or egg yolk to mayonnaise it helps the oil and vinegar to stay smoothly blended together.

Enriching other foods You can add a beaten egg to mashed potato or a milk pudding to improve the food value and make the dish more nutritious.

Glazing If pastry or scones are brushed with beaten egg and milk they will have a shiny golden brown appearance when cooked.

Page 50 tells you about the different methods of egg production.

The food value of eggs

Eggs are a valuable food as they contain many nutrients. They contain all the nutrients that would have been necessary for a chick to develop from the egg. These nutrients include protein, fat, vitamins A, B, and D, calcium, and iron.

Tests for freshness

1   A fresh egg is heavy because none of its moisture has evaporated through the shell. If you put it into a bowl of water it will sink to the bottom. A less fresh egg will rise in the water because of air in the shell. A stale egg will come right up to the top of the water. This is because so much of its moisture has evaporated through the shell and has been replaced by air, making it lighter.

Stale egg

Fresh egg

2   If you break a fresh egg on to a plate, the yolk will be firm and prominent. You will be able to see two different parts in the white. The inner part of the white will be thick and gluey. If the white is watery and thin then the egg is not very fresh.

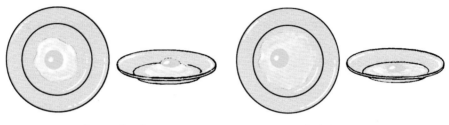

A very fresh egg　　　　　　　*A stale egg*

Buying and storing eggs

Eggs are graded for size: extra large, large, medium, or small. Egg cartons usually have a 'display until' date and a 'best before' date, and individual eggs are now often date-stamped. They will keep fresh for two or three weeks and should be kept in a refrigerator in their carton. If you want to boil them or use them for cake-making, they are best taken out of the fridge for at least 30 minutes. If they are at room temperature, they are less likely to crack when boiled, they will mix more easily into a cake, and they can be whisked more quickly for a meringue or sponge.

Recipes using eggs

When whisked – Swiss roll, sponge sandwich cake, sponge fruit flan or gateau.

To set a mixture – quiche Lorraine, cheese and onion flan.

Glazing – most pastry dishes, e.g. sausage rolls, meat or fruit pies, scones.

Binding – fish cakes.

Coating – fish cakes, fish, baked chicken joints, chilladas.

To emulsify – mayonnaise.

Other recipes – stuffed eggs, egg and cress sandwiches, lemon curd, Victoria sandwich and other cakes, pineapple upside-down pudding, steamed puddings.

QUESTIONS

1   Eggs are used for many different purposes in cooking. Describe the five purposes for which you think they are most often used.
2   List the nutrients which eggs contain.
3   Describe, with the help of a diagram, why a very fresh egg sinks in a bowl of water.
4   When buying eggs in a supermarket, how would you know which are freshest?
5   Why is it better not to cook with eggs straight from the refrigerator?

Milk

Milk is a valuable and useful food. It contains all of the nutrients that babies need; they live and thrive on a diet of nothing but milk for several months. Because it contains so many nutrients it is a good food for older children and adults too.

The food value of milk

Milk contains these nutrients:

- protein
- carbohydrate, in the form of a little sugar
- fat, the creamy part of the milk
- vitamins, especially retinol (vitamin A) and riboflavin (vitamin B_2)
- minerals, especially calcium and phosphorus

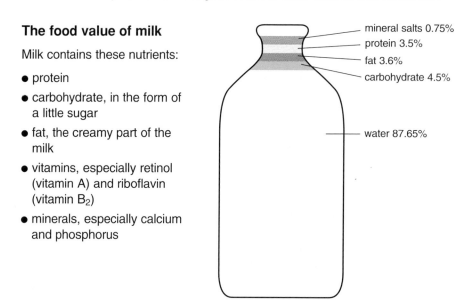

mineral salts 0.75%
protein 3.5%
fat 3.6%
carbohydrate 4.5%

water 87.65%

Different kinds of milk

Pasteurized

Milk is pasteurized to kill any harmful bacteria. That is, it is heated to 71°C for 15 seconds, then quickly cooled to below 10°C. Pasteurized milk will keep fresh for 2–3 days in a fridge. It is the kind of milk most often used for drinking, on cereals, and in cooking.

Pasteurized milk may be full cream, semi-skimmed, or skimmed. The difference between them is in the amount of fat, in the form of cream, they contain. Semi-skimmed and skimmed milk has had some of the creamy 'top of the milk' skimmed off before it is put into bottles or cartons. This makes it lower in fat and therefore lower in calories. Either of these is a good choice for anyone cutting down on animal fats or reducing their calorie intake.

Type of milk	kcal per 100 ml	g of fat per 100 ml	of which saturates
Full cream	67	3.9	2.6
Semi-skimmed	48	1.6	1.1
Skimmed	34	0.1	0.1

Freezing

Both semi-skimmed and skimmed milk can be frozen provided it is in cartons. Full cream milk does not freeze well as it tends to separate. You may have seen milk which has been standing outside in the snow and has frozen. When it thaws it separates and is not very appetizing. Never freeze any kind of glass bottle, as the liquid will expand as it freezes and crack the bottle.

UHT (ultra heat treated) or long life milk

The milk is heated to a very high temperature, about 132°C, for 1 second. It will keep for several months unopened so is useful to keep in the store cupboard. It is usually packed in 1 litre cartons, and will keep for 2–3 days in a fridge once it has been opened. The heat treatment affects the taste of the milk and most people prefer pasteurized milk for everyday use.

Soya milk

Soya milk is used by vegetarians and vegans. It comes in ½ or 1 litre cartons and will keep for a few months unopened. It is made by soaking soya beans in water, then straining them. It can be used in hot drinks and for cooking.

Storing fresh milk

You must be particularly careful when using milk to make sure that everything is scrupulously clean. Milk is an ideal food for bacteria to breed in and cause food poisoning. Keep milk *clean*, *cool*, and *covered*.

1   Never leave milk standing in the sun on your doorstep. Bring it in and put it in a cool place as soon as possible. The sun's heat will not only make the milk go off more quickly, but will destroy some of the vitamin B and vitamin C.
2   Do not mix milk from different days together. Put new milk into a clean jug, or leave it in the bottle or carton, which usually has a sell-by date.
3   When you wash a milk jug or bottle, first rinse it in cold water. Hot water will 'set' the milk on to the jug. After rinsing in cold water, wash in hot soapy water, then rinse out and drain or dry with a clean cloth.
4   Do not store milk near strong-smelling foods such as onions or fish, as the milk will quickly pick up the smell.

Dried and canned milk

1   *Dried milk* can be sold in tins, packets, or plastic bottles, in powder form. The water is removed and the dry powder will keep for a long time. Dried milk may be 'whole' dried milk, with its full fat content, or it may be skimmed to remove the fat before drying. Sometimes skimmed milk powder has vegetable fat added.
2   *Evaporated milk.* Some of the water in the milk is removed to make it more concentrated, then it is canned. It is useful as it has a flavour which many people like and can be used on puddings instead of cream or custard. It can be whipped to make it thicker and fluffy, as in jelly whip, p. 223. It is a useful source of vitamins A and D.
3   *Condensed milk* is milk which has been evaporated and has had a lot of sugar added to it. It is very thick and sweet and may be used for making puddings or sweets. You can buy it in a tube to take camping; it keeps for a long time as there is so much sugar in it.

Dishes made with milk

Mushroom soup (p. 133), sweetcorn and potato soup (p. 134), leek and potato soup (p. 134).

Fish and cheese sauce (p. 138), cheese and vegetable flan (p. 175), toad in the hole (p. 147), Yorkshire pudding (p. 147), lasagne (p. 157), macaroni cheese (p. 155), quiche Lorraine (p. 197), cauliflower cheese (p. 188).

Gingerbread (p. 205), jelly whip (p. 223), fruit fool (p. 222), rice pudding (p. 221), custard (p. 171), pancakes (p. 220).

Products made from milk

These include cream, butter, yoghurt, and cheese.

Cream is available in different forms. The thickness of the cream depends on the amount of butterfat it contains.

Single cream must have a butterfat content of at least 18%. It cannot be whipped and is used for pouring.

Whipping cream must have at least 35% butterfat. It is pasteurized and can be whipped.

Double cream has at least 48% butterfat, and can be whipped.

Clotted cream (Devonshire cream) has at least 55% butterfat.

Crème fraiche is a thickened French cream with a culture added. It can be used for cooking or spooning onto fruit or puddings.

Fromage frais can be eaten on its own or used instead of cream in desserts or savoury recipes. It can be bought plain or fruit flavoured (like yoghurt).

Tinned cream has at least 23% butterfat. It has been sterilized in the tin and will keep for several months. It cannot be whipped.

UHT cream is heat-treated so that it has a long shelf life. It is sold in foil-lined cartons. Some UHT creams can be whipped, others cannot; this is usually marked on the carton.

Frozen whipped cream is already whipped and is sold in waxed cartons or polythene bags.

Soured cream is not cream which has gone sour but is a specially prepared cream with a tangy flavour, which may be used in meat, fish, or other savoury dishes, or in salad dressings.

Butter is made from cream. It may be salted or unsalted. It has a very good flavour, either spread on bread or used for cooking, but as it is expensive and high in saturated fats it is sometimes replaced by margarine. Butter should be kept covered in the fridge or a cool place so that it does not go rancid. It should be stored away from strong smelling foods as it quickly picks up any smell.

Yoghurt is made from either skimmed milk or whole milk, with a specially added culture of bacteria. Sometimes it has fruit or sugar added. Unsweetened yoghurt can be added to meat or fish dishes, or used instead of milk or cream on cereals or fruit dishes. It will keep fresh for 4–5 days in the fridge, and is sold with a date stamp.

What will you put on your pudding?

	kcal	g fat per 100 g
Plain yoghurt	52	1.5
Fromage frais	102	7.4
Evaporated milk	151	9.4
Single cream	198	19.1
Crème fraiche	383	40.3
Double cream	449	48.0

QUESTIONS

1   What nutrients does milk contain?
2   What happens to milk if it is left on the doorstep in the sun?
3   Describe exactly what these terms mean:
    (a) pasteurized, (b) semi-skimmed, (c) UHT.
4   You want to keep a store of milk at home for emergency use. Suggest four ways you could do this, and give the advantages of each way.
5   What kind of milk is a suitable choice for someone trying to lose weight?
6   Name two kinds of milk suitable for someone on a low animal fat diet.
7   Describe how you would thoroughly wash a milk jug.
8   What is the difference between evaporated and condensed milk? Give two uses for each of them.
9   Plan the meals for a family for one day, including plenty of dishes made with milk.
10 What kind of cream would be suitable for each of these purposes:
    a) piping on to a cake or cold sweet to decorate it.
    b) keeping in store for a few weeks in the cupboard.
    c) pouring into coffee.
    d) putting into scones with strawberry jam for a 'Devonshire cream tea'.
    e) adding to a casserole.

Cereals

Cereals are the seed grains of grasses, so called after Ceres, the Greek goddess of the harvest. They include wheat, oats, barley, rye, maize or corn, and rice.

The cereal crop grown in any particular country is usually a very important staple food in that country. Examples are rice in India and China, and wheat, used for flour for making bread, in western countries.

Cereals are useful foods because they are easy to grow and easy to store. They are inexpensive compared with animal foods and they are filling and nutritious.

Food value

Cereals are a valuable source of carbohydrate, vegetable protein, B vitamins, and minerals. Whole grain cereals are a good source of NSP (dietary fibre).

Wheat

The most important cereal in the UK is wheat. The wheat is milled to make flour, which is then used for bread, a staple British food.

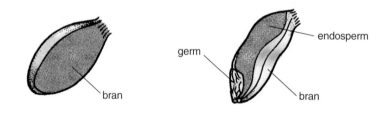

Grain of wheat

Different types of flour contain different parts of the whole grain of wheat.

Wholemeal flour is the whole grain of wheat ground up to produce flour. It is said to have '100% extraction rate'. This means that 100% of the grain is included in the flour. Nothing is taken away or added.

Brown or wheatmeal flour has between about 80% and 90% extraction rate. Some of the roughest outer layers of bran are removed during milling to make a smoother flour.

White flour has an extraction rate of only about 70%. All the outer layers of bran are removed, leaving a smooth white flour.

You can buy white flour as either plain or self-raising (SR) flour. Self-raising flour is just plain flour with a raising agent (baking powder) added to it. Strong plain flour is always used for making bread. It contains a large amount of *gluten*, which becomes stretchy when mixed into a dough (see p. 224). This enables the bread to rise well and to hold a good firm shape once it is risen.

'Hovis' or *'Vit-be'* flour is white flour with extra amounts of wheat germ added. This makes it a good source of the B vitamins which are in the wheat germ.

Brown or white bread?

You can buy or make bread from wholemeal, brown, or white flour. From the point of view of the nutrients they contain they are much the same. Although some of the nutrients in wholemeal flour are removed in the milling of white flour, all white flour in the UK is enriched with thiamin (vitamin B_1), niacin (B_3), iron, and calcium to make up for these losses.

The main advantage of wholemeal flour or bread is the large amount of NSP (dietary fibre) which it contains. This is a very important part of the diet. However, those people who prefer to eat white bread can include other high-fibre foods in their meals instead, for example whole breakfast cereals, bran breakfast cereals, pulses, vegetables, and fruits (see p. 12). Many people prefer the flavour and texture of wholemeal bread.

Other cereals

Oats Traditionally these are widely grown and used in Scotland, for porridge, haggis, and oatcakes. Oats are most often prepared as 'rolled oats'. These are crushed between heated rollers to crush and partly cook them. They are the kind usually used in porridge, muesli-type breakfast cereals, and biscuits.

Barley Most barley grown in the UK is used for malt, or for animal foods. You can also buy polished 'pearl barley', used for thickening soups and stews.

Maize or corn is used to make cornflakes, cornflour, and pop-corn. It is used also as a vegetable, as sweetcorn or corn on the cob.

Sago and tapioca are not cereals but they are starchy foods used for milk puddings, in the same way as rice and semolina. Sago is made from the pith of the trunk of the sago palm. Tapioca is made from the root of the cassava plant.

Semolina is produced from the starch in hard wheat when it is coarsely milled.

Arrowroot is prepared from a root. It is used for making a clear glaze for fruit flans, as it becomes transparent when boiled.

Rice and ground rice See p. 152.

QUESTIONS

1 What nutrients do most cereal foods contain?
2 Draw and label the diagrams of a grain of wheat.
3 Describe what is meant by wholemeal, brown, and white bread.
4 What kind of flour is used for breadmaking?
5 What kind of flour contains extra wheat germ?
6 Would you give your family wholemeal, brown, or white bread to eat? Explain your reasons carefully.

Vegetables and fruit

You can buy a great variety of fresh fruit and vegetables in the shops and markets today. There is usually a good selection of home-produced and imported fruit and vegetables to choose from. They are useful foods because:

1 There are so many to choose from that they can add a great variety of colour, flavour, and texture to meals.
2 They are a good source of many vitamins and minerals.
3 Many of them are inexpensive and widely available.
4 Many can be eaten either raw or cooked.
5 They fill us up but are low in calories, so they are not likely to make us put on excess weight.
6 They can be bought fresh, frozen, tinned, or dried.

Vegetables

Most vegetables can be roughly grouped as:
Root vegetables – e.g. potatoes, carrots, turnips, swedes.
Green vegetables – e.g. cabbage, sprouts, lettuce, watercress.
Pod or *pulse vegetables* – e.g. peas in their pods, broad beans, runner beans.
When dried they are known as pulses, e.g. dried peas, lentils, red kidney beans (see p. 158).

Choosing and storing vegetables and fruit

1 Look for fruit and vegetables which are in season (that means, at the time of year when they are growing plentifully). They will be cheap, easily available, and in good condition. This is the time to buy them to freeze for use later in the year.
2 Root vegetables should be firm and smoothly shaped so that they are easy to peel. They should not have a lot of dirt clinging to them.
3 Green vegetables should be firm, crisp, and a good colour. Avoid any which are soft, wilted, or discoloured.
4 Store vegetables in a cool, dark place. Do not buy large quantities of vegetables at one time as they soon lose their freshness.

5   The flavour of frozen, tinned, and dried vegetables and fruit is seldom as good as that of the freshly-picked kind, but they do have some advantages.
    a) The food value is usually as good as in fresh fruit and vegetables.
    b) They need little time spent in preparation.
    c) There is no wastage.
    d) Their cost remains the same all the year round.
    e) They can be stored for use when you cannot obtain the fresh variety.

The food value of vegetables and fruit

This varies quite a lot, depending on the type of fruit or vegetable. In general, the main value of most fruit and vegetables in the diet is in the minerals, vitamins, and NSP (dietary fibre) which they contain.

Protein There is a small amount in all vegetables and fruit, and good amounts in pod vegetables and pulses (beans, lentils, and peas).

Carbohydrate Potatoes and pulse vegetables supply a useful amount of carbohydrate.

Vitamin A is found in the form of beta-carotene in yellow, orange, and red fruit and vegetables (e.g. carrots, tomatoes, peaches) and in green vegetables. The beta-carotene is converted by the liver into vitamin A.

Vitamin B Some of the B vitamins are found in potatoes, pulses, and green vegetables.

Vitamin C Fruit and vegetables are our main source of vitamin C. Blackcurrants, tomatoes, oranges, lemons, and grapefruit are particularly rich sources. Vitamin C is very easily destroyed so vegetables must be carefully prepared and cooked to retain as much Vitamin C as possible when you eat them (see p. 31).

Antioxidants Vegetables and fruits are very good sources of the antioxidant vitamins beta-carotene, vitamin C, and vitamin E, which help prevent the harmful effects of free radicals (see p. 29).

QUESTIONS

1   Why are fruit and vegetables useful to anyone on a slimming diet?
2   Name three root vegetables, three green vegetables, three fresh pod vegetables, and three pulse vegetables.
3   Why should you look for fruit and vegetables in season?
4   Describe what you would look for when buying (a) root vegetables, and (b) green vegetables.
5   What are the points for and against choosing fresh vegetables rather than frozen or tinned?
6   Name the nutrients you would expect to find in (a) potatoes, (b) tomatoes, and (c) lemons.
7   What useful role do antioxidants play in the diet?
8   Name three vegetables and three fruits which you would expect to supply useful amounts of beta-carotene.
9   Describe how you would prepare and cook Brussels sprouts, so that they contain as much vitamin C as possible when you serve them.

Recipes

For recipes using fruit see the section on puddings, pp. 217–223. There are lots of other recipes using vegetables or fruit, especially in the sections on starters and soups, vegetarian recipes, and pulses: spicy chick peas (p. 164), chilli bean casserole (p. 166), savoury cheese potatoes (p. 166), three bean bake (p. 160), vegetable curry (p. 152), stuffed peppers (p. 168), stir fried vegetables and noodles (p. 168), ratatouille (p. 167), vegetable samosas (p. 169), avocados (p. 130).

In several of the recipes below, butter is added to the cooked vegetables, for flavour and finish. For a lower calorie and lower fat recipe, leave out the butter.

Boiled potatoes   *Serves 3*   Ⓥ

500 g potatoes

Method

Scrub the potatoes in cold water, then peel them thinly. Rinse and cut into even-sized pieces. Put into a pan and cover with cold water. Bring to the boil and simmer with the lid on until soft, about 20 minutes. Test with a skewer or a small sharp knife. Drain, and return to the pan briefly to dry off. Serve in a vegetable dish.

Boiled potatoes can also be cooked with their skins on.

Creamed potatoes Cook as above, but mash the cooked potatoes in the pan. Add 15 g butter or margarine, a tablespoon of milk, and seasoning, and beat until smooth and creamy. Serve in a vegetable dish, garnished with parsley.

Baked potatoes   Ⓥ

| Large potatoes, 1 for each person | Oil (optional) |
| (use medium potatoes if time is short) | Butter and parsley |

Method

1   Light the oven, Gas 6, 200°C. Place the shelf near the top of the oven.
2   Scrub the potatoes. Brush with oil (if using) and make a slit in the top of each.
3   Bake, on a baking tray for about 1 hour until soft. Test carefully with a skewer.
4   Cut a cross in the top, add a knob of butter and a sprig of parsley.
5   Serve in a vegetable dish, on a coloured napkin if you have one.

To save time, cook in a microwave oven (see p. 170). For a better finish, pre-cook in a microwave oven, then crisp for 10 minutes in a very hot oven.

Cheese-filled baked potatoes   *Fills 2 large potatoes*   Ⓥ

2 baked potatoes	1 tablespoon milk and 25 g butter
50 g grated cheese (or cottage,	2 teaspoons chopped parsley or chopped
curd, or cream cheese)	spring onion (optional), pepper

Method

1   Cut the potatoes in half lengthwise. Scoop out the potato from the centre leaving a shell 0.5 cm thick.
2   Mix the potato and filling ingredients together in a small bowl, and pile into the shells. Bake for a futher 10 minutes (or 2 minutes in the microwave).

Roast potatoes   *Serves about 3*   ⓥ

500 g old potatoes   50 g oil or dripping

Method

1 Light the oven, Gas 6, 200°C. Put the oil or dripping in a roasting tin near the top of the oven.
2 Scrub and peel the potatoes, cut to even-sized pieces. Dry and place in the hot fat, using a little of this to baste the potatoes.
3 Bake for about 1–1½ hours until soft and golden brown. Baste occasionally during cooking. Serve in a vegetable dish.

Potatoes are often roasted in the fat around a joint or chicken. They will cook more quickly if boiled for ten minutes before roasting.

New potatoes   *Serves about 3*   ⓥ

500 g new potatoes   Butter, parsley

Method

1 Half fill a pan of water and put on to boil.
2 Wash the potatoes, scrape, and rinse. Put into the boiling water and simmer gently for about 20 minutes until cooked. Test with a skewer.
3 Drain, using the pan lid, and return to the pan with the butter. Shake the pan gently, to coat the potatoes in melted butter.
4 Serve in a vegetable dish, sprinkled with a little parsley.

Buttered carrots   *Serves about 3*   ⓥ

250 g carrots   Parsley
25 g butter

Method

Peel the carrots, rinse, then cut into neat 'sticks' or rings. Put into a pan, and add enough water to cover the carrots. Bring to the boil, then simmer very gently with the lid on for about 15 minutes until tender. Drain, then return to the pan with the butter. Shake gently until the carrots are glazed, then serve, garnished with a little parsley.

For a change, add a tablespoon of orange squash with the butter.

Courgettes and mushrooms   *Serves 4*   ⓥ

500 g courgettes   Parsley
100 g button mushrooms   Salt and black pepper
25 g butter and 1 tablespoon vegetable oil

Method

1 Wash and dry the courgettes, and cut into 0.5 cm slices. Fry in butter and oil in a large pan for about 3 minutes on each side until soft and golden brown.
2 Wipe and slice the mushrooms and add to the pan for a few minutes, adding salt and pepper. Chop the parsley.
3 Put into a warm serving dish and sprinkle with the parsley.

Brussels sprouts *Serves about 3* Ⓥ

250 g sprouts
25 g butter

Method
Put a pan of water, about one third full, on to boil. Remove any coarse outer leaves from the sprouts. Cut a cross through the stalk of each sprout. Wash in cold water. Put into boiling water and simmer very gently with the lid on for 10–15 minutes. Drain very thoroughly. Return to the pan with the butter and shake gently to coat the sprouts. Serve neatly in a vegetable dish.

Cabbage *Serves about 3* Ⓥ

About 250 g cabbage
25 g butter

Method
Put a pan of water, about one third full, on to boil. Remove any coarse outer leaves and the stalk from the cabbage, wash it, then shred finely. Cook in the boiling water for about 10 minutes until tender. Drain very thoroughly. Return to the pan with the butter. Serve in a vegetable dish.

Cauliflower *Serves 3-4* Ⓥ

Wash the cauliflower, remove the leaves. Either leave it whole, cutting a cross through the stalk, or cut it into sprigs. Half fill a pan with water, and bring to the boil. Add the cauliflower and simmer very gently for about 15 minutes until tender. Drain and serve in a vegetable dish.

Cauliflower cheese *Serves about 3* Ⓥ

1 cauliflower   25 g margarine
250 ml milk   75 g cheese, grated
25 g flour   Salt, pepper, pinch of mustard

Method
Cook the cauliflower as above. Make the cheese sauce: put all the ingredients except the cheese into a pan. Bring to the boil, whisking all the time. Stir in most of the cheese until it is melted. Pour over the cauliflower. Sprinkle with the rest of the cheese and brown lightly under a hot grill.

Peas *Serves about 3* Ⓥ

500 g fresh garden peas in pods   25 g butter

Method
Shell the peas. Put a pan about one third full of water on to boil. Put the peas into the boiling water and simmer very gently with the lid on for about 15–20 minutes until tender. Test by tasting one of the peas. Drain and return to the pan with the butter. Shake gently to glaze the peas then serve in a vegetable dish. Frozen peas should be simmered for 2–3 minutes only.

Salads

Salads are made with raw or cold cooked vegetables and sometimes fruits. All the ingredients for the salad should be very fresh, crisp, and in good condition. Wash all the vegetables carefully but thoroughly in cold running water and shake gently to dry. Do not leave them soaking in water. A dressing served with a salad adds to the flavour and the food value. The two given below are both quick and easy to make. A salad may be made either as an accompaniment to the main dish in a meal, or as a complete dish in itself. There are recipes for both kinds below.

Some ways of preparing vegetables for a salad

Tomato 'waterlilies' Use a sharp knife with a narrow blade.

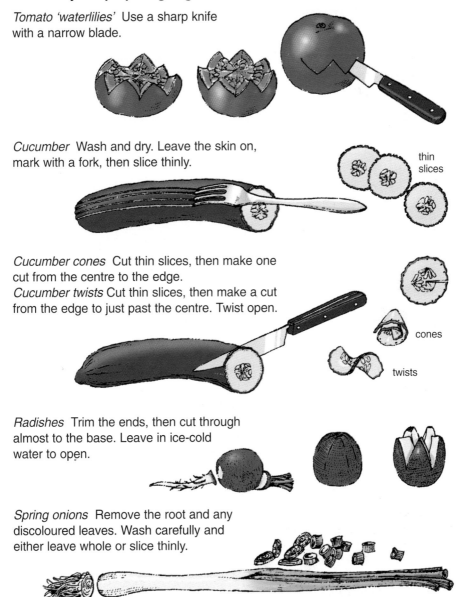

Cucumber Wash and dry. Leave the skin on, mark with a fork, then slice thinly.

thin slices

Cucumber cones Cut thin slices, then make one cut from the centre to the edge.
Cucumber twists Cut thin slices, then make a cut from the edge to just past the centre. Twist open.

cones

twists

Radishes Trim the ends, then cut through almost to the base. Leave in ice-cold water to open.

Spring onions Remove the root and any discoloured leaves. Wash carefully and either leave whole or slice thinly.

French dressing (v)

1 tablespoon vinegar or lemon juice
2 tablespoons salad oil
Pinch of salt   Pinch of sugar
Pinch of dry mustard   Shake of pepper

Method
Put all the ingredients into a jam jar with a screw top, or a plastic beaker with a leak-proof lid. Shake well together until thoroughly mixed. Shake again just before use.

Mayonnaise (v)

Using a blender or food processor
1 egg (at room temperature, not cold)   ½ level teaspoon sugar
125 ml salad oil   ½ level teaspoon salt
1 tablespoon vinegar or lemon juice   Shake of pepper
½ level teaspoon mustard

Method
Put all the ingredients into the blender and mix on maximum speed for about 1 minute. If you want to make the mayonnaise a little thicker, add a little more oil through the lid. To make it thinner, add a little vinegar.

Side salads

Tomato salad   *Serves 4* (v)

4 tomatoes
⅓ small onion or 2 spring onions
Parsley
French dressing (see recipe)

Method
1 Wash and dry the tomatoes. Slice and arrange neatly on a flat dish.
2 Chop the onion finely. Wash and chop the parsley.
3 Sprinkle the onion over the tomato. Spoon the French dressing over the tomatoes about 20 minutes before serving.
4 Sprinkle with chopped parsley.

Cucumber salad   *Serves about 3* (v)

Half a cucumber
French dressing (see recipe)
Parsley

Method
1 Wash and slice the cucumber, and arrange neatly on a shallow dish. Wash and chop the parsley. Make the French dressing.
2 Ten minutes before serving, shake the French dressing and spoon over the cucumber. Sprinkle with the parsley.

Lettuce and cucumber salad   *Serves about 3*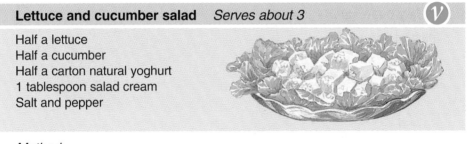

Half a lettuce
Half a cucumber
Half a carton natural yoghurt
1 tablespoon salad cream
Salt and pepper

Method

1   Wash the lettuce and gently shake it dry. Wash and peel the cucumber, and cut it into small dice.
2   Mix the yoghurt and salad cream, add a little salt and pepper, stir in the diced cucumber.
3   Put the lettuce on to the serving dish, spoon the cucumber mixture into the centre.

Potato salad   *Serves about 3*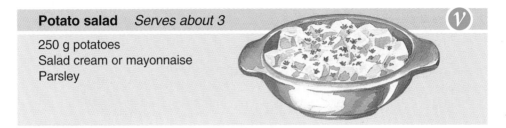

250 g potatoes
Salad cream or mayonnaise
Parsley

Method

1   Peel the potatoes, cut into 1 cm dice. Put in a pan, and cover with cold water. Add a tablespoon of oil, and simmer very gently for about 5 minutes until tender.
2   Drain and cool. Carefully mix in enough salad cream to coat the potatoes.

Serve in a vegetable dish garnished with parsley.

Mexican salad   *Serves about 3*

1 red or green pepper
100 g small button mushrooms
2 tomatoes
½ cucumber
French dressing (see recipe)

Method

1   Wash the mushrooms, remove the peel and stalks. Cut into neat slices about 0.5 cm thick. (You can include the stalks in the salad or not, as you prefer.)
2   Peel the cucumber and cut into 1 cm dice. Wash the tomatoes, and cut into wedges.
3   Wash the pepper, cut in two, and remove the seeds and stalk. Cut into small pieces.
4   Make the French dressing and combine it with all the salad ingredients, mixing them gently until they are coated.
5   Serve in a salad bowl.

Kidney bean salad   *Serves about 4*

400 g tin kidney beans
½ a small onion or 2 spring onions
French dressing
Parsley

Method

1   Drain the kidney beans very thoroughly in a sieve.
2   Peel the onion and chop it finely. Wash and chop the parsley.
3   Make the French dressing and spoon carefully over the beans.
4   Put the beans into a vegetable dish or salad bowl and sprinkle with the chopped onion and parsley. Serve chilled.

Butter bean salad Make in exactly the same way but use butter beans instead of kidney beans.

Coleslaw   *Serves about 3*

Half a firm white cabbage
1 medium carrot
1 eating apple
Salad cream or mayonnaise
Parsley or cress to garnish

Method

1   Put aside some large cabbage leaves for serving.
2   Shred the cabbage and the peeled carrot on the large side of the grater. Peel and core the apple and grate it.
3   Mix the cabbage, carrot, and apple, and add enough salad cream or mayonnaise to bind them together.
4   Serve neatly in a small vegetable dish, inside the cabbage leaves.
5   Garnish with a little parsley or cress.

Rice salad   *Serves about 3*

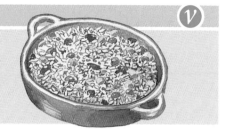

75 g long grain rice
1 large tomato
25 g frozen peas
25 g sweetcorn
Parsley

Method

1   Cook the rice in boiling, salted water for 11 minutes. Drain and cool.
2   Cut the washed tomato in two, remove the pips. Dice the tomato.
3   Simmer the peas gently in boiling salted water for 3–5 minutes. Drain and cool.
4   Wash and chop the parsley.
5   Carefully mix all the ingredients and serve in a vegetable dish. You could add a little French dressing if you like.

You can vary the vegetables which you add to the rice, according to your taste.

Main-course salads

Cottage cheese and pineapple salad   *Serves 2*

Half a lettuce
250 g cottage cheese
A few slices or chunks of pineapple
2 tomatoes
Cress

Method

1   Wash the lettuce carefully under cold running water, and gently shake dry. Wash the cress. Wash and slice the tomatoes.
2   Chop the pineapple and mix with the cottage cheese.
3   Arrange the lettuce to cover two plates. Put the cottage cheese in the centre of each plate. Put the slices of tomato around the edge of the cottage cheese and place a little cress in the centre of each salad.

Tuna fish salad   *Serves 4*

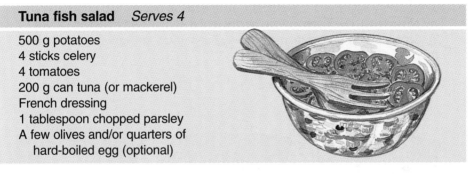

500 g potatoes
4 sticks celery
4 tomatoes
200 g can tuna (or mackerel)
French dressing
1 tablespoon chopped parsley
A few olives and/or quarters of
    hard-boiled egg (optional)

Method

1   Wash and peel the potatoes, cut to even sized pieces, cover with cold water, and simmer for about 20 minutes until cooked. Drain and slice.
2   Slice the celery and tomatoes. Drain and flake the fish. Chop the parsley.
3   Make the French dressing.
4   Put layers of ingredients into the salad bowl, sprinkling with the French dressing. Top with a layer of tomatoes and sprinkle with chopped parsley.

Sardine and tomato salad   *Serves 2*

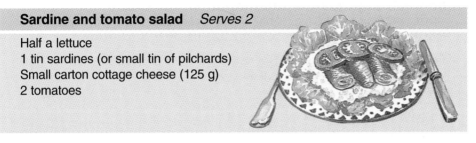

Half a lettuce
1 tin sardines (or small tin of pilchards)
Small carton cottage cheese (125 g)
2 tomatoes

Method

1   Wash the lettuce under cold running water. Gently shake dry. Slice the tomatoes.
2   Use the lettuce to cover 2 medium sized plates. Put half the cottage cheese into the centre of each and place the sardines on top.
3   Garnish neatly with the tomato slices.

Making pastry

Shortcrust pastry

Recipe for 100 g pastry	ⓥ

(this means pastry made with 100 g flour)

100 g plain flour, pinch of salt   25 g block margarine
25 g lard or white cooking fat   Cold water to mix, about 4 teaspoonfuls

Method
1 Sieve the flour and salt into a bowl. Add the margarine and lard (or white cooking fat) to the flour, and cut into small pieces.
2 Rub the fat into the flour using your fingertips, until the mixture looks like breadcrumbs. Do not rub it in too much or it will start to stick together and will be very difficult to roll out later.
3 Add the water a little at a time and mix to a firm, smooth dough.
4 Knead it very lightly until it is smooth. To knead the pastry: turn edges to centre and press firmly (1). Keep turning pastry round and turning edges to centre (2). Continue until underside and edges of pastry are smooth and free from cracks (3). Then turn underside to top.

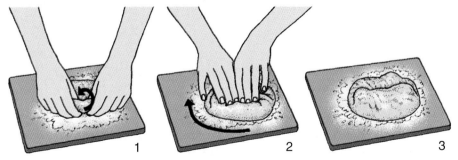

1   2   3

5 Roll out thinly and use as required. Bake in a hot oven (about Gas 6, 200°C).

Shortcrust pastry made with brown flour
Shortcrust pastry made with brown flour has a delicious, nutty flavour, and is particularly good for savoury flans and pies. For best results use either wheatmeal flour or a mixture of half wholemeal and half white flour. You may find that you need to add a little more water than usual.

Food processors are very good for rubbing fat into flour. You can mix more than you need, and store it in bags in the freezer.

Tips for making pastry

1 Keep everything cool, ingredients and utensils.
2 Handle very lightly.
3 Do not over-rub the fat into the flour.
4 Do not add too much water.
5 Roll out smoothly and evenly.
6 Bake in a hot oven.

Decorating pastry

To finish the edges of a pie or tart

Press the edges together with the fingers, and use a knife to 'knock up' the edges. Flute the edges with the left thumb and the knife.

To brush the tops of pies before cooking, for an attractive finish

For a sweet pie, such as apple, use egg white and caster sugar, or milk and caster sugar. For a savoury pie, such as corned beef and potato, use beaten egg and milk.

To make decorations for the top

Pastry leaves: roll out the trimmings and cut diamond shapes from 2 cm strips of pastry. Mark with a knife.

Use a scone cutter to make rounded leaves:

Tassels for a meat pie:

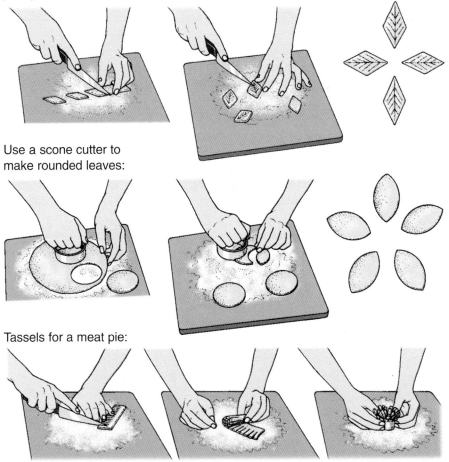

To line a flan ring

*Fluted flan ring
for sweet fillings*

*Plain flan ring for
savoury fillings*

1 Make the pastry and roll out to a circle about 5 cm larger than the flan ring.
2 Grease the flan ring and baking tray. Place the ring on the tray.
3 Place the rolling pin in the centre of the pastry. Fold one side over and lift the pastry into the ring.
4 Press it firmly but gently against the base and sides. Be very careful not to stretch or make a hole in the pastry.
5 Use a rolling pin to remove the excess pastry from the top of the ring. Leave the flan in the fridge or a cool place while you prepare the filling.

To bake a flan case blind means to bake it before the filling is added. Place a large piece of greaseproof paper over the pastry in the flan ring. Add dried beans to weight the pastry down and stop it rising (or you can use foil, without the beans). Bake at Gas 6, 200°C, on the top shelf for about 15 minutes. Remove the paper and beans, or the foil, and the flan ring. Return to the oven for a further 5 minutes to dry the pastry out.

greaseproof paper

beans

QUESTIONS

1 Write out and learn the basic ingredients for shortcrust pastry.
2 What are the rules to remember if you want to make a good pastry?
3 Suggest a suitable finish for brushing the top of (a) a plum pie, (b) a bacon and egg pie.
4 Suggest suitable decorations you could make with pastry trimmings for (a) a chicken and mushroom pie, (b) a gooseberry pie.
5 Describe what is meant by baking a pastry case blind.

Recipes using shortcrust pastry

Apple pie *Serves about 4*

Shortcrust pastry
200 g plain flour
Pinch of salt
50 g margarine
50 g lard or white cooking fat

Filling
500 g cooking apples
100 g sugar

Method
1 Light the oven, Gas 7, 220°C. Position the shelf at the top of the oven. Grease a pie plate about 20 cm in diameter.
2 Make the shortcrust pastry, and divide into two, one piece slightly larger than the other. Use the larger piece to line the pie plate.
3 Cut the apples into quarters, remove the peel and core, and slice thinly.
4 Place the apple on the pastry and sprinkle with the sugar. Damp the edges and cover with the other piece of pastry. Make two slits in the top. Seal the edges and decorate the pie if you like (see p. 195).
5 Brush with milk, or egg and milk, and sprinkle with sugar. Place the pie on a baking sheet and bake for 30–35 minutes until the pastry is golden brown and the apples are cooked.

For a change you could add a level teaspoon of cinnamon or mixed spice to the apple, and/or a tablespoon of dates or dried fruit. You could use a different kind of fruit, or a can of pie filling.

Quiche Lorraine *Serves about 4*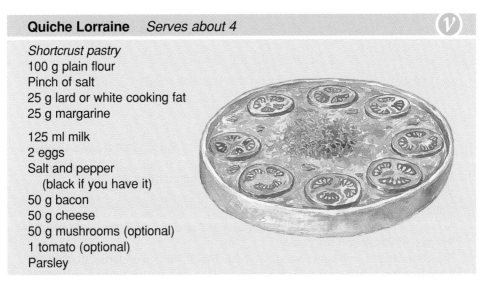

Shortcrust pastry
100 g plain flour
Pinch of salt
25 g lard or white cooking fat
25 g margarine

125 ml milk
2 eggs
Salt and pepper
   (black if you have it)
50 g bacon
50 g cheese
50 g mushrooms (optional)
1 tomato (optional)
Parsley

Method
1 Light the oven, Gas 5, 190°C. Place the shelf just above the centre. Grease a flan ring, about 18 cm in diameter, and a baking sheet (or use a sandwich cake tin).

2   Make the shortcrust pastry and use it to line the flan ring.
3   Cut the rind off the bacon and cut into small pieces. Fry for a few minutes in a small pan. Wash and chop the mushrooms and add to the pan for a further couple of minutes. Grate the cheese.
4   Put the bacon, cheese, and mushrooms into the flan. Beat the eggs and milk, and add just a little salt and pepper. Pour into the flan.
5   Slice the tomato and carefully place on top of the flan.
6   Bake for 30–40 minutes until golden brown and firm to touch. Remove the flan ring for the last ten minutes. Garnish with a little parsley and serve hot or cold with a salad.

Cheese and onion flan Make and bake in exactly the same way, but instead of the bacon, add 1 onion, chopped and fried in 15 g margarine until soft.

Both these flans are very good if the pastry is made with brown flour. Use either wheatmeal flour or a mixture of wholemeal and white flour (50 g of each) for best results.

Sausage rolls

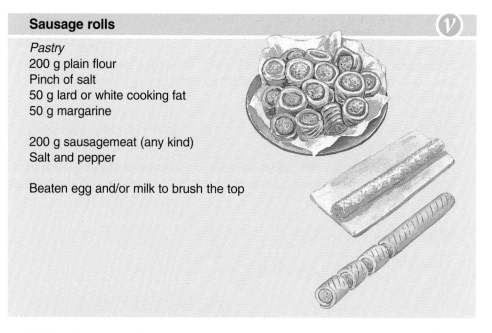

Pastry
200 g plain flour
Pinch of salt
50 g lard or white cooking fat
50 g margarine

200 g sausagemeat (any kind)
Salt and pepper

Beaten egg and/or milk to brush the top

Method
1   Light the oven, Gas 6, 200°C. Position the shelf at the top of the oven. Grease a baking tray.
2   Make the shortcrust pastry and roll it out. Cut it into a rectangle about 30 cm x 25 cm.
3   Cut in two, lengthwise.
4   Add some salt and pepper to the sausagemeat and roll it out the same length as the pastry. Place it on the pastry.
5   Brush the edges with water and seal them. Place the join underneath. Cut into 5 cm lengths, mark the tops with a knife, and brush with the beaten egg and/or milk.
6   Place on the baking tray and cook for about 20 minutes until golden brown.

Serve them hot or cold.

Cake-making

Tins

You should use a tin very close to the size given in a recipe. If the tin is much larger, the mixture will be spread more thinly and could end up like a biscuit. If the tin is too small, the cake could rise and spill over the edge.

Lining tins

When you are making cakes it is important to prepare the tins carefully, to ensure that the cakes can be removed from the tins without breaking. The best way to line the tin depends on its shape and on the mixture you are using.

To line a sandwich cake tin or a loaf tin
It is usually only necessary to line the bottom of the tin. The sides can be greased with margarine. Stand the tin on a piece of greaseproof paper, draw around the base of the tin, and cut the paper on the pencil line.

To line a Swiss roll tin, base and sides
Place the tin on a sheet of greaseproof paper and draw a pencil line around the base of the tin. Cut the paper about 1.5 cm away from the pencil line. At the corners, cut into the pencil line. Place the paper neatly into the tin and the corners will fit smoothly against the sides and base.

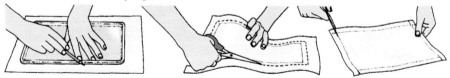

To line a deep cake tin
Place the tin on the greaseproof paper, draw around the base, and cut out this piece. For the sides, fold a sheet of greaseproof paper into two, lengthwise. Turn up about 2 cm at the folded edge. Make diagonal cuts on this fold. Place the paper inside the tin as shown then place the circle on to the base.

Methods of cakemaking

There are four basic methods of mixing the ingredients together when you make a cake. The method you use depends on the type and amounts of ingredients you are using. The methods are: *rubbing-in, creaming, melting,* and *whisking*.

All-in-one creaming method

This is used for cakes which have more fat and sugar compared to flour, usually about equal weights of each. For example, a Victoria sandwich cake might have:

100 g self-raising flour	100 g caster sugar
100 g margarine	2 eggs

These are called 'rich' cakes and they keep fresh for longer than plain cakes because of the extra fat. The flour is sieved into the bowl, then the other ingredients are all added and beaten together with a wooden spoon until the mixture is light-coloured and fluffy. The following ingredients are used:

Self-raising flour This means there is no need to add extra baking powder.

Margarine Soft margarine in a tub is very easy to cream. Block margarine is also suitable and easy to use, provided it is not used straight from the refrigerator.

Caster sugar This is better than granulated, because it has smaller crystals, which blend more easily into the mixture.

Eggs should be at room temperature, not chilled. For perfect results, weigh the eggs, then use an equal weight of each of the other ingredients. For example, if the 2 eggs weigh 120 g, use 120 g each of the flour, margarine, and sugar.

The all-in-one creaming method is quicker and simpler than the traditional creaming method and it is easier to achieve perfect results every time.

As well as the recipes below, this method is also used to make pineapple upside-down pudding (p. 220), steamed sponge pudding (p. 219), Hungarian chocolate biscuits (p. 214), and crunchy bran biscuits (p. 214).

The traditional creaming method

Using this method the fat and sugar are creamed together until light and fluffy. The eggs are whisked, then gradually beaten into the mixture, and then the flour is gently folded in.

Victoria sandwich cake

100 g self-raising flour
100 g caster sugar
100 g soft margarine
2 eggs (medium)
Jam to sandwich the cake

Method

1 Light the oven, Gas 4, 180°C. Place the shelf in the centre. Grease 2 sandwich cake tins, 18–20 cm in diameter, and line them with greaseproof paper.
2 Sieve the flour into a bowl. Add the sugar, margarine, and eggs and beat well with a wooden spoon (or mixer) until the mixture is light-coloured and fluffy.
3 Divide between the tins and smooth the top. Bake for 20–25 minutes, until firm and golden brown. Turn on to a wire tray to cool, then sandwich with jam.

To make a larger cake use 3 eggs and 150 g each of flour, sugar, and margarine. It will take longer to cook (30–40 minutes at Gas 3, 170°C) but can be cooked in the same two 18–20 cm tins.

Fairy cakes

125 g self-raising flour
100 g margarine
100 g sugar, preferably caster
2 eggs

Method
1. Light the oven, Gas 5, 190°C. Place the shelf just above the centre. Place 18 paper cases into a bun tray.
2. Sieve the flour into a bowl, add all the other ingredients, and beat well with a wooden spoon until light and fluffy.
3. Divide between the paper cases and bake for about 20–25 minutes until well risen, firm, and golden brown.

Queen cakes Make exactly as above, but add 50 g currants or sultanas to the mixture.

Cherry cakes Make exactly as above, but add 50 g cherries which have been washed, dried, and chopped.

Butterfly cakes Make some Fairy cakes as described above. Make some butter cream by sieving 100 g icing sugar, adding 50 g margarine or butter and 2 teaspoons milk, and beating together until smooth and light. Slice the tops off the cakes, cut each top in two to make 'wings'. Put a little butter cream on each case and replace the wings. Sieve a little icing sugar over the top of the cakes.

Chocolate cake

15 g cocoa
100 g self-raising flour
75 g margarine
75 g caster sugar
2 eggs
1 level tablespoon golden syrup

Butter cream
100 g icing sugar
50 g margarine or butter
1 level tablespoon cocoa (optional)
½ teaspoon vanilla essence

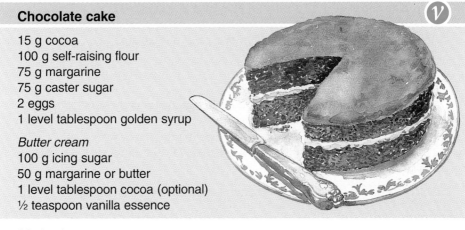

Method
1. Light the oven, Gas 3, 170°C. Place the shelf near the centre. Grease two 15 cm or 18 cm sandwich cake tins and line them with greaseproof paper.
2. Sieve the flour and cocoa into a bowl, add the margarine, sugar, eggs, and syrup, and beat well until very light and fluffy.
3. Divide between the two tins and bake for 25–30 minutes until firm. Cool on a wire tray, then sandwich with the butter cream. Sieve a little icing sugar over the top.

To make the butter cream
Sieve the icing sugar into a bowl, with the cocoa if you are using it. Add the butter and vanilla essence, and beat well.

Cakes made with oil

These are quick and easy to make, but may have less flavour than cakes made with butter. They are a good choice for anyone cutting down on animal fats.

Victoria sandwich ⓥ

150 g self-raising flour
1 level teaspoon baking powder
125 g sugar (caster if possible)
100 ml oil

2 medium eggs
3 tablespoons milk or water
1 teaspoon vanilla essence

Method
1 Light the oven, Gas 4, 180°C. Put the shelf just above the centre. Line two 18 cm cake tins with greaseproof paper. (Or use one 20 cm tin and cook for longer).
2 Sieve the flour and baking powder into a bowl. Add all the other ingredients and beat well for 2 minutes. Pour into the tin or tins (the mixture will be quite soft).
3 Bake for about 30 minutes (40 minutes if in one tin) until firm and golden brown.
4 Leave in the tin for 5 minutes, then turn onto a wire tray to cool.

To finish the cake, simply sandwich it with jam.

Orange cake ⓥ

Two Victoria sandwich cakes

Butter cream
100 g icing sugar
50 g soft margarine
1 teaspoon orange zest
1 teaspoon orange juice

Glacé icing
75 g icing sugar, sieved
1 tablespoon orange juice
1 teaspoon orange zest

Method
1 Make the butter cream: beat the ingredients together until light and fluffy.
2 Sandwich the cakes with the butter cream.
3 Make the glacé icing: mix all ingredients together until smooth.
4 Spread the glacé icing over the top of the cake. Do not move the cake until the icing has set or you will crack it.

Lemon cake: use the juice and zest of a lemon instead of an orange.

Sultana tray bake ⓥ

250 g self raising flour
100 ml oil
2 eggs

125 g sugar (caster if possible)
1 tablespoon water
100 g sultanas

Method
1 Light the oven, Gas 4, 180°C. Line a tin about 16 x 28 cm with greaseproof paper. Put the shelf just above the centre.
2 Sieve the flour into a bowl. Add the oil, eggs, sugar, and milk, and beat well. Stir in the sultanas. Pour into the tin.
3 Bake for 30–35 minutes until firm and golden brown. Cool on a wire rack.

The melting method

This method is less often used than the others. The fat and syrup or treacle are melted in a pan and poured into the flour and other dry ingredients. Plain flour is usually used, with bicarbonate of soda as the raising agent. The bicarbonate of soda has quite a strong taste and darkens the colour of the cake, so is suitable for recipes like gingerbread. The ginger flavour covers the taste, and the dark colour improves the appearance of the gingerbread. These cakes usually improve with keeping, developing a good flavour and becoming more moist.

Many of these recipes use black treacle or golden syrup.

An easy way to weigh and pour syrup Take the lid off the tin and put the tin into a small pan with water half-way up the side. Bring the water to the boil, then turn off the heat. Leave the tin in the water to warm. It will become runny and easy to pour.

To clean the sticky tin Press the lid back on very firmly. Put the whole tin into hot soapy water, and clean with a brush or cloth. Dry.

Gingerbread ⓥ

150 g plain flour	100 g black treacle or golden syrup
2 rounded teaspoons ground ginger	25 g butter
1 level teaspoon mixed spice	1 egg
1 level teaspoon bicarbonate of soda	3 tablespoons water or milk
25 g sugar (any kind)	

Method
1   Warm the treacle with the lid off as above.
2   Light the oven, Gas 4, 180°C. Place the oven shelf just above the centre.
3   Line a tin 16 x 28 cm with greaseproof paper.
4   Sieve the flour, ginger, spice, and bicarbonate of soda into a bowl. Add the sugar.
5   Carefully pour the warm treacle into the weighing scales, then pour it into the flour.
6   Melt the butter in the pan, then add to the flour. Add the egg and water, and beat until smooth. Pour into the tin.
7   Bake for about 20 minutes until firm. Cool on a wire tray, then cut into squares.

Easy mix fruit cake ⓥ

100 g butter or margarine	200 g wholemeal flour
100 g brown sugar	1 level teaspoon baking powder
250 g mixed dried fruit	2 eggs
1 rounded teaspoon bicarbonate of soda	1 rounded teaspoon mixed spice
125 ml water	

Method
1   Put the butter, sugar, fruit, bicarbonate of soda, and water into a saucepan. Bring to the boil, simmer gently for five minutes. Leave to cool.
2   Light the oven, Gas 4, 180°C. Position shelf in centre of oven.
3   Grease and line a Swiss roll tin, about 16 x 28 cm.
4   Mix flour, baking powder, and mixed spice, and add them to the pan. Beat the eggs and add to the pan. Pour the mixture into the tin.
5   Bake until firm, about 30 minutes. Leave in tin for 5 minutes. Cool on a wire tray.

Flapjacks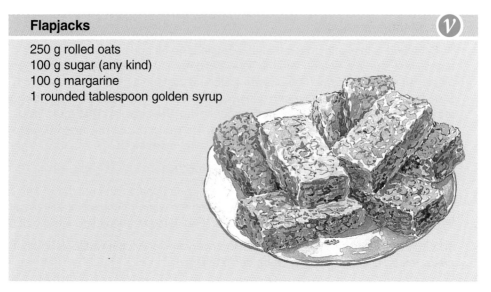

250 g rolled oats
100 g sugar (any kind)
100 g margarine
1 rounded tablespoon golden syrup

Method

1 Light the oven, Gas 5, 190°C. Put the shelf in the centre of the oven.
2 Grease a tin 16 x 28 cm with margarine.
3 Put the oats and sugar into a bowl, and mix together.
4 Put the margarine into a small pan. Add 1 rounded tablespoon of golden syrup, and warm on a very low heat. As the syrup warms it will come off the spoon.
5 When the margarine is melted, pour over the oats and mix well. Press into the tin and flatten the top.
6 Bake for 20−25 minutes. The flapjack will not be crisp until it cools, so do not cook until it is crisp or it will be too hard. Cool in the tin for 5 minutes then mark into fingers.

Parkin

150 g black treacle
200 g plain flour
1 level teaspoon bicarbonate of soda
1 rounded teaspoon mixed spice
1 rounded teaspoon cinnamon
1 rounded teaspoon ground ginger

200 g medium oatmeal
(or porridge oats would do)
100 g sugar
150 g butter or margarine
100 ml milk
1 egg

Method

1 Light the oven, Gas 4, 180°C. Put the oven shelf just above the centre. Line a tin, 16 x 28 cm, with greasproof paper.
2 Put the treacle to warm (see p. 205).
3 Sieve the flour, bicarbonate of soda, spice, cinnamon, and ginger, into a mixing bowl, and mix well. Stir in the oatmeal and sugar.
4 Carefully measure the warm treacle into the weighing scales, then pour it into the flour.
5 Melt the butter or margarine very gently in a small pan (or microwave). Pour it into the flour. Add the milk and the egg.
6 Stir the mixture until it is well mixed and smooth. Put it into the tin and bake for 30−40 minutes, until firm to the touch. Cool on a wire tray.

The whisking method

This method is used for making sponge cakes. Sponge cakes contain no fat, so they soon become stale. They should be eaten within a day of being made. The ingredients used are flour, eggs, and caster sugar only.

Flour Self-raising flour is used to give extra lightness, though plain flour could be used. It must be well sieved.

Sugar Caster sugar is essential for this light mixture.

Eggs should be at room temperature. If cold, they will take longer to whisk.

Method

1 Put the eggs and sugar into a mixing bowl. Using an electric mixer, whisk until they are thick, white, and creamy. Test carefully to see if the mixture is ready. It should hold the mark of the beater trailed over the mixture for at least 10 seconds. This is called 'ribbon texture'.

2 Use a metal spoon to fold the sieved flour *gently* into the mixture, a little at a time. This must be done very lightly and carefully, but thoroughly.
3 Pour the mixture into the prepared tin, and bake in a fairly hot oven, about Gas 6, 200°C.

Swiss roll

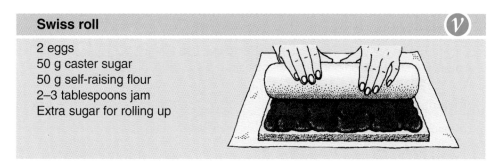

2 eggs
50 g caster sugar
50 g self-raising flour
2–3 tablespoons jam
Extra sugar for rolling up

Method

1 Light the oven, Gas 6, 200°C. Place the shelf near the top of the oven.
2 Line a Swiss roll tin, 16 x 28 cm, with greaseproof paper. Grease the paper. Sieve the flour on to a plate.
3 Whisk the eggs and sugar until thick (see above). Gently fold in the flour using a metal spoon. Pour into the tin.
4 Bake for 8–10 minutes, until golden brown and firm. Do not overcook, or it will break when you try to roll it up.
5 While the cake is baking, spread the extra sugar over a piece of greaseproof paper. Place a sharp knife and a palette knife beside the paper. Warm the jam.
6 When the Swiss roll is cooked, tip it on to the sugared paper. Peel off the lining paper. Trim the edges of the Swiss roll.
7 Spread quickly with the warm jam then roll it up, using the paper to help you. Cool on a wire rack.

If your Swiss roll tin is larger, about 22 x 30 cm, use 75 g caster sugar, 3 eggs, and 75 g SR flour.

Sponge fruit gateau

2 eggs
50 g caster sugar
50 g self-raising flour
Half a tin of fruit, such as mandarin oranges
    or pineapple, or a few fresh strawberries
About 50 g toasted coconut raspings,
    or grated chocolate for the sides
Small carton double or whipping cream

Method

1   Light the oven, Gas 6, 200°C. Place the shelf near the top of the oven.
2   Line a Swiss roll tin, 16 x 28 cm, with greaseproof paper. Grease the paper. Sieve the flour on to a plate.
3   Whisk the eggs and sugar until thick (see p. 207). Gently fold in the flour using a metal spoon. Pour into the tin.
4   Bake for 10–15 minutes, until firm. Then remove the paper and cool on a wire tray.
5   Drain the syrup from the fruit. Whip the cream and keep it cool.
6   When the cake is cold, cut it into 2 or 3 equal sized pieces and sandwich them together with a little cream. Spread a little cream on the sides (not the top).
7   Put the coconut raspings/grated chocolate on to a piece of greaseproof paper. Dip the sides of the cake into this to coat them.
8   Spread a little cream on to the top of the cake, arrange the fruit on this, then decorate with piped cream.

If your Swiss roll tin is larger, about 22 x 30 cm, use 3 eggs, 75 g caster sugar, and 75 g self-raising flour to make the cake.

Sponge sandwich cake

3 eggs
75 g caster sugar
75 g self-raising flour
2 tablespoons jam
Small carton double
    or whipping cream (optional)

Method

1   Light the oven, Gas 5, 190°C. Place the shelf just above the centre.
2   Line two 15 cm or 18 cm sandwich cake tins with greaseproof paper. Grease the paper and the sides of the tin.
3   Sieve the flour on to a plate.
4   Whisk the eggs and sugar until thick (see p. 207). Gently fold in the flour using a metal spoon. Pour into the tins.
5   Bake for 20–30 minutes until firm and golden brown. Leave in the tins for a few minutes, then turn out to cool.
6   Sandwich with jam (and whipped cream if you use it).

Chocolate sponge cake Make and bake exactly as above, but use 50 g flour and 25 g sieved cocoa instead of 75 g flour.

Sponge flan case

2 eggs
50 g caster sugar
50 g self-raising flour

Method
1 Light the oven, Gas 6, 200°C. Position the shelf above the centre.
2 Grease a 20 cm sponge flan tin with melted lard or margarine. This must be done very thoroughly. Flour the tin lightly.
3 Sieve the flour on to a plate. Whisk the eggs and sugar until thick (see p. 207). Gently fold in the flour with a metal spoon. Pour into the tin.
4 Bake for about 20 minutes until firm and golden brown. Leave in the tin for a few minutes, then turn on to a wire tray to cool.

Sponge fruit flan

Flan case
2 eggs
50 g caster sugar
50 g self-raising flour

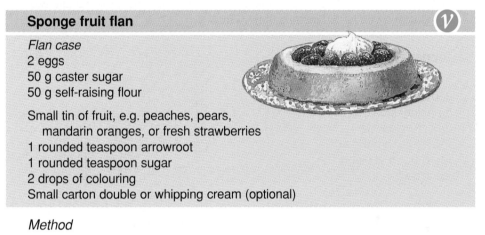

Small tin of fruit, e.g. peaches, pears, mandarin oranges, or fresh strawberries
1 rounded teaspoon arrowroot
1 rounded teaspoon sugar
2 drops of colouring
Small carton double or whipping cream (optional)

Method
1 Make a sponge flan case exactly as described above.
2 Drain the syrup from the fruit into a measuring jug. Add enough water to make 125 ml liquid.
3 Arrange the fruit neatly in the flan case.
4 Put the syrup, arrowroot, and sugar into a small pan. Bring to the boil, stirring all the time, and boil until transparent. Add the colouring if you wish, e.g. pink for pears.
5 Use a metal spoon to coat the fruit with this glaze.
6 When completely cold, decorate with the whipped cream if you are using it.

Apple sponge flan

Flan case	*Filling*
2 eggs	500 g cooking apples
50 g caster sugar	75 g sugar
50 g SR flour	Small carton double or whipping cream (optional)

Method
1 Make the sponge flan case exactly as described above.
2 Cut the apples into quarters, remove the peel and core, slice.
3 Put into a pan with about 4 tablespoons water and simmer very gently with the lid on until soft. Add the sugar and beat until smooth. Put in the flan case.
4 When the flan is completely cold, decorate with the whipped cream.

Cold drinks

Lemonade

2 lemons
50 g sugar
500 ml water

Method
1 Wipe the lemons with a clean damp cloth. Peel the rind very thinly and put into a jug or basin with the sugar. Pour on the boiling water, and leave until cold.
2 Strain into a glass jug, through muslin or a nylon sieve.
3 Add the lemon juice and some ice cubes and serve.

Orange squash Make in exactly the same way as the lemonade, but use two oranges and one lemon instead of two lemons.

Ginger and lemon punch

1 teabag or 1 rounded teaspoon tea
250 ml boiling water
50 g granulated sugar
250 ml cold water
1 lemon, 1 orange
Small bottle of ginger ale
Ice cubes

Method
1 Make the tea with the boiling water. Leave to infuse for 3 minutes, then pour into a large jug or basin. Add the sugar and stir to dissolve. Add the cold water and leave until cold.
2 Cut the orange and lemon into halves. Remove two slices from each and save for decoration. Squeeze the juice from the orange and lemon halves. Add to the tea.
3 Strain into a glass jug, add the ginger ale and ice cubes, and float the lemon and orange slices on the top.

Chocolate cream   *Makes 2–3 large glasses*

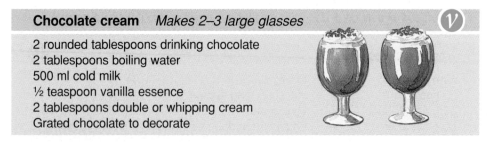

2 rounded tablespoons drinking chocolate
2 tablespoons boiling water
500 ml cold milk
½ teaspoon vanilla essence
2 tablespoons double or whipping cream
Grated chocolate to decorate

Method
1 Dissolve the drinking chocolate in the boiling water.
2 Whisk in the milk and vanilla essence. Pour into glasses.
3 Whip the cream until thick.
4 Just before serving, spoon or pipe the cream on to the milk and sprinkle with a little grated chocolate.

Sandwiches

Sandwich fillings

Cheese and chutney – grated cheese with chutney or sweet pickle.

Egg and cress – chopped hard boiled egg, mixed with salad cream and cress.

Cooked meat and coleslaw – ham, chopped pork, corned beef, etc., with a little coleslaw (see p. 192).

Cottage cheese and pineapple – chop the drained pineapple.

Cottage cheese and spring onion – chop the spring onion.

Cream cheese and cucumber – chop the cucumber.

Cream cheese and chopped walnuts.

Chopped pork and salad cream – chop the pork, mix with the salad cream.

Sardine and tomato – drain the sardines, mix with slices of tomato.

Salad – use a mixture of salad ingredients, with or without a little salad cream.

Making sandwiches

When you are making sandwiches, spread the butter or soft margarine right to the edges of the bread. There are many different kinds of bread available: wholemeal, brown, or white, and different shaped loaves and rolls. Make sure the sandwiches have plenty of filling. The filling should be moist so that the sandwiches don't taste dry. Serve them on a dishpaper, well garnished with cress, parsley, or lettuce to add some colour.

Afternoon tea or 'dainty' sandwiches
Use thinly sliced white or brown bread with the crusts removed, cut into small squares, fingers, or triangles. Garnish with cress or parsley.

Open sandwiches
Use bread buns, halved. Choose a moist filling which will not fall off, and colourful garnishes.

Vienna rolls or loaves
These look attractive if they are split along the side, well buttered, and filled with a moist filling. Use slices of tomato, cucumber, or hard-boiled egg, with lettuce or cress to add colour.

Toasted sandwiches
Most sandwiches can be toasted except those with lettuce or salad in the filling. Use any of the fillings above, or try grilled bacon and fried mushrooms, or any other filling.

Biscuits and scones

Biscuits are easy to make at home and they usually have a better flavour than the bought variety. When you are making them, follow these rules for good results.

1   Grease the baking tray carefully, as biscuits are fragile and may break easily when you lift them off the tray.
2   Leave them to cool on the tray for a minute or two after removing them from the oven. Then cool on a wire tray.
3   Do not crowd them together on the baking tray, as some recipes will spread a little in the oven.
4   Make sure that you do not use too large a baking tray for your oven. If you do, the biscuits will not brown evenly and some may be overdone and dark before others are cooked.
5   Biscuits do not go crisp until they are cool, so do not leave them in the oven until they are crisp, or they will be overdone.

A food processor is ideal for making biscuits. Use it for rubbing the fat into the flour, then making a dough to roll out.

Lemon or orange biscuits

100 g self-raising flour
50 g butter or margarine
50 g caster, icing, or granulated sugar
    (plus a little extra to sprinkle on the tops)
1 egg
1 level teaspoon lemon or orange rind

Method
1   Light the oven, Gas 4, 180°C. Place the shelf in the centre of the oven. Grease a baking tray.
2   Separate the egg yolk from the white. Wash the lemon or orange, then grate the rind finely.
3   Put the flour into a mixing bowl. Rub in the butter, then stir in the sugar and lemon or orange rind. Add the egg yolk and mix to a smooth dough.
4   Knead lightly, then roll out thinly. Cut into about 15 biscuits with a medium-sized cutter.
5   Place on the baking sheet, brush with the beaten egg white, and sprinkle with a little sugar.
6   Bake for 12–15 minutes until pale gold. Leave to cool on the baking tray for a couple of minutes, then cool on a wire rack.

Currant biscuits Leave out the lemon or orange rind, and add 25 g currants when you add the sugar.

Cherry biscuits Leave out the lemon or orange rind, and add 25 g cherries (washed, dried, and chopped) when you add the sugar.

Spice biscuits Leave out the orange or lemon rind, and add 1 level teaspoon mixed spice when you add the sugar.

Digestive biscuits ⓥ

75 g wholemeal flour
15 g plain flour
Good pinch of salt
½ level teaspoon baking powder

15 g oatmeal or porridge oats
40 g butter or margarine
40 g sugar, preferably caster
3 tablespoons milk

Method

1 Light the oven, Gas 5, 190°C. Place the shelf in the centre. Grease a baking tray.
2 Sieve the plain flour, salt, and baking powder into a bowl, and mix well. Stir in the wholemeal flour and oatmeal.
3 Rub in the butter, stir in the sugar. Add the milk and mix to a stiff dough.
4 Roll out thinly and cut into about 12 biscuits with a medium-sized cutter.
5 Place on the baking tray and bake for 15–20 minutes until pale golden brown.

Shortbread biscuits ⓥ

150 g plain flour
100 g butter or margarine
50 g sugar (preferably caster)
Some extra sugar to sprinkle on the top

Method

1 Light the oven, Gas 3, 170°C. Place the shelf just above the centre of the oven. Grease a baking tray.
2 Put the flour into a bowl, rub in the margarine, stir in the sugar.
3 Squeeze together firmly with your fingers until the mixture forms a dough. Do not add any liquid.
4 Roll out to about 1cm thick. Cut into circles with a medium-sized cutter, or cut into fingers.
5 Carefully place on the baking tray. Bake for about 15–20 minutes until pale golden brown. The biscuits will not be crisp until they are cool.
6 Lift on to a wire tray to cool. Sprinkle with a little sugar.

Cheese biscuits or straws ⓥ

150 g plain flour, white or brown
100 g butter or margarine
75 g cheese

½ level teaspoon salt
½ level teaspoon mustard
Pepper

Method

1 Light the oven, Gas 4, 180°C. Grease a baking tray.
2 Grate the cheese finely.
3 Using a wooden spoon, beat the butter until soft. Work in the cheese, seasoning, and flour, and form into a dough. Cover with polythene, and leave in a cool place for 10–20 minutes.
4 Roll the pastry on to a lightly floured surface to 5 mm thick, and cut into biscuits 3 cm across or straws 5 mm wide and 8 cm long.
5 Place on the baking sheet and mark with a fork. Bake for about 15 minutes, until light golden brown and slightly crisp. Carefully place on a wire rack to cool.

Crunchy bran biscuits

50 g sugar
50 g margarine
1 egg
100 g wholemeal flour
50 g wheat bran
1 rounded teaspoon baking powder

Method

1 Light the oven, Gas 5, 190°C. Place the shelf in the oven centre. Grease a baking tray.
2 Cream the sugar and margarine until soft, then beat in the egg.
3 Mix all the other ingredients thoroughly in a bowl, then add to the margarine and sugar. Knead into a dough.
4 Divide into about 20 pieces, each the size of a walnut. Roll between the palms of the hands until smooth.
5 Place on the baking tray, well apart, and flatten slightly.
6 Bake for about 20 minutes until crisp and brown.

Hungarian chocolate biscuits

100 g plain flour
25 g cocoa
100 g margarine
50 g sugar
½ teaspoon vanilla essence

Chocolate butter cream
50 g icing sugar
25 g butter or margarine
1 level teaspoon cocoa + 1 teaspoon hot water

Method

1 Light the oven, Gas 4, 180°C. Place the shelf near the top of the oven. Grease a baking tray.
2 Sieve the flour and cocoa together on to a plate.
3 Cream the margarine, sugar, and vanilla essence. Stir in the flour and mix well.
4 Divide into about 16 pieces, each the size of a walnut. Place well apart on the baking tray. Flatten each one with a fork dipped in cold water.
5 Bake for 15 minutes. Cool on a wire tray.
6 When cool, sandwich with the butter cream. To make the butter cream: mix the cocoa with the hot water. Sieve the icing sugar into a small basin, add the butter and cocoa, and beat together until smooth and soft.

Melting moments Replace the 25 g cocoa with another 25 g flour. Roll each biscuit in 50 g rolled oats (porridge oats). Decorate each with a small piece of cherry. (You do not sandwich these together with butter cream.)

Viennese creams Replace the 25 g cocoa with another 25 g flour. Sandwich with plain butter cream, leaving out the cocoa.

Scones

Scones take only a short time to make and to bake. They should be eaten quite soon after being made as they contain little fat and so go stale quickly. Scones should be light, well risen, and golden brown. Follow these rules for successful scone-making.

1 The scone dough should be quite soft.
2 The scones should be at least 2 cm thick before they are put into the oven.
3 The scones should be cooked at the top of a hot oven.

Plain scones

250 g self-raising flour
40 g margarine
125 ml milk

Method
1 Light the oven, Gas 7, 220°C. Position the shelf at the top of the oven. Grease a baking tray.
2 Sieve the flour into a bowl. Rub in the margarine.
3 Pour in the milk, and mix to a fairly soft, but not sticky, dough.
4 Knead lightly, then roll out. The dough *must* be at least 2 cm thick. Cut into rounds using a medium cutter and place on the baking tray.
5 Brush with a little milk, then bake for 12–15 minutes until golden brown. Cool on a wire tray.

Currant scones Make and bake in exactly the same way, but add 25 g sugar and 75 g currants to the mixture after you have rubbed in the margarine.

Cheese scones Make and bake in exactly the same way as the plain scones, but add 75 g grated cheese, ½ level teaspoon mustard, and a pinch of salt to the mixture after you have rubbed in the margarine.

Wholemeal scones

125 g wholemeal flour   40 g margarine
125 g plain flour   125 ml milk
2 level teaspoons baking powder

Method
1 Light the oven, Gas 7, 220°C. Position the shelf at the top of the oven. Grease a baking tray.
2 Put the wholemeal flour into a mixing bowl. Sieve in the plain flour and baking powder, and mix well. Rub in the margarine.
3 Save a little milk to brush the tops, pour the rest into the flour. Mix to a soft but not sticky dough.
4 Knead lightly then cut into 3. Shape each into a round and roll out to 2 cm thick. Place on the baking sheet. Cut each one almost through into quarters.
5 Brush tops with milk, then bake for 15–20 minutes until firm and well risen. Cool on a wire tray.

Victoria scones

250 g self-raising flour
50 g margarine
50 g sugar
1 egg plus enough milk to make
    125 ml of egg and milk altogether
3 glacé cherries

Method

1   Light the oven, Gas 6, 200°C. Position the shelf near the top. Grease a baking sheet.
2   Sieve the flour into a bowl. Rub in the margarine and stir in the sugar.
3   Keep 2 teaspoonfuls of egg and milk to brush the tops. Pour the rest into the flour and mix to a soft dough. Knead it lightly until smooth.
4   Cut into 3 pieces and shape each to a round. Roll out to 2 cm thick. Place on the baking sheet.
5   Cut across the top, almost into quarters. Brush with beaten egg and milk, and put a piece of cherry on to each quarter.
6   Bake for about 15–20 minutes until golden brown.

Dropped scones

125 g self-raising flour
15 g margarine
50 g sugar
1 egg + 4 tablespoons milk
A little oil for girdle or frying pan

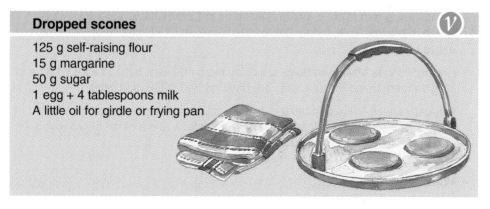

Method

1   Sieve the flour into a bowl, rub in the margarine, and stir in the sugar.
2   Beat the egg and milk and add to the flour a little at a time, beating with a whisk until smooth.
3   Heat the girdle or frying pan with a little oil.
4   Drop tablespoons of the mixture on to the girdle or pan, and cook for about 3 minutes on each side. Cook about three at a time.
5   When the scones are cooked, pile them into a clean tea towel to keep them warm and moist. Serve as soon as possible.

Puddings

There are several recipes here for traditional English puddings. These are usually fairly high in fat and sugar, so we should not eat them too often. A healthy compromise is to have fruit or low-fat yoghurt through the week, and a pudding on Sunday or for a special meal.

Hot puddings

As well as the recipes given here, you will find others in the pastry section. Custard is served with most hot puddings, so the recipe is given here first of all.

Custard

250 ml milk
2 level tablespoons custard powder
1 level tablespoon sugar

Method
1   Put a little of the milk into a jug or basin, add the custard powder and sugar, and mix until smooth and free from lumps.
2   Bring the rest of the milk to the boil and pour on to the mixture, stirring all the time.
3   The mixture may be thick enough now. If it is not, return it to the pan and simmer gently, stirring all the time until thickened.

Fruit crumble   *Serves about 4*

500 g fruit (for example, apple, plum, rhubarb,
    gooseberry, blackberry and apple, apricot)
About 75–100 g sugar

Crumble topping
100 g flour
50 g margarine
50 g sugar

Method
1   Light the oven, Gas 6, 200°C. Place the shelf just above the centre of the oven.
2   Quarter, peel, and core the apples, or prepare the other fruit. Slice roughly and put in a pan with a lid, with 5 tablespoons water. Simmer very gently until the fruit is cooked, 10–20 minutes.
3   Meanwhile, make the crumble topping: put the flour into a mixing bowl, rub in the fat, stir in the 50 g sugar. Carefully taste the fruit, and add sugar depending on how tart the fruit is.
4   Pour the fruit into an ovenproof dish, cover with the crumble, and bake for 15–20 minutes, until golden brown. (Or cook in a microwave on High for 4 minutes.)
5   Serve with custard.

You could put the fruit and sugar uncooked into the crumble, but it would take 40–50 minutes to cook, at Gas 5, 190°C.

Pineapple upside-down pudding *Serves about 4* (v)

1 small can pineapple rings
2 glacé cherries
About 2 tablespoons golden syrup
100 g self-raising flour
100 g soft margarine
100 g caster sugar
2 eggs

Method
1 Light the oven, Gas 4, 180°C. Place the shelf in the centre of the oven.
2 Grease a deep 18 cm cake tin or a 20 cm sandwich cake tin.
3 Cover the bottom of the tin with a thin layer of golden syrup. Drain the pineapple rings and place them on the syrup with half a cherry in the centre of each ring.
4 Sieve the flour into a bowl. Add the margarine, sugar, and eggs, and beat well until light and fluffy. Spread this mixture carefully over the pineapples.
5 Bake for about 45 minutes until firm. Turn out on to a plate.

Serve with either custard or pineapple sauce.

Microwave method
Use a special plastic microwave dish (18–20 cm) or a round glass or china dish with straight sides. Cook for about 7 minutes, turning halfway through if your microwave has no turntable. Stand for 3 minutes before turning out.

Pineapple sauce Put the syrup from the tin of pineapples into a measuring jug. Add enough water to make 250 ml liquid. Put this into a small pan and add a rounded teaspoon of arrowroot or cornflour, a rounded teaspoon of sugar, and 2 teaspoons of lemon juice. Bring this to the boil, stirring all the time, until thick.

Pancakes *Serves about 4* (v)

100 g plain flour	Sugar, preferably caster
1 egg	1 large lemon (or about 3 tablespoons lemon juice)
250 ml milk	Lard or oil for frying

Method
1 Put the flour into a bowl. Drop the egg in the centre, add a little milk, and beat well with a whisk until smooth. Whisk in the rest of the milk a little at a time. *Or* blend all the ingredients for about 30 seconds until smooth.
2 Cut the lemon in two and squeeze out the juice.
3 Put a pan of water to heat, with a plate on top. This is to keep the pancakes warm until they are all made.
4 Heat a little lard or oil in a frying pan (use just enough to cover the bottom). A small pan (about 15 cm diameter) is best, but use whatever size you have.
5 When the fat is hot, pour in just enough batter to cover the bottom of the pan. Cook for 2 or 3 minutes until the bottom of the pancake is golden brown, then toss or turn it over and cook the other side.
6 Put it on to the plate to keep hot. Sprinkle it with a little lemon juice and sugar. Cook the rest of the pancakes.
7 When they are all cooked, roll each one up and serve on a warm serving dish.

Rice pudding   *Serves 3–4*

50 g pudding rice
50 g sugar
500 ml milk
15 g butter

Rice pudding cooked in a pressure cooker takes only 30 minutes to prepare and cook, and makes a very creamy pudding. You could use the traditional method below, but it takes 2 hours to cook.

Method

1 Melt the butter in the pressure cooker. Add the milk and bring to the boil. Add the washed rice and sugar and bring to the boil again.
2 Adjust the heat so that the milk continues to just boil in the bottom of the pan. Do not alter the heat again.
3 Put the lid and H pressure weight on the pan. Bring to pressure then cook for 12 minutes. Allow the pressure to reduce at room temperature.
4 Stir the pudding well and pour in to a serving dish. If you wish, brown the top under a grill or at the top of the oven.

Traditional method

1 Light the oven, Gas 2, 150°C. Place the shelf in the centre or below. Grease a 750 ml ovenproof dish.
2 Put the rice into a sieve and wash it under cold running water. Put it into the dish and sprinkle it with sugar. Pour the milk over. Dot with the butter.
3 Bake for about 2 hours until the rice is soft and the top is golden brown.

Bread and butter pudding   *Serves 3–4*

3 slices bread, brown or white (crusts off preferred)
25 g butter
50 g dried fruit
1 level tablespoon sugar
350 ml milk
2 eggs
Nutmeg

Method

1 Light the oven, Gas 4, 180°C. Grease an ovenproof dish with a little of the butter. Use the rest of the butter to spread on the bread. Cut into slices.
2 Put a layer of bread in the dish, sprinkle with fruit and sugar. Continue these layers, ending with bread on top.
3 Beat the eggs. Warm the milk, but do not let it boil. Pour onto the eggs and mix. Pour the mixture onto the bread through a sieve, and sprinkle with ground nutmeg. Leave to soak for ten minutes if possible, but this is not essential.
4 Place the dish in a roasting tin with water coming half-way up the side.
5 Bake for 30–40 minutes, until set and golden brown.

Cold puddings

Fruit fool   *Serves 4*

500 g cooking apples, rhubarb, or other fruit
75 g sugar
About 5 tablespoons water
250 ml milk
1 rounded tablespoon custard powder
1 level tablespoon sugar
Grated chocolate to decorate

Method

1   Cut the apple into quarters, remove the peel and core; or wash the rhubarb. Cut into slices and put these into a small pan with the water.
2   Simmer very gently with the lid on until the fruit is soft. Remove from the heat and stir in the 75 g sugar.
3   Make the custard: put most of the milk into a pan, leaving about 4 tablespoonfuls in a jug or basin. Add the custard powder and sugar to the milk in the jug and mix until it is completely free from lumps. Bring the milk in the pan to the boil, then pour it into the jug, stirring all the time.
4   The custard may now be thick. If it is not, pour it back into the pan and bring to the boil, stirring all the time until thick.
5   Put the custard and the fruit into the blender, blend until smooth, then pour into glass dishes.
6   When it is cold, decorate with a little grated chocolate.

Fresh fruit salad   *Serves about 4*

1 apple (preferably red-skinned)
1 pear
1 banana
1 orange
50 g grapes
1 lemon
250 ml water
100 g sugar

Method

1   Make the syrup: dissolve the sugar in the water in a small pan. Boil for 1 minute, then pour into a large bowl to cool. Add the juice of the lemon.
2   Wash, quarter, core, and slice the apple and the pear, and add to the syrup.
3   Peel and slice the banana and orange, add to the syrup.
4   Wash the grapes, cut into two and remove the pips. Add to the syrup.
5   Serve the fruit salad when completely cold, with custard, cream, or yoghurt.

For a change, add different fruits such as strawberries, raspberries, or a kiwi fruit, peeled and thinly sliced.

For a quick-to-make fruit salad, open a can of mandarin oranges and add the prepared fresh fruit to it. You could leave out the fresh orange.

For a low-sugar fruit salad, use fresh orange juice instead of making a syrup.

Lemon cheesecake *Serves 4–5*

150 g digestive biscuits
75 g butter or margarine
225 g low-fat curd cheese or cream cheese
125 ml fresh double or whipping cream
50 g caster sugar
1 lemon

Method

1 Put the biscuits into a polythene bag and crush with a rolling pin, or use a blender to make them into crumbs.
2 Melt the butter in a pan, and stir in the biscuit crumbs. Use this to line the base and sides of a flan case or shallow dish, about 20 cm in diameter. Put in a cold place.
3 Wash the lemon. Grate the skin finely and squeeze out the juice.
4 Whip the cream until thick. Beat the cheese to soften it. Stir the cream into the cheese. Fold in the sugar, lemon rind, and lemon juice.
5 Spread the mixture over the crumbs and chill before serving.

Jelly whip *Serves 4–5*

1 small can evaporated milk
1 packet of jelly
Small carton of double or whipping cream (optional)
Grated chocolate or flake to decorate

Method

1 Put the jelly into a small pan and add 125 ml water. Warm gently, stirring until the jelly is dissolved. Do not allow it to boil.
2 Pour this into a large mixing bowl and add a further 125 ml cold water. Leave until completely cold.
3 Very slowly, pour the milk into the jelly, whisking all the time until the mixture is frothy. Pour into a serving dish. Leave in a cool place to set.
4 Decorate with whipped cream, and sprinkle with a little grated chocolate.

Dried fruit salad

100 g dried apricots
100 g prunes
100 g dried figs

Method

1 Wash the fruit well in cold water, put into a large pan, and cover with cold water. Leave to soak overnight.
2 Put the pan on to heat and bring to the boil. Simmer very gently for 20 minutes. Cool for 5 minutes, then spoon into a serving dish.

This is delicious served warm or cold, either as a pudding or as a change for breakfast. It is high in NSP, low in fat, and has enough sweetness in the fruit without any added sugar.

Cooking with yeast

Making your own bread and rolls at home is very satisfying. It saves quite a lot of money and need not take long. You can prepare and cook bread buns or pizza in an hour, if you work very quickly and have all your equipment (including the room you work in) very warm.

The flour to use

Choosing the right flour for making bread is essential if you want good results. Always use *strong flour*, which is labelled 'strong' or 'bread' flour.

Strong flour is made from hard wheat, often imported from North America or Canada. It contains more of a substance called *gluten* than does the softer wheat grown in the UK. When gluten is mixed with water and kneaded it becomes stretchy, elastic, and strong. The dough rises easily and can hold the bubbles of carbon dioxide gas which the yeast produces. In this way it forms a strong framework for the bread and gives a well-shaped loaf with a good texture.

Strong, wholemeal, brown, and wheatmeal flour are all suitable for bread-making, as they are ground from hard wheat (see cereals, p. 182). They produce bread which is an excellent source of NSP (dietary fibre). They always need a little more liquid for mixing than white flour to produce a soft, pliable dough.

Yeast

Yeast is a living, unicellular fungus. If it is killed by excess heat it will not work and make the bread rise, so it must be carefully treated.

How the yeast works

In the right conditions the yeast cells will reproduce and increase in number. As they do this, alcohol and carbon dioxide gas are produced. The bubbles of gas are held in the stretchy framework of the dough and so the dough grows in size. Once it has increased in size sufficiently to give a light, well-risen loaf, it is put into a hot oven, the yeast is killed, and the dough does not rise any further.

Yeast needs moisture and food to grow. When you make bread, water or milk in the dough provide moisture. Sugars in the flour provide food. Warmth helps the yeast grow more quickly, but is not essential. Bread dough will rise in a refrigerator overnight and this cool rise produces a well-shaped loaf.

Too much warmth or heat will kill the yeast cells so you must be careful to avoid mixing the yeast with hot water or leaving it to rise in too hot a place.

The type of yeast to use

Quick-acting dried yeast is the simplest to use, as it can be stirred straight into the flour. (It does not need to be mixed with water first.) As it is easy to buy, cheap, and simple and quick to use, it has been used in all the following recipes. When you use this kind of yeast, the water temperature should be around 43°C, to help the dough to rise as quickly as possible. A thermometer is useful for this.

Fresh yeast is easy to use but is not available in many shops. You would use 15 g in each of these recipes. Measure out the water or milk for your recipe and make sure that the temperature is correct (blood heat). Add the yeast and stir until it is dissolved. Then use this liquid according to the recipe.

Ordinary dried yeast (not the quick-acting kind – do not confuse the two types). This has to be mixed with water and left until it is frothy (about 15 minutes) before you can use it and so it is not so quick and convenient to use.

Oil and salt

A tablespoon of oil has been added to these recipes, but you could instead rub 15 g of margarine or lard into the flour. The fat helps the bread to keep fresh, but it is not essential. Salt is added to bring out the flavour of the bread. It also helps to prevent the dough from being too sticky.

The water temperature

It is important that you use water which is at the right temperature for the kind of yeast you are using. For the quick-acting dried yeast used in these recipes it should be quite warm, 43°C, for the quickest rise. For fresh or ordinary dried yeast it should be just lukewarm or at blood heat. If you dip your finger into the water it should feel neither hotter nor cooler than your finger. If the water is too hot, the yeast may be killed and the bread dough will not rise. If the water is too cold, it will rise much more slowly.

When you add the water to the flour the mixture should be fairly soft and sticky at first. If it is too dry and hard it will be difficult to knead and the bread may be heavy. As flours vary in the amount of water they absorb, you may have to add a little more than the recipe states. Wholemeal and brown flours particularly may need a little more water to ensure a soft pliable dough.

Kneading

This is an important part of breadmaking. It makes the gluten stretchy and strong so that the dough can rise easily and hold its risen shape. Knead the dough as vigorously as you can, pulling and stretching it to develop the gluten. If you have a large electric mixer you can use a dough hook attachment. A food processor is ideal for kneading small quantities of dough, up to 250 g or 500 g of flour depending on the model. You just put all the ingredients into the bowl and process for 3–4 minutes.

Leaving the dough to rise

Dough can be left to rise in the tins in a warm place or on the kitchen table, or in the refrigerator for a slower rise. In a warmer place the dough will rise more quickly, but too high a temperature may kill the yeast. The dough should be covered loosely during rising to prevent a hard skin forming on the surface. Wrap the tin loosely in a polythene bag. A supermarket carrier bag is ideal.

Traditional method

In recipes using larger quantities you can leave the dough to rise in the mixing bowl after you have kneaded it. Once it has doubled in size you knead it again lightly, shape it into loaves, leave it to rise again to the top of the tin, then bake it.

Baking

Bread should be baked in a hot oven, Gas 8, 230°C. The heat causes the bread to rise a little more at first, then the yeast cells are killed and the bread is baked and 'set' in its risen shape. Test the bread to see if it is cooked by turning it out of the tin and tapping it underneath. If it is cooked it will sound crisp and hollow. Leave it to cool on a wire tray.

To get an attractive finish, brush bread with beaten egg and milk and sprinkle with poppy seeds before baking.

General instructions for making bread using quick-acting dried yeast

1 Mix the flour, salt, and yeast.
2 Measure the water, and add the oil.
3 Mix the flour and liquid, and knead well.
4 Shape into loaf or rolls.
5 Cover and leave to rise.
6 Bake in a hot oven.

To achieve good results in the shortest time possible

1 Use quick-acting dried yeast.
2 Use water at the right temperature, 43°C, warmer than blood heat.
3 Keep everything warm, including the room and the mixing bowl.
4 Use a food processor or mixer with a dough hook for mixing and kneading.
5 Stir in oil rather than rub in margarine.

QUESTIONS

1 Why is it essential to use strong flour for breadmaking?
2 What is gluten?
3 What are the conditions for yeast to grow?
4 Explain how the yeast causes the dough to rise.
5 What kind of yeast would you prefer to use? Why?
6 How would you store fresh yeast in a freezer?
7 How much dried yeast would you use instead of 15 g fresh yeast?
8 Why is it necessary to knead bread dough?

Recipes

Bread *To make a small loaf, quick method* Ⓥ

250 g strong white, brown,
   or wholemeal flour
1 level teaspoon salt
1 rounded teaspoon quick-acting
   dried yeast (½ sachet)
150 ml water
1 tablespoon oil

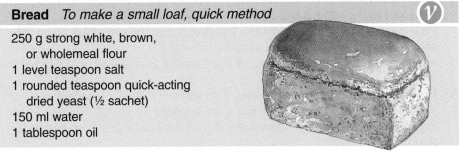

Method

1 Light the oven, Gas 8, 230°C. Place the shelf just above the centre of the oven. Grease a small loaf tin.
2 Put the flour into a bowl, add the salt, stir in the yeast.
3 Put 4 tablespoons of boiling water into a measuring jug. Add enough cold water to make 150 ml. Add the oil.
4 Stir the water into the flour and mix together. The dough must be soft at this stage. If it seems dry, add another 2–3 tablespoons of water.
5 Knead firmly for 10 minutes, then shape into a loaf. To shape, turn the edges to the centre and press firmly. Repeat until smooth (1).
6 Place the dough in the tin, smooth side up. Put the tin into a large polythene bag (2). Leave in a warm place until the dough has risen up to the top of the tin (3).
7 Bake for about 40 minutes. To see if the loaf is cooked, remove it from the tin and tap it underneath. It should sound crisp and hollow. Cool on a wire rack.

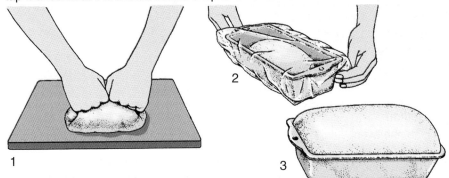

Quick bread buns Ⓥ

250 g strong white, brown,
   or wholemeal flour
1 level teaspoon salt
1 rounded teaspoon quick-acting
   dried yeast (½ sachet)
150 ml water
1 tablespoon oil

Method

1 Light the oven, Gas 8, 230°C. Place the shelf near the top of the oven. Grease a 20 cm sandwich cake tin.

2 Put the flour in the bowl, stir in the salt, stir in the yeast.

3 Put 4 tablespoons of boiling water into a measuring jug. Add enough cold water to make 150 ml. Add the oil.

4 Pour into the flour and mix together. The dough must be soft at this stage. If it seems dry, add another 2−3 tablespoons of water.

5 Knead firmly for 10 minutes, then cut into 8 pieces. Shape each into a bread bun and arrange in the tin.

6 Put the tin into a large polythene bag, then leave in a warm place to rise.

7 When the buns have risen to the top of the tin, bake for 15−20 minutes. To see if they are cooked, tap them underneath. If done they will sound crisp and hollow. Cool on a wire rack.

Pizza   *For a quick cheese pizza see p. 174*   (v)

For a quick cheese pizza see p. 174

Dough
250 g strong wholemeal, brown, or white flour
1 level teaspoon salt
1 rounded teaspoon quick-acting dried yeast (½ sachet)
150 ml water
1 tablespoon oil

1 tin tomatoes (or 250 g fresh tomatoes)
100 g cheese
Salt, pepper, pinch of oregano or mixed herbs
50 g mushrooms
1 onion
1 tablespoon oil
Tin of sardines, pilchards, or anchovies (optional)

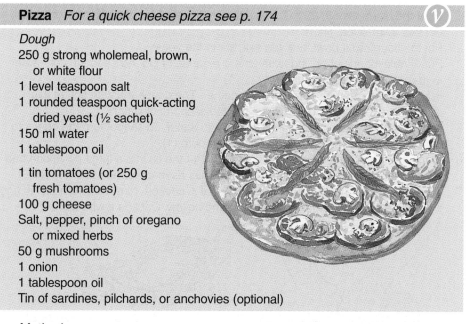

Method

1 Light the oven, Gas 7, 220°C. Place the shelf near the top of the oven. Grease a baking sheet.

2 Put the flour, yeast, and salt into a bowl.

3 Put 4 tablespoons of boiling water into a measuring jug. Add enough cold water to make 150 ml. Add 1 tablespoon oil.

4 Pour into the flour and mix to a soft dough. Add a little more water if necessary. Knead for 5 minutes. Roll out to a large circle, about 23 cm in diameter, put on a greased baking tray, and leave in a warm place while you prepare the filling.

5 Peel and chop the onion, and slice the mushrooms. Fry in the oil until soft. Drain the tomatoes, or slice if fresh ones. Grate the cheese. Brush the pizza dough with oil right to the edges.

6 Put the tomatoes, cheese, onion, and mushrooms over the dough, and add a pinch of oregano or mixed herbs and a little salt and pepper. Arrange the fish on top if you are using it.

7 Bake for about 30 minutes, until the base is cooked. Cool on a wire tray. Serve with a salad.

Jams and preserves

Making jam at home is an ideal way of preserving fruit in season for use throughout the year. Good home-made jam has a very fruity flavour, a clear bright colour, and a firm set, and will keep well.

Jam is made from two main ingredients, fruit and sugar. The fruit must contain plenty of pectin and acid if the jam is to set properly. Some fruits contain plenty of pectin and acid, so the jam will set easily. These are often the hard, sour fruits such as plums or damsons. Other fruits contain less pectin and acid, so to make sure that the jam sets well you have to add pectin or acid in some form.

Fruits which contain plenty of pectin and acid and so set easily	Fruits with a moderate amount of pectin and acid	Fruits with low pectin and acid content which do not set well
Gooseberries Apples Plums, damsons Black and redcurrants	Blackberries Raspberries Apricots	Strawberries Rhubarb Cherries

Pectin

Pectin is a gum-like substance found in the cell walls of ripe fruit in varying amounts. In under-ripe fruit it is in the form of pectose which can be turned to pectin when the fruit is stewed with an acid. In over-ripe fruit the pectin has turned to pectic acid and has lost its setting properties. This means that you should choose fruit which is either ripe or under-ripe for making jam. Avoid fruits which are over-ripe as results are likely to be poor.

If the fruit you are using is low in pectin you can add to it either:

1   some fruit of a kind with plenty of pectin, e.g. apples to blackberries, gooseberries or blackcurrants to strawberries; or
2   pectin in powder or liquid form, e.g. 'Certo' (buy from a chemist or supermarket).

Acid

Acid is needed in jam to:

1   convert any pectose to pectin and so help the jam to set;
2   improve the flavour and colour of the jam;
3   prevent hard crystals of sugar forming in the jam when you store it.

If you are using fruits which are low in acid, you can add it in the form of one of the following, before you start to cook the fruit:

1   lemon juice (about 2 tablespoons to each 1 kg of fruit);
2   citric acid, tartaric acid, or cream of tartar (½–1 level teaspoon for each 1 kg fruit) (buy from a chemist or supermarket).

Sugar

Use granulated sugar as it is cheapest and gives good results. You can buy special preserving sugar. This is meant to dissolve more easily and to produce a little less scum, but it is more expensive and not really necessary.

General method for making jam

1 Prepare the jam jars.
2 Prepare the fruit according to what kind it is and cook gently until completely soft.
3 Add the sugar and dissolve thoroughly.
4 Boil vigorously until setting point is reached.
5 Pour into the jars, cover, and label.

To prepare the jam jars

It is essential that these are clean, dry, and warm. Wash them thoroughly in warm, soapy water, rinse, and drain. Dry the outsides with a clean tea-towel. Warm the jars by standing them on a wooden board on the floor of a *very* low oven or by placing them above a warm cooker.

To test for setting point

Once the sugar has dissolved in the cooked fruit, you boil the jam vigorously until setting point is reached, usually in about 15–20 minutes. You have to test the jam to see if it has reached this point. There are several tests:

1 *The wrinkle test* This is the simplest method. Place a small saucer in the fridge. When you think that the jam may have reached setting point, remove it from the heat. Put a small teaspoon of jam on to the cold plate and let it cool a little. Push the jam with your fingertips over the plate. If it wrinkles on the surface the jam should set. If not, boil for a little longer and test again.

2 *The flake test* Use a clean, dry, wooden spoon to remove a little jam from the pan. Allow it to cool slightly. Gently pour the jam over the side of the spoon. If it comes off in wide flakes it is ready. If it pours off the spoon in a thin trickle it is not.

A good flake *Jam not ready*

3 *The thermometer test* The jam should reach a temperature of 104–105°C before it has the sugar concentration of 65% which is necessary for it to set. Keep the thermometer in a pan of boiling water beside the jam pan. It enables you to check it for accuracy (the water boils at 100°C) and makes the thermometer easier to clean.

Removing scum

Scum is just made up of small bubbles of air which have been caught up in the sticky, boiling jam. It is harmless, but spoils the appearance of the jam. Once the jam has reached setting point, remove it from the heat. Stir in a small piece of butter or margarine. This will disperse most of the scum from the jam. If any remains, remove it with a metal spoon.

Filling the jars

This should be done while the jam is very hot, unless you are making strawberry jam or marmalade. With these, you allow the jam to cool for 15 minutes in the pan, so that all the fruit does not rise to the top of the jar.

Fill the jars very carefully, as hot jam can scald your hands badly. Use a jug to scoop the jam out of the pan. Scrape the bottom of the jug on the edge of the pan, then pour the jam into the jars. Fill them right to the top, as jam shrinks when it cools.

Stand the jars on a board or baking tray and position each one right at the edge of the pan before you fill it. This keeps the outside of the jars clean and avoids splashes. Never hold a jar in your hands while pouring hot jam into it.

To cover the jars

As soon as you have filled them, place a waxed disc over the jam, wax side down. Damp the cellophane covers in a saucer of water, on one side only. Place the dry side down, and secure with an elastic band. You can use jars with screw-top lids instead of cellophane tops.

Remove any splashes from the outside of the jars with a damp cloth. Label the jar with the name of the jam and the date.

If you want to decorate the jars with small circles or squares of cotton fabric, place these over the cellophane cover or screw-top, and secure with an elastic band. Store the jam in a cool, dry, dark place.

Common faults in making jam	Possible causes
Jam will not set.	Jam has not been boiled for long enough and so has not reached setting point.
	Fruit is over-ripe.
	Fruit is low in pectin or acid and you have not added anything to counteract this, e.g. lemon juice, cream of tartar.
Jam goes mouldy or ferments.	Not enough sugar.
	Storing in a damp, warm place.
Crystals in the jam.	Jam has been boiled too long.
	Too little acid.
Jam is thick and stiff.	Jam has been boiled for too long past setting point.
Fruit is tough and hard.	Fruit was not properly cooked before sugar was added.

QUESTIONS

1 What four ingredients are necessary for making well-set jam?
2 What is pectin?
3 Why is over-ripe fruit unsuitable for jam-making?
4 If you are making jam using fruit which is low in pectin and acid, how can you ensure the jam will set?
5 Describe the 'wrinkle test' for setting point.
6 How would you prepare the jars to be used for jam?
7 What precautions would you take to avoid scalds when you are pouring hot jam into the jars?
8 What results would you expect if:
   a) you boiled the jam for too long?
   b) you boiled the jam for too short a time?
   c) you made strawberry jam without adding any ingredient except sugar?
   d) you stored jam in a cupboard which was slightly damp?

Recipes

Strawberry jam   *Makes about 1.25 kg*

1 kg strawberries
1½ level teaspoons cream of tartar *or* 2 tablespoons lemon juice
900 g sugar
15 g butter or margarine

Method

1 Hull and wash the strawberries. Cut them in half and put them in the pan with the cream of tartar or lemon juice.
2 Simmer very gently in their own juice for about 20 minutes, until the fruit is soft. Add the sugar, stir until dissolved, then boil rapidly until setting point is reached.
3 Add the butter, and stir it around the pan. Allow the jam to cool for 15 minutes to prevent the fruit rising in the jars.
4 Carefully pour into the warm jars, cover, and label.

Plum jam   *Makes about 2.5 kg*   (V)

1.5 kg plums
450 ml water
1.5 kg sugar
15 g butter or margarine

Method

1   Wash the plums in a colander. Put them into a pan with the water. Simmer gently until the plums are cooked, about 15 minutes.
2   Add the sugar, and stir until it is dissolved. Boil briskly until setting point is reached.
3   Take from the heat and remove all the stones with a perforated spoon. Stir in the butter to remove the scum.
4   Pour into clean, warm jars, cover, and label.

Raspberry jam   *Makes about 1.25 kg*   (V)

1 kg raspberries
1 kg sugar
15 g butter or margarine

Method

1   Put the raspberries into the pan, and simmer very gently to extract the juice.
2   Add the sugar, and stir over a low heat until all the sugar is dissolved.
3   Boil quickly until the jam is at setting point. Stir in the butter to remove the scum.
4   Pot, cover, and label.

Lemon curd   *Makes about 500 g*   (V)

50 g butter or margarine
3 eggs
200 g sugar
1 large or 2 small lemons

Method

1   Melt the margarine or butter in a double pan. If you do not have a double pan, place a large bowl over a pan of water.
2   Wash and dry the lemon. Grate the rind finely, then squeeze out the juice. Add this to the pan. Then add the sugar.
3   Beat the eggs and add to the pan. Stir with a wooden spoon until the mixture is thick enough to coat the back of the spoon. Keep the water just *below* boiling point.
4   Pour into clean, warm, small jars. Keep in a cold place and eat within 2 weeks.

Marmalade   (V)

You can make good marmalade quickly, cheaply, and easily using cans of pre-sliced oranges and lemons. You simply follow the instructions on the can, adding only sugar.

Further reading and useful addresses

General reading

The balance of good health, BAPS, Health Publications Unit, DSS Distribution Centre, Heywood Stores, Manchester Road, Heywood, Lancashire, OL10 2PZ.

The Ministry of Agriculture, Fisheries, and Food (MAFF) publishes a series of booklets, including *About food additives, Food allergy, Foodsense, Healthy eating, Healthy eating for older people, Organic food, Understanding food labels.* These are available free from Foodsense, London, SE99 7TT.

Reference books

Dietary fats: a nutrition briefing paper
(Health Education Authority, 1994)

Dietary reference values for food energy and nutrients for the United Kingdom
(HMSO, Report number 41, 1991)

Manual of nutrition, 10th edition
(MAFF, 1995)

The composition of foods, 5th edition, McCance and Widdowson
(Royal Society of Chemistry and MAFF, 1991)

Useful addresses

Food and Drink Federation
6 Catherine Street
London
WC2B 5JJ

Vegetarian Society
Parkdale
Dunham Road
Altrincham
Cheshire
WA14 4QG

Index

Recipe index